The World of Culinary Supervision, Training, and Management

Noel C. Cullen, Ed.D., CMC, AAC

Prentice Hall
Englewood Cliffs, NJ 07632

Library of Congress Cataloging-in-Publication Data

Cullen, Noel C.
    The world of culinary supervision, training, and management / Noel
C. Cullen.
        p.   cm.
    Includes index.
    ISBN 0-13-348897-7
    1. Food service management.   2. Cooks.   I. Title.
TX911.3.M27C85   1996
647.95'068—dc20   95-4000
                                                                   CIP

Acquisitions editor: Robin Baliszewski
Editorial/production supervision and interior design: Tally Morgan,
    WordCrafters Editorial Services, Inc.
Cover design: Marianne Frasco
Manufacturing buyer: Ed O'Dougherty

 © 1996 by Prentice-Hall, Inc.
A Simon & Schuster Company
Englewood Cliffs, NJ 07632

Printed in the United States of America
10   9   8   7   6   5   4   3

0-13-348897-7

Prentice-Hall International (UK) Limited, *London*
Prentice-Hall of Australia Pty, Limited, *Sydney*
Prentice-Hall Canada Inc., *Toronto*
Prentice-Hall Hispanoamericana, S.A., *Mexico*
Prentice-Hall of India Private Limited, *New Delhi*
Prentice-Hall of Japan, Inc., *Tokyo*
Simon & Schuster Asia Pte. Ltd., *Singapore*
Editora Prentice-Hall do Brasil, Ltda., *Rio de Janeiro*

Dedication

To my wife, Linda,
whose constant encouragement and practical support
was always provided in a loving way

Contents

**PART THREE
MANAGEMENT AND CHEF
SUPERVISORS**

LIST OF TABLES

"CHEF TALK" CONTRIBUTORS

Contributor	**Title**
Scott Almendinger President and Publisher Journal Publications Rockland, ME	Management by Thought, 59
Heiko Bendixen, CMC, AAC Director of Foodservice Showboat Hotel and Casino Atlantic City, NJ	Fixing a Problem, 307
L. Edwin Brown, AAC Executive Vice President American Culinary Federation St. Augustine, FL	What Is a Chef?, 8
Charles Carroll, CEC Executive Chef The Balsams Grand Resort Hotel Dixville Notch, NH	Team Building, 75
Alfonso Contrisciani, CEC Assistant Professor College of Culinary Arts Johnson & Wales University Providence, RI	Leadership in a Busy Kitchen, 147
Noel Cullen, Ed.D., CMC, AAC Boston University Boston, MA	My First Day, 228 Pioneer Apprentice, 89 Power and Authority, 142 Teaching Old Dogs New Tricks, 169 Using the Correct Language, 289
Bert P. Cutino, CEC, AAC Co-owner, The Sardine Factory Restaurant on Cannery Row Monterey, CA	Plan the Work and Work the Plan, 263

*Certification levels of the American Culinary Federation are:

CC:	Certified Cook	CCE:	Certified Culinary Educator
CSC:	Certified Sous Chef	CEC:	Certified Executive Chef
CCC:	Certified Chef de Cuisine	CMC:	Certified Master Chef
CWPC:	Certified Working Pastry Chef	CMPC:	Certified Master Pastry Chef
CWC:	Certified Working Chef	AAC:	Member American Academy of Chefs

Ken Wade, CEC, AAC
Chef/Operator
Jupiter Foodservice
Jupiter, FL

Coaching, 17

Thomas L. Wright
Vice President
College of Culinary Arts
Johnson & Wales University
Providence, RI

Total Quality Communication, 114

Foreword

Culinary supervision, training, and management are indeed timely subjects. After reading *The World of Culinary Supervision, Training, and Management*, I find that the subject of culinary management is one that is rarely talked about, much less practiced. Chefs in supervisory positions are not often trained to manage a staff. Because of this, a chef often overcompensates by being too much of a boss, giving orders and never listening to the other members of the kitchen team. This book fills a void in the industry and brings the matter of supervision in the kitchen to the fore.

Noel Cullen offers a unique perspective, of the chef as supervisor and mentor. He demonstrates the value and the importance of everyone understanding and striving for teamwork within a foodservice/restaurant setting. He effectively explores the concept of total quality management and total quality communication, brand-new concepts in the foodservice industry. Total quality management in kitchens is fast becoming a valuable tool, as more attention is focused on customer satisfaction.

This book is aimed at teaching chefs how to implement the concept of teamwork in a kitchen environment. I believe this book will be a valuable resource for any chef who is faced with the challenge of managing a dynamic and diverse kitchen staff.

Ferdinand E. Metz, CMC
President, The Culinary Institute of America

Preface

WHY THIS BOOK WAS WRITTEN

Increasingly, the role of the chef requires not only high-quality culinary skills, but also skill sets that enable the supervision, leadership, and management of people and their work environment. This book is written primarily for chefs, sous chefs, chefs de cuisine, executive chefs, and all others who wish to garner the necessary knowledge, skills, and attitudes required to supervise foodservice workers. Additionally, this text may be used by chefs who are seeking supervisory skills development in order to climb the certification ladder of the American Culinary Federation Educational Institute. It is also designed for use by chef educators as a textbook suitable for inclusion in the curriculum of colleges and institutions offering culinary arts degree programs.

The chef supervisor is often a front-line cook who has been promoted from the ranks who may or may not have had any formal training in the techniques of supervision, training, or management. The first of its type, this book was written by a chef for chefs and provides a quick reference to the tried-and-true techniques of supervising and managing people in the increasingly complex foodservice work place. The emphasis throughout the book is on successful "total quality" chef supervision and the role chefs must assume if the foodservice industry is to reach its goal of total customer satisfaction.

An overview of the modern foodservice industry shows that the traditional duties of the chef have been expanded. No longer is "chefing" a singularly male preserve or purely a "craft-skills"-only position. Chefs now must lead the culinary operation by utilizing excellent supervision, training, and management techniques. They must display competency in leadership, communication, and training along with first-class technical skills in safety, sanitation, nutrition, and of course, the culinary area.

This refocusing of the traditional role of the chef is driven by the requirement to lead people and provide a work climate that fosters teamwork in the kitchen. Greater emphasis is now placed on quality, at all levels of culinary practice, which results in customer satisfaction and retention along with *employee* development and retention. Employee turnover in the foodservice industry, particularly in the kitchen, has too often been attributed to poor back-of-house supervisory skills.

TOTAL QUALITY RESPECT

Employee abuse, usually verbal, was often excused as "venting" due to the "pressure cooker" nature of the kitchen. This behavior is inexcusable under any circumstances. Successful chef supervisors are great leaders and coaches. They set standards of performance with a total quality respect for those they supervise and train.

ORGANIZATION OF THE BOOK

The World of Culinary Supervision, Training, and Management provides answers to many questions about supervising and training people in the foodservice industry. It has been designed to present different aspects of supervisory management as they affect the chef. The book is written against the background of the total quality management movement, and is the product of the author's 25 years of practical experience in the foodservice industry as a chef, sous chef, executive chef, educator, and food and beverage manager. Part I details the elements of supervision and total quality management. Part II is directed to all aspects of training as they affect the chef supervisor. Part III outlines management skills and functions with which a chef supervisor is involved. Chapters have been organized to include information necessary for the creation of the motivational, training, and coaching environments.

Sections entitled "Chef Talk" feature topics that deal with culinary supervision and present various management experiences by leading chefs in the United States. In these segments the featured chefs give anecdotes related to chapter topics.

ACKNOWLEDGMENTS

This book would not have been possible without the support and practical help of many people. I am particularly grateful to Robin Baliszewski for her gentle and professional directions. Special thanks to my teaching assistants at Boston University's School of Hospitality Administration: Nichole Accettola,

Christine McDermott, and particularly the outstanding Scott Wicke for the countless hours he spent in the library.

My warmest appreciation to Ferdinand Metz for writing the Foreword to my text. Sincere gratitude to my chef friends who contributed so generously of their time and experiences in the "Chef Talk" sections.

To my wife Linda, who typed and made sense of my ramblings, and my son Darragh for his understanding, my loving thanks.

I wish also to thank everyone at Prentice Hall and WordCrafters, including Rosemary Florio and Tally Morgan.

I would like to acknowledge the following reviewers for their astute observations, comments and assistance:

Kirk Williams, CCE, LederWolff Culinary Academy, Sacramento, CA

John D. Britto, CEC, Delta College, Stockton, CA

Thomas L. Wright, Johnson & Wales, Providence, RI

Michael A. Piccinino, Shasta College, Redding, CA

Jeanne Curtis, Newbury College, Brookline, MA

Noel C. Cullen, Ed.D., CMC, AAC
Boston University

Part 1   The Chef as Supervisor

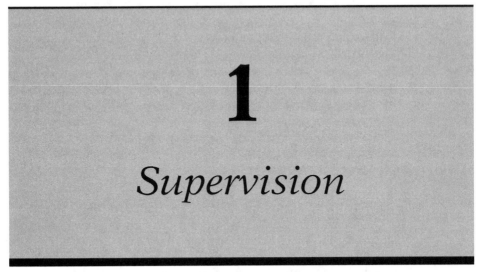

1

Supervision

Outline

- Introduction
- Supervision defined
- Attributes of the successful chef supervisor
- Chef supervisory role models
- Duties and functions of the chef supervisor
- The chef supervisor and TQM
- Elements of kitchen supervision
- Concept of authority
- The evolution of supervisory chefs
- Conclusions
- Summary
- Discussion questions

Objectives

When you complete this chapter, you should be able to:

1. Identify the central position the chef supervisor occupies in assisting management to reach the goals of total quality management.

2. Identify and discuss the attributes, skills, duties, and functions of the chef supervisor.

3. Outline the key elements and ingredients of a desirable kitchen work environment.

4. Understand the difference between culinary skills and human skills and the role each plays in the supervisory and management process.

5. Indicate trends and new dimensions associated with the development of the chef supervisor.

6. Recognize the role chef supervisors play with regard to management, customers, and team members.

INTRODUCTION

Webster's New World Dictionary 1988 defines the word *chef* as follows: 1. a cook in charge of a kitchen, as of a restaurant; lead cook, 2. any cook. The literal English translation from French means "chief" or "director." The universally accepted definition in the foodservice industry is that the chef is the chief cook in the kitchen; the word *supervisor* is not yet generally applied to them. However, in today's modern foodservice industry the chef is not only expected to be a first-class culinarian who can create gastronomic masterpieces, but also a supervisor who can motivate and lead the kitchen team toward the goals of total quality management (TQM) and be able to do this in a way that will maximize profits and please the customer. And all of this must be accomplished in a compressed time period in a potentially stressful environment. It is therefore essential that chefs who supervise kitchen operations today be equipped with the finest culinary skills along with the highest quality supervisory, training, and management skills. The following chapters will explore, outline, and develop the elements that contribute to making the modern chef supervisor. This book is not about cooking or food cost controls, but it does concern itself with the recipes and ingredients that make up the modern culinary supervisor, who is a combination of culinarian, leader, coach, trainer, and manager.

The qualifications for the chef supervisor's job are impressive. Chefs need to be technically competent and know the aspects that make up professional culinary practices: the processes, equipment, and quality standards. Technical competency also means knowing the foodservice organization's rules and the statutory regulations that govern the kitchen, from safety and sanitation standards to government regulations and labor laws. Chefs are selected to be supervisors because, among other things, they are good workers. Chef supervisors who fail do not do so because they lack technical culinary skills, but because they are unable to get others to work effectively. They lack good people skills. Therefore, potentially all chefs are supervisors because of the necessity to work with others to satisfy guests.

Some foodservice organizations are content with a kitchen staff that functions traditionally. Other managers, using the same number of people doing similar tasks with the same equipment and technology, manage to improve productivity dramatically by establishing a climate where people are willing to give their best and work in teams. When chefs acquire supervisory skills, they too can become outstanding supervisors who can build great culinary teams.

SUPERVISION DEFINED

Simply put, a supervisor is anyone in the position of directing the work of others and who has the authority that goes with this responsibility. The legal status is defined by the Taft-Hartley Act, which states that a supervisor is

> any individual having authority, in the interest of the employer, to hire, transfer, suspend, lay off, recall, promote, discharge, assign, reward or discipline other employees, or responsibility to direct them, or to adjust their grievances, or effectively to recommend such action, if in connection with the foregoing the exercise of such authority is not merely routine or clerical in nature, but requires the use of independent judgement.*

The knowledge and skills required to be a successful chef supervisor fall into four broad skill categories: personal, interpersonal, technical, and administrative.

Supervision in a kitchen requires not only a highly skilled chef but one who has the vision to know what to do, the necessary skills to know how to do it, and the ability to get it done by empowering other people to carry out quality standards of performance. Supervision, therefore, concerns those chefs who have the ability to communicate, plan, organize, train, lead, coach, and correct and at the same time stimulate the kitchen team to meet the establishment's goals and objectives. These objectives are achieved through supervising people in an effective and caring way and by creating a motivational environment in the kitchen and ensuring that necessary resources are available so that quality meals can be produced that meet and exceed customer expectations every time.

Philip Crosby, one of the founding "gurus" of total quality, states that "in the final equation, the supervisor is the person the employee sees as the company. The type of work accomplished and the attendance maintained by employees are very much indications of their relationship with the supervisor" (1).

Crosby suggests that the good supervisor can overcome, at least to some extent, the poor management practices of a weak company. At the other extreme, the weak supervisor can offset the good management practices of a good company.

---

*Alfred W. Travers. *Supervision Techniques and New Dimensions*. Prentice Hall, Englewood Cliffs, 1993, p. 13.

The role of supervision generally has changed. No longer can supervisors expect to control people. In the past some chefs were viewed as autocratic. Today, this chef supervisory role has shifted to one of coach. The effectiveness of the chef as coach and supervisor is measured not just by customer satisfaction and customer retention but also through the ability of the kitchen staff to carry out the workload to meet and exceed set standards of quality. Poor chef supervisory skills impact not only on the quality of the food produced but also on the work climate and the kitchen team, the results of which are unhappy customers and high levels of employee turnover.

ATTRIBUTES OF THE SUCCESSFUL CHEF SUPERVISOR

Successful chef supervisors who see themselves as coaches undoubtedly make a greater impact in the foodservice industry. New business and management philosophies clearly advocate the supervisor as a coach and outline a modern approach to supervision. Bill Marvin, in his book *The Foolproof Foodservice Selection System*, suggests a new focus for supervisors:

> to acting as facilitator, as enablers, and as people whose jobs are the development of people and their skills. When the foodservice staff starts to look at the person in charge more as a coach, their impression of their jobs change. When the supervisory positions in your operation carry the title of coach, I believe supervisors will approach their work from a fundamentally different direction . . . the coach's job could be defined as achieving success through the activities of others. (2)

What, then, are the attributes of chef supervisors who see themselves as coaches? As in all good coaching, the coach tries to get the best possible performance from the team through motivation, training, leadership communication, and demonstrating respect for all the team players with an acute awareness of their different strengths and weaknesses. Being sympathetic and approachable is clearly an asset. Unfortunately, in many instances these qualities are not traditionally associated with chefs. In the past chefs were viewed as supervisors who ruled the kitchen with a rod of iron.

Apart from excellent practical culinary skills, excellent chef supervisors develop the following "mise-en-place" as part of their personal inventories:

- Positive mental attitude
- Enthusiasm toward work
- Innovativeness in dealing with problems
- Honesty and sincerity
- Awareness of employee problems
- Respect and courtesy in communicating with employees

- Impeccable personal hygiene and grooming
- Technical competence
- High motivation with the ability to motivate others
- Consistency
- Assertive and action-oriented personality
- Tolerance of diversity in the kitchen
- Ability to trust others
- Constant search for new ways to enhance skills
- Ability to praise others when deserved
- Leadership by example
- Team building skills
- Loyalty toward organizational goals and employees
- Love of cooking
- Ability to maintain control
- Good listening skills
- Desire to please the customer
- Good persuasive skills and interest in imparting knowledge

Chef supervisors, perhaps more than any other category of supervisor, need to be able to bring all of these qualities to the kitchen work environment and be able to coach and supervise under the pressures of busy meal service periods. Additionally, the chef supervisor should have the ability to understand the feelings, attitudes, and motives of others, communicate effectively, and establish good relations with the kitchen team and all other departments in the foodservice organization. These attributes apply whether the chef is employed in a restaurant, hotel, institution, club, the military, education, or any other foodservice organization.

CHEF SUPERVISORY ROLE MODELS

Professionalism and ethics are not only desirable in the chef supervisor but also essential. Ethics refers to the moral principles of individuals and society. Together with professional practice, ethics is concerned with the determination of right and wrong in human behavior. A code of ethics is particularly important in the foodservice industry. Employees and employers are affected by poor ethical and professional standards on the part of chef supervisors, but more importantly the health and safety of the public is at stake.

An ethical code of professional practice is necessary for both employees and supervisor: "It serves as a framework in which various other standards can be evaluated" (3). Issues of professional practices include policies such as hiring/firing, confidentiality, stealing, lying, malicious gossip, harassment, racial, gender, or ethnic slurs, and any action that causes the loss of human dignity.

Additionally, the chef supervisor should administer a code of professional practice fairly and without bias to all employees regardless of their position, gender, and ethnic or religious backgrounds.

History has provided us with examples of outstanding chef supervisors as role models. These chefs, renowned for their culinary prowess and advancement of culinary art through new gastronomic creations, new techniques of cooking, improvements in kitchen design, and contributions in nutrition, are an inspiration. Yet, when we examine why these chefs are role models, it is not surprising to discover that they were also excellent managers, supervisors, trainers, and coaches with great legacies of passing onto others their knowledge, skills, and high personal and professional standards.

Antoine Careme, who came from humble beginnings in the postrevolution era of France, was probably the first role model for chefs. The sixteenth child of a workman, Careme had few advantages. He entered the kitchen as an apprentice chef at the age of 10. He taught himself how to read and write and wrote several books before his death at the age of 50. From his writings we get a sense of his professionalism. Describing a banquet, he provides a glimpse of the awful working conditions chefs had to endure at that time (4):

> Imagine yourself in a large kitchen such as that of the Foreign Minister at the moment of a great banquet [Talleyrand was Foreign Minister at the time]. There one sees twenty chefs at their urgent occupations, coming, going, moving with speed in this cauldron of heat. Look at the great mass of live charcoal, a cubic meter for the cooking of the soups, the sauces, the ragouts, the frying and the bain maries. Add to that the heap of burning coals in front of which bears a sirloin weighing 45–60 lbs, and another two for fowl and game. In this furnace everyone moves with tremendous speed; not a sound is heard; only the chef has the right to make himself heard, and at the sound of his voice everyone obeys. He concludes by saying . . . "Honor commands, we must obey even though physical strength fails. But, it is the burning charcoal which kills us."

Careme's power and influence is due not only to his writings and culinary creations, which still survive today, but also to his character and personality. His professionalism throughout his life asserted a new prestige for the chef. He was an innovator and simplifier who demonstrated all the elements of being an outstanding chef leader and supervisor.

Alexis Soyer, born in 1809, lived almost exactly as long as the great Careme. Soyer's greatest days were as the chef at London's Reform Club. He also gained fame by being invited to go to Crimea, where he did for military cooking what Florence Nightingale did for nursing. His dynamic contributions in the area of culinary arts and management included development of a luxury restaurant during the Great London Exhibition, a soup kitchen, and a cookbook priced for the poorer classes. He also invented a military cooking stove that was still in use during World War II. Soyer was an outstanding example of a chef leader. He could hold his own among the professional class of his time as much by his own personal qualities as by his culinary skills. He helped to further enhance the image of the chef through his writings and his superb organizational skills and leadership abilities.

Auguste Escoffier, known as the "King of Chefs" and the "Chef of Kings," dominated the first quarter of the 20th century and continues to influence chefs and the culinary arts to this day. Escoffier is perhaps still the greatest role model for chefs as a culinarian and as one of the greatest chef supervisors and coaches of all time.

He was a man whose talents dovetailed into the trends of his times and who was fortunate to be linked with a man who was perhaps the greatest hotelier of all time, Caesar Ritz. In the early part of the 20th century, economic and social forces were changing, as were the dining and wining habits of society. Escoffier sensed perfectly the needs of these times and was prepared not only to go with trends but to anticipate them. He refined and simplified classic cuisine and created dishes that have become part of the classic cuisine repertoire. He was a supreme organizer. It was he who created the "Partie System," a system that streamlined the work flows and processes of the foodservice industry.

Escoffier was a pioneer in the movement toward exquisite simplicity. He believed in the simple concept that food should look like food. Other firsts attributed to Escoffier include (5):

1. He required cooks to wear the newly fashioned jacket and check trousers.
2. He insisted on the highest standards of personal hygiene from his employees.
3. He was an advocate of education and strongly supported schooling for his employees.
4. He moved the kitchen out of its traditional location in basements.
5. He demonstrated a high level of personal professionalism.
6. He discouraged his staff from smoking and drinking.

His obvious wisdom and professionalism explain why *Le Guide Culinaire* is still the most esteemed textbook of the professional chef in the world. Escoffier was not a prisoner of the classic traditions. Clearly a man of great foresight, his writing encouraged change so as to meet evolving culinary trends, a process that still continues today. Having started his career at the age of 12 (in 1859) Escoffier retired from active duty at the Carlton in London in 1921. He was then 74 years old and had practiced his art for over 62 years. Throughout the history of foodservice, there is no better example of professionalism. Escoffier remains today the supreme example of the professional chef with impeccable ethical standards—a leader who constantly sought to elevate and raise the image and prestige of the culinary profession. He achieved this through superb culinary art *and* brilliant supervisory, organizational, and "coaching" ability, all directed to the gastronomic satisfaction of his customers.

To be a leader, no matter what field of endeavor you are in, it is necessary to adopt a code of professional ethics to which others will aspire. It has been said that those preparing food for consumption by the public require higher ethical standards than those in the manufacturing sector. Food workers lacking in professional ethics are a threat not only to the image of the food-service industry but more importantly to the health and safety of the public. True culinary professionalism will always embrace high ethical standards.

Chef Talk: "What Is a Chef?

Somewhere between the innocence of the new pot-washer and the majestic indignation of the local tycoon (who wants a special dinner tonight and you're booked solid) there is a harassed, tormented, overworked, underpaid, pitiful creature known as the "chef."

The chef is also the manager, the cook, the boss, and the supervisor.

Chefs come in all sizes, shapes, and conditions. You find them everywhere—upstairs, downstairs, at the range, in the freezer, checking portions, repairing equipment, in the kitchen, in the dining room, in the supply room, in the office, or in the pantry.

A chef is patience with a clenched fist, humor with fingers crossed, experience with scars on hands, imagination with a recipe, and a childlike trust in the honesty of guests.

A chef has the work capacity of a computer, the energy of a lion, the curiosity of a cat, the lungs of an umpire, and the enthusiasm of a child at a circus.

A chef loves big parties, prompt arrivals, full tables, quick turnovers, cheerful employees, happy patrons, clean dining rooms, good waiters and waitresses, and free publicity.

They aren't much for clutter, clatter, waste, carelessness, mistakes, delays, gripes, accidents, complaints, deadbeats, burned food, drunks, or employees who don't show up for work.

Chefs are amazing creatures. When you want them, you can't find them; when you don't, they are looking over your shoulder.

You can keep them out of sorts, but you can't keep them out of your hair. You can frustrate their desires, but you can't frustrate their drive. You can top their jokes, but you can't top their performance. They are our inspiration, our example, our parent image, our critic, our conscience, and our despair.

But when the dining rooms are full and the guests are smiling, the chef is the personification of benevolence and lovable magnanimity.

And when they go to the last great banquet, St. Peter will smile a warm welcome, bow, and ask, "Are you sure you have a reservation?"

L. Edwin Brown, Executive Vice President, American Culinary Federation, St Augustine, FL
Paraphrased from "What Is a Boy" by Alan Beck.

DUTIES AND FUNCTIONS
OF THE CHEF SUPERVISOR

In the past chef supervisors reported mainly to the food and beverage manager. In many foodservice establishments the manager supervised food and beverage operations, of which kitchen operations were a major portion. The food and beverage manager, or some higher level of management, usually evaluated the chef supervisor on the limited criteria of the achievement of a 30 percent food cost, along with the smooth production of meals with a minimum level of customer complaints. If this was achieved, then the manner by which it was achieved was left up to the chef. All major decisions regarding menu positioning and the recruitment, orientation, training, and termination of employees were within the manager's domain. Today, that is not the case. The functions of the chef as a supervisor, trainer, coach, and manager have widened considerably.

As decision making is pushed downward, the modern chef, in addition to being a highly skilled culinarian, must also be many other things: a people developer, supervisor, coach, and team builder, in short a front-line leader with a major role to play in the development of the foodservice establishment.

The traditional notion of the chef supervisor was that this person supervised the foodservice operation from the back door to the front door—primarily responsible for receiving food products at the back door and then their processing by a kitchen team into a customer meal at the front door.

Issues of quality management of the product in this process were given only cursory attention. Quality human resources management involving kitchen staff as a team was not a major concern. This system was authoritarian by nature; directives and orders were given, with little or no input from employees and even less interest in what the customers had to say. The modern chef supervisor is a team leader who exhibits a different style than those who were content with simply supervising or managing the kitchen.

This historical portrayal of the chef supervisor as an unreasonable temperamental artist has no place in the modern foodservice industry. It never had a place there, and it would not, quite correctly, be tolerated by management or staff today. Foodservice workers, like other workers, need to be recognized as contributing team members and want to know what is expected of them by their chef supervisor. As in other areas of industry, kitchen employees need an open and communicative environment where they can develop a sense of belonging and where there is even-handed and fair treatment by the chef supervisor. They want to give their best, and it's up to the chef supervisor to ensure that this work climate is provided. This is vital because a chef supervisor's success depends upon his or her staff.

Today's chef supervisor is a customer-driven professional skilled in all aspects of high-quality food production and supervisory skills. The principal driving force behind the modern chef is customer satisfaction—managing the culinary operation from the front door to the back door rather than the other way around. One of the main reasons customers stop patronizing a foodser-

Chef Talk: "The Autocrat"

There was a time when chefs believed it was necessary to act out the often portrayed image of the crazy, unreasonable, temperamental chef. This disposition often manifested itself in undesirable traits such as shouting, throwing things around the kitchen, and arguing loudly with waiters, other chefs, and managers. The kitchen area was a hostile domain. These old-style chefs were not approachable; they were aloof and generally indifferent to employees. I particularly remember, as an apprentice chef, that I "knew my place" as a lowly trainee and was expected not to converse with those higher than me. In fact, open communication was not the order of the day. The pecking order was through the supervisory layers; chef, chef de partie, sous chef, and finally the head chef. Heaven forbid if you had to ask for time off within your scheduled time. I came to work scared and left scared for the first year of my apprenticeship. Back then, the head chef practically had the power of life or death over each member of the kitchen staff. I believe that if the work climate in the kitchen had been different then and more conducive to communication I would have learned a lot more and probably could have contributed more to the operational goals. That head chef was eventually dismissed, and the day he left the kitchen staff had a party.

Noel C. Cullen, Ed.D. CMC AAC Boston University, Boston, MA

vice establishment is an attitude of indifference by the staff. It makes little sense to prepare food that customers don't want. The chef should be aware of customers' preferences and be trained in all the contributing elements of customer satisfaction.

There are many new and not so new elements of supervising the functions involved in food production. Many of these ideas have swung with the pendulum of different management faddisms over the years, such as rationalization, down-sizing, risk management, yield management, management by objective, and so on. However, several will remain part of a chef supervisor's arsenal of skills.

THE CHEF SUPERVISOR AND TQM

Take all the evidence together and a clear picture of the successful company in the next century and beyond emerges. It will be (6):

- Flatter
- Populated by more autonomous units

- Oriented toward differentiation
- Quality conscious
- Service conscious
- More responsive
- Much faster at innovation and
- A user of highly trained, flexible people as the principle means of adding value

Traditionally the foodservice industry has been a follower rather than a leader in the area of management and supervisory theories. Most management models were developed with the manufacturing industry in mind. The hospitality and foodservice industries were strongly people oriented and sold services to and made a profit from people. They were less inclined to embrace these new theories of management, which were not always people centered.

Marketing has always been based on the four P's: price, product, place, and promotion. Now a fifth P has been added: *people*. Most of the initiatives and outcrops of the quality management movement involve the expenditure of time and an investment in developing people. The overreliance in the past on the narrow technical skills of supervision produced a supervisor not overly endowed with leadership qualities. Control was more of an issue than coaching and team building; certainly the old style chefs were big on control and power. Total quality management will only thrive in a business environment that espouses a culture conducive to a total quality process.

According to Mike Hurst, owner of 15 Street Fisheries in Fort Lauderdale and former president of the National Restaurant Association, "the foodservice sector of the hospitality industry, now at 9 million employees, will grow to 12 million in the U.S. by the year 2000."* As the foodservice industry grows, there will be a greater need for chefs with people skills along with great culinary talent and a strong customer focus. These elements will produce a formidable combination in any chef supervisor.

At the heart of TQM is the conviction that it is possible to achieve error-free quality product most of the time. This assertion is phrased in various ways as getting it right the first time, working smarter, or zero defects. Total quality management is not only about external customers, it is also about internal customers. In his book *The Essence of Total Quality Management*, John Bank observed (7):

> There is also the internal customer, the person within the company who receives the work of another and then adds his or her contribution to the product or service before passing it on to someone else. In a restaurant, the chef has the waiters and waitresses as internal customers and the chef must meet their requirements if they are all to please the guest.

*From a speech delivered at ACF National Convention, Orlando, FL, 1993.

Total quality management, as it applies to the foodservice industry and in particular the kitchen, is here to stay. It is a commitment to quality applied to all aspects of a foodservice organization's operations, which include quality food specifications, customer satisfaction focus, training techniques, leadership, communication, planning, organizing, championing employees, and team building, all combining not only to produce highly satisfied customers who will promote the business by telling others of their satisfaction and returning again, but most importantly to produce a highly motivated kitchen team.

We can no longer view the duties of a chef to be only mildly customer oriented; they have widened considerably and require that the chef supervisor become aggressively involved in getting the customer's viewpoint through either focus groups or formal surveys. This involves tapping the brainpower of every foodservice worker. Increased customer awareness and new supervisory and management skills all combine to mold the modern chef. It is therefore important that the chef supervisor be secure enough in his or her level of understanding of this refocused role to delegate and trust kitchen team members to carry out the workload to the required quality standards. There is no magic to being a good chef supervisor. It just takes some understanding of human behavior combined with the timely application of effective leadership.

ELEMENTS OF KITCHEN SUPERVISION

Supervising

Supervision can be best described as the most effective and timely use of personnel and materials to achieve the goals of customer satisfaction and retention by maintaining a highly motivated, well-trained kitchen team. Within this process the chef supervisor actively participates in the employment of chefs and other kitchen support team members.

Part of this process is the recruitment and interviewing of potential kitchen team members. Procedures for recruitment may vary. Placing advertisements in newspapers, magazines, or trade journals is the preferred method, while others recruit employees directly from culinary schools and colleges or through professional headhunter organizations. Checking job applicants' resumes and references and interviewing these applicants fall within the chef supervisor's functions. Other elements of the chef supervisor's general duties include:

- Preparation of new employee induction/orientation programs
- Assessment of training needs
- Preparation of training objectives
- Development of standards of performance
- Implementation of total quality standards

- On-going and continuous training and team building
- Coaching and correcting employees
- Setting high standards of personal hygiene and grooming
- Setting excellent standards of conduct and fairness
- Developing and encouraging teamwork
- Providing decisive leadership
- Building and fostering professional pride
- Providing timely employee feedback on performance
- Encouraging a desire to meet and exceed customer expectations
- Demonstrating a total quality respect for all kitchen team members

Planning

Following the successful invasion of Europe by Allied forces during World War II it was suggested to the supreme commander of the successful invading forces, General Eisenhower, that he must have had an outstanding plan to have carried out such a massive operation, moving thousands of men and equipment with all the ancillary support of materials and men. His response to this question was most enlightening: "The plan is nothing, but planning is everything" (8).

In addition to the obvious need to plan menus, considerable planning is required to run a smooth, efficient foodservice operation. The first step in all good planning is to plan time to plan. The major areas of planning for the chef supervisor include:

- Planning and forecasting workloads
- Preparing employee work schedules
- Ascertaining guest satisfaction levels
- Planning equipment repair and replacements
- Determining food and supply inventories
- Developing employee empowerment programs
- Planning future personnel levels
- Providing effective communication with team members and other departments
- Determining training needs
- Setting standards of performance
- Conducting employee performance appraisals

Organizing

When plans have been made, it is necessary to organize people and materials to secure the successful fulfillment of these plans. This happens through good organizational ability on the part of the chef supervisor by using the available resources and being prepared to adapt as circumstances and conditions warrant. Typical organizational goals of a kitchen department are:

- Organizing the kitchen team to produce and serve meals in the most efficient, economical, and effective fashion and utilizing each team member within a limited time period and within criteria of effort and productivity
- Organizing and determining the five of W's of empowerment: who, what, where, when, and why
- Defining job tasks, analyses, and descriptions
- Preparing task lists to accomplish the planned goals
- Determining relationships with each member of the kitchen team together with management, other departments, and customers
- Organizing support areas of purchasing, receiving, storage, and stewarding
- Organizing training sessions
- Organizing and implementing employee empowerment and reward systems
- Organizing and implementing recycling programs

Coaching

This means guiding and correcting kitchen staff to perform their jobs in a way that is compatible with the goals and objectives of the organization. It means the creation of an environment in which staff feel comfortable enough to give of their best. Good coaching requires excellent communication and leadership skills, but more importantly it requires chef supervisors who trust people. They should be consistent and not subject to wild mood swings; be fair at all times, firm when appropriate, approachable, and friendly; and possess an overriding commitment to the "team" concept. Additionally, the chef supervisor is the linking pin to two groups: management and players. A good coaching style involves:

- An interest in people attaining personal goals
- Sincerity, honesty, fairness, and impartiality
- Sensitivity and respect for different cultures
- Strong ethical and moral values
- Respect for the dignity of every individual in the team
- An emphasis on the future rather than the past
- A positive people attitude
- Praising where praise is due
- Correcting mistakes without apportioning blame

Forming a team within the kitchen, developing the skills of its members, and enabling them to work together are the initial steps in any TQM program. These first steps must be sustained by continuous analysis of results along with the corresponding adjustments and improvements to the changing objectives of the kitchen's total quality plan. The chef supervisor therefore must be an adept coach who is constantly improving and applying good coaching techniques toward the kitchen team so as to meet the needs of the situation and the customer's gastronomic satisfaction.

Team Building

Kitchen employees can be developed into teams with the help of a committed chef supervisor. Within an effective kitchen team each member plays an assigned role. When the members integrate their skills to build on strengths and minimize weaknesses, foodservice quality objectives are assured of success. On the other hand, when the kitchen staff are poorly led and work as individuals, they will often fail. Unfortunately, many chef supervisors fail to recognize their roles as team builders. In the past many failed to understand how to transform their employees into productive teams.

Effective teamwork has no level. It is just as important among top executives as among kitchen employees. If the chef supervisor does not place high value on teamwork, it will not occur. Teamwork takes conscious efforts to develop and continuous effort to maintain. Some of these conscious efforts include the following:

- Kitchen staff and the chef supervisor commit to support each other to make the team successful.
- Team members understand priorities and support one another when difficulties arise.
- Communication is open. The expression of new ideas, improved work methods, and articulation of problems and concerns are encouraged.
- Problem solving is more effective because the collective expertise of the kitchen team is available.
- Performance feedback is more meaningful because team members understand what is expected and can monitor their performance against expectations.
- The team is recognized for outstanding results as are individual team members.
- Kitchen team members are encouraged to test their abilities and try out new ideas.
- Learning to work as a team in one department is good preparation for interacting as a team with other foodservice departments.
- Collective wisdom is virtually always superior to individual wisdom, and the team and the individual are recognized and rewarded equally.

A foodservice organization can serve its customers only as well as it serves its employees. The organization therefore must be committed to developing and supporting a highly motivated team. The chef supervisor as a team builder:

- Has confidence in the team
- Is approachable and friendly
- Is eager to help team members become more effective
- Is supportive and careful to avoid ego and emotionally threatening behavior
- Removes stress in the team
- Empowers each team member with *real* authority to make decisions
- Is flexible in leadership style relative to the individual situation
- Helps each team member to develop his or her talent
- Is a teacher as well as a supervisor and is willing to share growth and recognition with others

Championing

Organization celebration is the process of honoring individuals, groups, events, and achievements in a creative, meaningful, and positive manner. The term *championing* has replaced *control*, which implies an authoritarian narrow focus. If all the stated goals of supervision, planning, organization, coaching, and training have been accomplished, then controlling, or oversupervision of employees, is not necessary. Chef supervisors should champion the kitchen team—make heroes out of them, sing out their praises, turn "controlling" into a positive celebration of the kitchen staff's success and accomplishments. The chef supervisor should tell everybody of the team's success—give them a party, send them flowers, birthday cards, let them know they are appreciated, celebrate their successful performance. Central to the goals of championing is the investment in team building, training, and coaching and a belief that in the correct work environment the kitchen team will give their best and exceed organizational goals.

Communication

This is an integral and crucial element of the supervision process. Quality supervision often breaks down or fails as a result of poor communication. Communication is the lifeblood of supervision. All elements of supervision and management require effective communication. This process involves a sender and a receiver exchanging and understanding information so that the information can be received and understood.

Communication is the foundation for understanding, cooperation, and action. A good communication system maintains a two-way flow of ideas,

Chef Talk: "Coaching"

Building a successful kitchen team requires a great deal of patience and a lot of time and effort. Ten years ago when I took over at Harpoon Louie's (six million dollars a year in sales), I found a kitchen staff without a single professional chef on board. My first step was to recruit four experienced chefs who had worked with me before and understood what had to be done.

With the four on board a foundation was set. The professional chef's uniform was mandatory for all kitchen cooks. The fryer cooks, broiler cooks, and all other cooks were terminated and those who were interested in becoming professional chefs were rehired as apprentices. No specialized positions were offered until such time as all the cooks had become competent in all areas of the kitchen.

Hiring procedures were developed and implemented. Crucial to these new procedures was the hiring of kitchen team members who had a real and genuine interest in cooking. We started our formal apprenticeship program soon after under the auspices of the American Culinary Federation Educational Institute.

Constant coaching, in-house cooking classes, and encouragement to our apprentices to compete in professional chef competitions were key to bonding the team together. Once the team was in place and working, employee retention became a priority. As is common in other establishments, financial reward alone does not guarantee retention. It is vital to be sympathetic to the needs of the team, which can be very demanding, but with careful motivation a team spirit can be maintained.

Respect is key. It has a tremendous bearing on what type of coach you are. Unskilled employees in the kitchen are a vital part of the foodservice operation. How these team members are treated reflects dramatically on their performance level. The coach must be sure to communicate with these team members on a regular basis—coaching, correcting, and offering words of encouragement. Chefs who have had to wash their own pots know how important these team members are and have a great deal of respect for them. I very clearly see myself as a coach rather than a manager. Today kitchen staff should be led rather than managed or directed. Without a team approach at our restaurant we would not be successful.

Kenneth G. Wade, CEC AAC, President, Jupiter Foodservice Inc., Florida opinions, information, and decisions. The first step in any effort to open communication is the establishment and maintenance of a climate that encourages the free exchange of ideas. It is the umbrella under which all effective supervision lies.

Delegation

Delegation means granting to a kitchen team member the authority to oversee specific tasks and responsibilities and letting other team members know that these responsibilities have been delegated to this team member.

Telling a team member to perform a task is not delegation; it is work allocation. It may be sufficient for simple, short-term jobs, but more complex tasks that require a sustained effort should be delegated.

Before delegating the chef supervisor should determine the following:

- Does the team member understand the purpose of the task?
- Is the value of the task recognized by the team member?
- Is the workload too much for just one person?
- Has the employee been provided with detailed step-by-step instructions?
- How will satisfactory completion of the tasks be evaluated and measured?

Chef supervisors should not "delegate" those portions of their work they consider unpleasant, unimportant, or risky. Kitchen team members are seldom deceived by the chef supervisor's efforts to "dress up" the task. What usually results from such practice is resentment, demotivation, and a considerable amount of effort on the part of the team member to avoid or off-load the task.

In addition, before delegating it is useful to check the following:

- Acceptance and understanding of the task
- If a reason for delegation was given
- If the task delegated was a worthwhile and whole task
- If the team member can be trusted and encouraged to do the job correctly
- If checkpoints were built in to check progress
- If knowledge was shared by pinpointing possible problems
- If information was withheld that could have simplified and speeded up the tasks
- If sufficient training, encouragement, coaching, and leadership were provided to make the team member look good and succeed

Delegation by the chef supervisor encourages cooperation among kitchen team members, demonstrates trust in the team, and builds morale. The advantage of delegation is that the workload is spread in a planned sequential way. It allows more time for creating and planning. The chef supervisor who tries to do everything will not succeed. Support of the kitchen team is essential; it is impossible for a chef supervisor to prepare, cook, and present every meal every day. The chef supervisor who fails to delegate to other team members will be frustrated, unproductive, and be viewed as a weak leader by the entire kitchen team. (Note: See Chapter 8 on leadership.)

Empowerment

Empowerment is the process of enabling people to do what they have been trained for and are qualified to do. It means giving kitchen team members a part in the decision making. Empowering kitchen team members to take more initiative is viewed as essential to quality supervision and management. It has also become a key element in team building. There is no better way to have a vision shared and to generate commitment and loyalty than through empowerment. This comes from the combination of pushing down the decision-making process to give greater latitude to each employee and the provision of training that facilitates its inception.

In 1992, the Ritz Carlton Hotel Company won the Malcomb Baldridge National Quality Award. This was the first time a hotel company had won this award. Part of their winning strategy was called *applied employee empowerment*. According to Horst Shulze, The Ritz Carlton's Chief Operating Officer, "all our employees are empowered to do whatever it takes to provide instant pacification. No matter what their normal duties are, other employees must assist if aid is requested by a fellow worker responding to a guest's complaint or wish" (9).

Kitchen team members who are able to participate actively in decision making and express their ideas will share the company vision and become more productive. The biggest challenge to the concept of empowerment is its acceptance by chef supervisors. They must let go of the traditional power and control associated with the chef's position.

Empowerment means actively seeking ideas from team members on how to improve menus, methods of production, purchasing, quality and service of product, and the testing and tasting of dishes, encouraging innovation and allowing the team to implement their ideas. If all members of the kitchen team are empowered and come to realize that their opinions, views, and ideas are important, they will quickly take ownership of a particular innovation to which they have contributed and seek to continuously improve it.

Sanitation

Food safety is clearly an important issue for the chef supervisor. According to a Center for Disease Control and Prevention study, over six million people become ill from contaminated food annually in the United States, and almost 80 percent of these illnesses occur at foodservice establishments.

One food safety and self-inspection system that the chef supervisor should be thoroughly familiar with is the *Hazard Analysis Critical Control Point*, more commonly known as HACCP. There are many chances in the food preparation and serving flow for food to become contaminated. The HACCP system targets these areas. By emphasizing high-risk foods and handling procedures, the chef supervisor can reduce food contamination risks.

It is important, therefore, for the chef supervisor to adopt a proactive position relative to sanitation. All foodservice workers are potential disease spreaders. It requires the chef supervisor to analyze the procedures involved in the issues of food receiving, preparation, cooking, and storing, use of food leftovers, and effective supervision of sanitation. The foodservice operation should be looked at through a customer's eyes: What sanitation messages are being sent? Is the kitchen team clean and well groomed and trained in the prevention of food contamination? This important segment of the duties of the chef supervisor requires constant supervision.

Safety

The goal of excellent foodservice operation is to reduce the possibility of accidents in the kitchen. Accident prevention works best when it involves the participation and cooperation of all kitchen team members. A safety program should have incentives to encourage the entire team to work safely. Rewards may be given to kitchen team members who remain accident free. The issue of safety needs to be incorporated into induction and orientation training programs, and its importance needs to be stressed and emphasized thereafter on a continuous basis.

Technology

The chef supervisor must stay ahead of technological advances in equipment and machinery in order to be competitive and focused. New innovations in labor-saving devices and training devices become available each year, along with computer-managed information programs that allow more time for the chef supervisor to concentrate on developing and coaching kitchen team members to become more efficient team players.

Leadership

This is what drives TQM in all situations and at all levels. Leadership styles and skills are vital to making all the factors and elements of supervision in the kitchen work. Because almost everything necessary for high-quality supervision requires effective communication and leadership skills, these topics are treated in depth in Chapters 5 and 6.

CONCEPT OF AUTHORITY

The chef supervisor is the formal leader of the group by virtue of the authority of the position. Supervisory success for the chef, however, is dependent on more than this source of authority. It is dependent on many skills. The greater the chef supervisor's skill in developing a team, the greater the productivity and satisfaction of the whole kitchen team. When team-building skills are applied rather than solely authoritarian leadership, foodservice employees cooperate more with each other and other departments as well as developing better interpersonal relationships and a great team spirit. The requisites of authority are as follows:

- To require an obedience in which employees retain their freedom
- To strike a balance between itself and individual freedom
- To lead individuals towards growth
- To possess practical judgment skills
- To act as a uniting element of a group's common goals
- To enhance cooperative efforts
- To reserve the right and power to make decisions

For authority to be genuine, chef supervisors exercising that authority must know what they are requesting of team members and why they are making those requests. Authority for the sake of power is useless. It must seek to inspire desired outcomes from each person. Requests or demands made on employees without good reason often lead to anger and frustration on the part of both the employee and the chef supervisor. Remember, kitchen team members will respond more freely to a request than they will to an order.

THE EVOLUTION OF SUPERVISORY CHEFS

As has often been said, the primary difference between the United States and Japan in the area of human resource management is that in Japan people are managed as a true resource whereas in the United States people are managed as a cost center. While this is not entirely true, the concept of utilizing the collective human resources of an organization in a way that makes employees feel that they are participative members of a team is relatively new, certainly in the foodservice industry. Foodservice organizations often lagged behind the manufacturing industry in the provision of a work environment where employees are encouraged to contribute to decisions, which ultimately impacted on the single most important issue of customer satisfaction.

Chefs often complained that in many instances they were the last to be consulted on topics such as kitchen design, menu concepts, and supervision of kitchen employees. However, management often complained that chefs were difficult to deal with and did not want any part of issues chefs considered to be the food and beverage manager's responsibilities. Competition has increased, and foodservice organizations must now pursue a more discerning and diverse customer who has an acute awareness of first-class service, good food, and the value for money. There is therefore a need to have chef supervisors committed to a strong customer focus and, more importantly, to developing the kitchen team and the kitchen work environment to meet these new competitive challenges. In order to prepare the chef supervisor in modern approaches to the creation of a motivational kitchen environment, the following elements trace the evolution of two theories of people management. Additionally, this section of the chapter will examine the different trends, directions, and strategies that have evolved to meet the current foodservice business climate.

Hawthorne Studies

Begun in the 1920s, the Hawthorne studies represented an effort to determine what effect hours of work, periods of rest, and lighting might have on worker fatigue and productivity. These experiments were conducted by university professors Elton Mayo, Fritz Roethlisberger, and J. W. Dickson at the Western Electric Company's Hawthorne Works near Chicago, Illinois. These studies represented one of the first endeavors to evaluate employee productivity. The Hawthorne studies revealed that the attitudes employees had toward management, their work group, and the work itself significantly affected their productivity. Initially, the results of the research on the small study group baffled the researchers. Despite altering the work environment and measuring their productivity against this changing environment (reduction of rest periods and the elimination of rest time), the productivity of the study group increased continuously, and this group had fewer sick days than other workers who were not in the research group.

The leaders of the research group concluded that productivity increased, not as a result of any of their contrived stimuli, but rather as a result of the absence of any authoritarian supervision and the interest shown in employees by the researchers. The fact that they were being studied was sufficient for the workers to improve productivity. This phenomenon is still referred to by researchers as the Hawthorne effect: Change will occur simply because people know they are being studied rather than as a result of some form of treatment. However, the most important result of the Hawthorne studies was that people respond better when they have a sense of belonging.

The findings of the Hawthorne studies produced a new direction for people management. As a result of these studies a greater emphasis was placed on managing employees, with a concern for them as individuals. They also focused attention on the need for managers and supervisors to improve their communication skills and become more sensitive to employee needs and feelings. This new movement also emphasized the need for developing more participative employee-centered supervision.

In the 1940s, Renis Likert conducted research into the creation of a productive and desirable work climate. He observed four approaches to supervision and leadership (10). The first type was an authoritative approach that is potentially explosive. It involves high pressure on subordinates through work standards. It obtained compliance through fear techniques. This approach resulted in high productivity over short periods and low productivity and high absenteeism over longer periods. The second approach was authoritarian but benevolent in nature. The third approach was a consultative supervisor/employee approach. The fourth approach was group participative, in which the supervisor was supportive and used group methods of supervision, including group decision making. The last three approaches yielded high productivity, low waste, and low costs along with low absenteeism and employee turnover.

Likert also developed the "linking pin" concept, which focused on coordinating efforts through layers of middle management. It provided a formal structured approach. Central to its philosophy was the idea that each level of management is a member of a multifunctional team that includes the next upward level.

We can only guess at how long it took for this new supervision focus to permeate the foodservice industry. Supervision in kitchens has a long history of being authoritarian with a resulting high staff turnover. The rise of modern human resources management in the foodservice sector of the hospitality industry directly parallels the major demographic changes in U.S. society. Highly trained chefs, usually of European origin, were in high demand during the 1960s and 1970s. Most of these chef positions were in hotels. The foodservice industry grew during the 1970s and 1980s with the explosive growth of popular chain and fast-food restaurants. Trained chefs were in short supply. It was also during the 1970s and 1980s that the growth of culinary schools and programs was witnessed. In addition to the culinary education expansion, there was tremendous growth in restaurant, hospital, institutional, and industrial foodservice sectors, which also became more customer focused and sensitive.

New Trends

The employee-centered supervisory element of the chef's position became more important when there was an acute shortage of trained kitchen staff during the 1970s and 1980s. Culinary schools could not keep up with the demands for skilled chef graduates. During this period apprenticeship programs for chefs were introduced by the American Culinary Federation, which in turn required the chef supervisor to acquire instructor training skills. It was during this period that the chef as supervisor began to evolve, chefs became more aware of the needs of their predominantly American culinary college trained chefs, and the satisfaction of those needs became a vital part of the chef supervisor's job.

Chefs with supervisory and management skills recognized the necessity to recruit not only employees for their technical knowledge but also those chefs who matched a particular culture fostered by the foodservice organization. Career development, training, leadership, and participation were seen as retention tools that contribute to fostering employee loyalty to the foodservice organization.

The 1980s was a very exciting time for the U.S. foodservice industry. The economy was strong with rapid job growth. These good times brought about a change in American dining habits with a higher level of gastronomic sophistication. People were traveling more and consequently gained more exposure to different cuisines. There was even a glamor associated with being a chef. This changed in the 1990s. Now for a chef to be successful, it was necessary to possess additional skills, along with a new attitude to food production, which had to be customer driven and focused on quality. Also, chefs were now required to provide a motivational kitchen environment, one which kitchen team members could "buy into."

CONCLUSIONS

Quality permeates every aspect of what a chef does, from the aspect of culinary art to total quality supervision. These are watchwords for the modern chef: quality in cooking and quality respect toward other kitchen team members. This must be driven by meeting and exceeding customers' satisfaction levels through quality food production and service. This will produce the consummate professional chef supervisor. Quality is a continuous process, not a destination (11).

Chef supervisors are the middle persons, with responsibilities to senior management, customers, and other team members. By understanding the different elements that are part of a chef supervisor's role, it becomes easier to refocus efforts toward creating the motivational environment in the kitchen. Experience has shown that when all kitchen team members actively participate in the day-to-day decision making and are empowered with real authority, what results is not only a more pleasant and productive environment but also a more creative culinary one.

SUMMARY

The modern chef supervisor's skill sets include the abilities to coach and lead the entire kitchen team by creating the motivational environment. Successful chef supervisors see themselves as facilitators and enablers whose job it is to develop the kitchen team. This means demonstrating attributes that include an understanding of feelings and attitudes that motivate the entire kitchen team.

Chef supervisors should:

- Practice a code of ethics and administer this code fairly and without bias to all kitchen team members
- Emulate the outstanding chef role models history has provided, from Careme to Escoffier

- Apply the tenets of TQM and be customer satisfaction driven professionals
- Know, understand, and apply the elements of supervision and how these elements interrelate with the foodservice organization's goals, the other departments, and the kitchen team
- Know and understand the various steps in planning, organizing, coaching, team building, communicating, delegating, empowering, safety, sanitation, leadership, and technology
- Separate and know the concepts of authority, power, and leadership

The growth and professionalization of chefs have evolved from a purely craft skills area to a supervisory level. This evolution has occurred against the emerging development of the human resources management movement, from Hawthorne to Likert.

DISCUSSION QUESTIONS

1. List and explain the functions of the chef supervisor's job.
2. What skills and attributes do you consider important for the chef supervisor's success?
3. How has the role of the chef supervisor's job changed? How do these changes impact the concept of total quality management?
4. Why is an ethical code of conduct critical to a chef supervisor's job?
5. What is meant by the concept of front-door to back-door management as it relates to the chef supervisor's job?
6. What are the elements of kitchen supervision? Describe them.
7. What are the benefits of team building and empowerment within the foodservice industry?
8. What is the concept of authority?
9. What is meant by the evolution of the chef with regard to supervisory positions?
10. How does the chef supervisor's role impact upon management, team members, and customer satisfaction?

NOTES

1. Philip Crosby, *Quality Is Free*, McGraw-Hill, New York, 1978, p. 111.
2. Bill Marvin, *The Foolproof Foodservice Selection System*, John Wiley, New York, 1993, p. 12.
3. Anna Katherine Jernigan, *The Effective Foodservice Supervisor*, Aspen, Rockville, MD, 1989, p. 213.
4. *Larousse Gastronomique*, Hamlyn, London, 1971, p. 303.
5. Jerald Chesser, *The Art and Science of Culinary Preparation*, American Culinary Federation Educational Institute, St. Augustine, FL, 1992, p. 5.
6. Tom Peters, *Thriving On Chaos: Handbook for a Management Revolution*, Harper & Row, New York, 1988, p. 34.

7. John Bank, *The Essence of Total Quality Management*, Prentice-Hall, London, 1992, p. 17.

8. Dwight D. Eisenhower, *Great Quotes From Great Leaders*, Ed. Peggy Anderson, Lombard, IL, Great Quotations, 1989, p. 52.

9. Ritz Carlton publicity pamphlet, The Ritz Carlton Co., Boston, MA, 1993.

10. Arthur Sherman, George Bohlander, and Herbert Crudden, *Managing Human Resources*, 8th ed., South-Western, Cincinnati, OH, 1988, p. 352.

11. James A. Belasco, *Teaching the Elephant to Dance*, Crown, New York, 1990, p. 28.

2

Quality, Philosophy, History, Excellence, Reengineering, and Change

Outline

- Total quality management
- The foodservice customer defined
- Deming's principles of quality
- Philosophies, concepts, and strategies of management
- Scientific management: a historical perspective
- Management by objective
- The excellence movement
- Reengineering
- Change
- Conclusions
- Summary
- Discussion questions

Objectives

When you complete this chapter, you should be able to:

1. Describe the background, development, and essential elements of total quality management and outline its main characteristics and their implications for chef supervisors.
2. Define the customer within the wider context of the foodservice industry.
3. Identify the principles and philosophies of scientific management, management by objective, reengineering, and the elements of the excellence movement.
4. Understand the development, strengths, and weaknesses of different concepts of management.
5. Identify major trends and developments in the workplace that affect chef supervisors.
6. Understand the nature and importance of change and explain why people resist change.
7. Indicate the guidelines for overcoming resistance to change.

TOTAL QUALITY MANAGEMENT

W. Edwards Deming is often credited with the Japanese industrial domination of post–World War II. Deming brought his concepts of production, quality control, cost savings, and continuous improvement to Japan and is generally hailed as the father of modern Japanese industry. Deming may also be viewed as the catalyst for many of the changes made in the name of quality management in the United States: "Much has been written about Deming's work and his principles are widely quoted. However, we have also seen a wide range of interpretation of his ideas" (1).

Joseph M. Juran's impact on quality in Japanese industry was considered second only to Deming's. Juran defined quality as "fitness for use," meaning that the users of a product or service should be able to count on it for what they need. To achieve fitness for use, Juran developed a comprehensive approach to quality that spanned a product's life—from design through vendor relations, process development, manufacturing control, inspection and test, distribution, customer relations, and field service. His major vehicle for top management involvement was the annual quality program. Similar to long-range financial planning and the annual budget process, this program gave top management quality objectives and was especially important for internalizing the habit of quality improvement to ensure that complacency did not set in.

In addition to Deming and Juran, another important innovator and contributor to the quality movement, Philip B. Crosby, made the famous claim that quality is free (2). Crosby, like Deming, lists 14 points as part of any quality program (3):

1. *Management commitment*: Top management must become convinced of the need for quality improvement and must make its commitment clear to the entire company.

2. *Quality improvement team*: Management must form a team of department heads to oversee quality improvement. The team's role is to see that needed actions take place in its departments and in the company as a whole.

3. *Quality measurement*: Quality measures that are appropriate to every activity must be established to identify areas needing improvement.

4. *Cost of quality evaluation*: The controller's office should make an estimate of the costs of quality to identify areas where quality improvements would be profitable.

5. *Quality awareness*: Quality awareness must be raised among employees. They must understand the importance of conformance and the costs of nonconformance. These messages should be delivered by supervisors.

6. *Corrective action*: Opportunities for correction are generated by steps 3 and 4, as well as by discussions among employees. These ideas should be brought to the supervisory level and resolved there.

7. *Zero-defects planning*: An ad hoc zero-defects committee should be formed from members of the quality improvement team.

8. *Supervisor training*: Early in the process, all levels of management must be trained for their part of the quality improvement program.

9. *Zero-defects day*: A zero-defects day should be scheduled to signal to the employees that the company has a new performance standard.

10. *Goal setting*: To turn commitments into action, individuals must establish improvement goals for themselves and their groups. Supervisors should meet with their people and ask them to set goals that are specific and measurable.

11. *Error cause removal*: Employees should be encouraged to inform management of any problems that prevent them from performing error-free work.

12. *Recognition*: Public, nonfinancial appreciation must be given to those who meet their quality goals or perform outstandingly.

13. *Quality councils*: Quality professionals and team chairpersons should meet regularly to share experiences, problems, and ideas.

14. *Do it all over again*: To emphasize the never-ending process of quality improvement, the program (steps 1–13) must be repeated. This renews the commitment of old employees and brings new ones into the process.

Central to these business, supervisory, and management philosophies is continuous improvement at all levels. Total quality management, or TQM, can be equally applied to the foodservice industry and in particular the kitchen. The TQM theory can sound rather complex, but it is based on simple princi-

A Letter from GTE concerning TQM

Total quality management is the continuous improvement in every facet of business through teamwork.

At GTE we have formalized our already significant commitment to TQM. It challenges every employee, manager, and supervisor to work together to create the environment and culture that will provide products and services that meet or exceed customer expectations. It is imperative in the face of declining business and the increasing competitive environments that this culture will increase the efforts of all our people in continuous improvements in every aspect and process within our organization.

Total quality management is good business, and it makes sense. Therefore, I urge and challenge each of you, our valued suppliers, to em-

brace the philosophy and goals of TQM by striving for continuous improvement and providing material and services free of defects. Your wide range of expertise is essential to our mutual success. The end result of our efforts will be a new standard for delivering to our customers products and services of the very highest quality at the lowest possible cost.

As we proceed into the next century and beyond, TQM must influence everything we do. In the near future it is likely that many of you will be encouraged to participate in one or more improvement projects. Survival is at stake. Our goal is excellence. Committed to TQM, we will maintain and hopefully improve our position as suppliers and services in our respective fields.

I know that I can count on each of you as we look to the future. Working together we will succeed.

Armen Der Marderosian, GTE

---

ples. The customer is the boss in TQM. Reaching goals and constantly improving, organizing, and delivering a foodservice product right the first time are its tenets. The theory is also about investing in people: If the chef supervisor takes good care of the kitchen staff, then they will take good care of the customer. Quality can be defined as "anything that enhances the product from the viewpoint of the customer. Some aspects of quality are easily identified . . . other aspects of quality are not, but the absence of it stands out like Bermuda shorts worn to a black tie affair" (4).

THE FOODSERVICE CUSTOMER DEFINED

A foodservice customer is any person of any demographic group frequenting any commercial hotel, restaurant, or institutional, industrial, or military din-

Chef Talk: "Customer Driven"

In 1992, the James Beard Foundation awarded its outstanding service award to the Union Square Cafe of New York City. In his Summer newsletter, owner Danny Meyer described his gratitude and the honor of being chosen. He wrote about how proud he was of the whole Union Square team for displaying the essential pro-guest attitude that defines great service. He went on to say that "if service is an attitude, then surely you can taste its excellence in the food. Every cook in our kitchen excels at sharing a real love of food and sincerely cares that the guest enjoyed it. When a diner sends back an undercooked steak in most restaurants, it is common to hear the chef grumble about having to cook it all over again. At the Union Square cafe the only grumbling you'll ever hear is from a cook who is honestly upset that the guest wasn't satisfied."

Danny Meyer, Union Square Cafe, New York

ing establishment who is prepared to pay for wholesome, nutritious meals prepared by professionals utilizing first-class quality food products and outstanding culinary skills in a safe and sanitary kitchen and served by friendly, caring, efficient dining room staff. This customer is of any age and may be any of the following:

- Casual restaurant diner
- Hotel/motel restaurant guest
- Cafeteria diner
- Room-service guest
- Hospital patient
- Senior living home guest
- School or college diner
- Catered party guest
- Airline, train, or cruise passenger
- Fast-food diner
- Theme and recreation park diner
- Banquet diner
- Office/factory diner

- Upscale white tablecloth restaurant diner
- Delicatessen and supermarket customer

DEMING'S PRINCIPLES OF QUALITY

It is interesting to note that early in his career Deming worked at the Hawthorne Plant in Illinois during the summer months, the site of the famous human productivity studies discussed in Chapter 1. In *The Deming Management Method* Walton states, "Some of his ideas are rooted in his experiences at Hawthorne . . . where 46,000 men and women produced telephone equipment in sweatshop conditions, where workers were paid by the piece and docked if it failed inspection" (5).

Deming's 14 "quality" principles, upon which much of the TQM movement is based, recommend that each company or organization work out its own interpretations and adapt them to the corporate culture. While Deming's quality principles were primarily directed toward manufacturing industry, they have many applications to quality in the foodservice industry. These principles were developed following World War II and later were rediscovered in the United States.

In the foodservice industry, a quality service or product may be defined as one that fully meets the expectations and requirements of those who produce or use it. Continuous improvement in quality food production is fundamental for any success in the foodservice industry.

The following list demonstrates how Deming's 14 quality points may be adapted for application to a total quality kitchen operation (6).

1. *Create constancy of purpose toward the improvement of product and service.*
Commit the kitchen staff to continuous improvement. Create a common purpose; get the kitchen team to embrace continuous improvement. Get *all* the kitchen team involved, make each member responsible for improvements: dishwashers, purchasing agents, pantry persons, chefs, trainees, and apprentices. Develop key result areas for each person with assigned quality improvement, create a team atmosphere, and then set benchmarks on quality. Set the tone of the team and put it across with enthusiasm. Remind the kitchen team of it often.

2. *Management must take the leadership role in promoting change.*
Together with management, create a climate for change in the kitchen. Embrace change; make it your friend. Change with purpose, not just for the sake of change. Chef supervisors who embrace change will need to be supportive and train the kitchen team—be proactive rather than reactive. Create and live a vision for the kitchen department that will become a beacon for team building and effective supervision. Remember, the one constant is change and change can be a frightening concept for individuals who are accustomed to living in a comfort zone.

3. *Stop dependence on inspection to achieve quality. Build quality into the product in the beginning.*

Total quality chef supervisory management is dedicated to preparing meals and providing service in a way that provides high standards from the outset. Chefs should abandon the notion that they know more about what the customer wants than the customer; they must not be gastronomic snobs. Without foodservice customers, there would be no need for chefs.

This refocused direction applies equally to all foodservice establishments whether white tablecloth, health care, student dining, or fast-food establishments. Quality is perceived by the customer; *they* define quality, *not* the chef producing the meal. The customer is the boss. One dissatisfied customer leaving the restaurant will tell 12 friends who will tell 6 others who will tell 3 of their friends; eventually hundreds of people may hear about the poor meal and dining experience.

Involve the kitchen staff team in menu development; let them vote on new dishes before they are introduced onto the menu. Involve customers; have *them* taste test the menu items. Allow customers a vote on which dishes should be included on the menu. Ask the customers what they want and then provide it. If the meal looks fine and tastes fine to the chef preparing it, it does not necessarily mean that customers will also feel that way about it. They may not always be right, but they are always the customer, the person we want to continuously satisfy and retain, so that the foodservice business can grow and prosper.

Building quality into food preparation through team members at all levels is perhaps the single most important task of the chef supervisor. This can only be achieved through excellent coaching and team-building skills and instilling in the kitchen team a sense of pride and passion for quality food standards. It is upon the promise of high quality at all levels, provided through a motivated and a well-trained kitchen team, that the success or failure of the modern chef supervisor rests.

4. *Move to a single supplier for any one item. Create long-term relationships with suppliers.*

Chef supervisors should view suppliers and vendors as a vital part of the total quality improvement process in the kitchen. This means trusting suppliers and asking for their input. It means closer contacts and relationships with farmers and growers. More and more foodservice operators and chefs are dealing directly with local farmers and fishermen. Buying locally can give access to fresher and organically grown products. Suppliers can customize their products to meet the specific needs of a foodservice operation. Using single suppliers versus the use of two or more challenges the old strategy of playing one supplier against the other, using price and delivery as leverage and bargaining chips. As Bill Eacho stated, "Foodservice operators can improve quality and consistency, while at the same time lower costs by forming strategic partnerships" (7). While issues of price, quality, delivery, units of purchase, and credit terms will remain important business issues, quality product and

produce from suppliers based on your foodservice specifications are para-
mount. A quality end product begins with quality ingredients.

5. *Improve constantly the system of production and service and thus decrease costs.*

Quality equals profit and motivated kitchen team members can reduce
costs. Communicate the importance of each person's role in the quest for high-
quality standards. Support and explain decisions to help each kitchen team
member apply quality standards. On a weekly basis brief the team on progress,
policy, and points of action. As food quality improves through continuous
quality review, waste is reduced and costs decrease. Food cost reduction programs in and of themselves do not often lead to improved quality. On the other
hand, effective quality applications by informed team members leads to not
only improved quality but also lasting reductions in food and production costs
as well. Quality and costs are not opposites or trade-offs, with one being improved at the expense of the other. Instead both can be constantly improved.
Total quality improvement is a never-ending journey. It is therefore essential
for the chef supervisor to provide an atmosphere where total communication
can exist in the kitchen and where it is possible to tap constantly the collective
brainpower of the team.

6. *Institute training on the job.*

Train all kitchen team members, including the support team. Practice
equal training opportunities and gain support from management for the concept of on-the-job training. Set examples; coach employees to reach their potential. Diversity and multiculturalism are common to foodservice operations;
therefore, a good deal of on-the-job training is necessary. This training should
always be conducted in a sensitive and caring way. (See the chapters on training in Part II.)

7. *Institute leadership. The aim of supervision should be to help people and
machines do a better job.*

Chef supervisors must become better leaders. This requires delegating
authority, empowering kitchen team members to become independent decision makers, providing guidance, and creating a positive work environment.
Chef supervisors as role models, leaders, and trainers should provide the tools
and necessary coaching required for the rest of the team to operate a successful total quality kitchen. Use technology and machines to support the efforts
of the kitchen team, not just to replace them. Learn from successes and mistakes. Regularly walk around each team member's place of work, observe, listen, and praise. (See Chapter 8 on leadership.)

8. *Drive out fear, so that everyone may work effectively.*

The greatest fears of a kitchen team member are fear of the unknown and
of rejection or failure. What am I expected to do? How do I know if I am doing
a good job? Create an environment in which team members feel comfortable
in offering suggestions and ideas. Just because members of a group do not say

anything does not necessarily mean they have nothing to say. They may be shy or simply afraid to advance their ideas. Give constant feedback on team member performance. Feedback should be given only on issues of performance, not on the type of person the team member is. (See Chapter 3 on motivation, morale, and strokes.)

9. *Break down barriers between departments. Promote team building as people from different departments work together to solve problems and improve quality.*

Customers react holistically to quality and service. The dining experience involves other people besides the kitchen team. Quality food must be complemented by friendly, courteous service by staff dedicated to meeting and exceeding customer expectations. The service staff is the chef's internal customer and an integral part of the foodservice TQM drive. Customers recall the negative aspects of the dining experience before the more positive ones; therefore, negative and positive experiences don't go together. The animosity that has traditionally existed between dining room staff and kitchen staff has absolutely no place in TQM: "Within the world of TQM, a customer may be someone besides the end user of the product sold; it may be co-workers who supply one another with services" (8). Chefs must realize that the waiter is also a customer.

10. *Eliminate slogans, exhortations, and targets for the work force, asking for zero defects and new levels of productivity.*

Slogans containing production numbers only—numbers of meals served and degree of difficulty associated with the production of certain menu items—should be avoided as tools of measurement. Food cost percentage targets are important but should not be the major measurement tool for chefs in foodservice. Develop the kitchen team, emphasize people, not profit, hire kitchen staff with hospitality attitudes; technical skills are important, but good attitudes and a desire to please the customer by cooking the best meal possible are more important. Remember the reputation of the chef supervisor is on the last meal served to a customer, not on any previous accolades or gold medals won at food shows.

11. *Eliminate work quotas; substitute leadership.*

Practical experience has shown that during service time, quality in the kitchen is at its lowest. To improve the kitchen work environment, instead of labor-intensive, boring work sequences, rotate team members. Insure that no one is a prisoner of a particular station, area, or job. Design jobs and arrange work to encourage the commitment of individuals to the team. Communicate clearly so as to ensure quality performance standards; be understood and understand; be a good listener. Serve the team; care for their well being and safety; work alongside team members and deal with grievances promptly.

Leadership within the kitchen must replace the old heavy-handed style of chefs. There must be a recognition that team members will have initiative and creativity, that they can and will make valuable contributions to quality if provided a motivated work environment. Chef supervisors more and more will be required to lead a culturally diverse kitchen team, which will necessitate skills in understanding the special values of diversity so as to turn this diversity into a total quality strength. Deming continuously honed these principles. He states: "For years point seven was a mandate to institute supervision, of late I believe leadership is a better word" (9). (See Chapter 8 on leadership.)

12. *Remove barriers that rob managers, engineers, and the hourly paid worker of their right to pride of workmanship. Change the emphasis from numbers to quality.*

Almost all kitchen team members want to give their best. Chef supervisors should remove barriers in order to create a motivational environment. However, removing barriers alone will not create motivation; motivation comes from within each individual. Without motivational conditions in the kitchen, team members will operate at minimal performance levels. The most common demotivating barriers to quality performance are:

- Erratic mood swings by the chef supervisor
- Poor physical kitchen facilities
- High temperatures in the work environment
- Poor equipment
- Insufficient small wares
- Inappropriate floor surfaces
- Inconsistent treatment of individuals and no communication or feedback on job performance

In a total quality kitchen operation, chef supervisors must realize that elements that motivate them will probably hold true for each kitchen team member. The example that the chef supervisor sets greatly influences the productivity and motivation of the team. Most kitchen team members take considerable pride in their work performance and the meals they serve. Simply blaming kitchen team members for poor business numbers and lack of revenues makes no contribution to operational success. Quality equals profit in the promotion of pride, and a sense of self-worth will enhance profits. (See Chapter 3 on motivation, morale, and strokes.)

13. *Institute a vigorous program of education and self-improvement.*

Training and instructor skills are just as important to the chef supervisor as culinary technical skills. Invest in training; it will prove to be the greatest impetus toward the goals of continuous improvement. Total quality chef supervisors who arm themselves with instructor training skills and techniques and who use them in different planned training situations will win big with TQM. Training like TQM is not something done once; it has to be on-going, a way of life in the kitchen. At times learning can proceed irregularly. Expect periods with no perceptible progress in some individuals, but with changes taking place in the culture of the kitchen team and in other individuals. The single most unifying force in developing people and creating conditions for a real and genuine total quality product and motivated kitchen team is the planned implementation of sequential and progressive training programs. (See Part II on training.)

14. *Put everyone in the company to work to accomplish the transformation. Make it an all-pervasive common goal and support it.*

The type of transformation that is possible through initiating TQM as part of kitchen operations is enormous. However, it cannot be maintained unless the entire organization and the various supporting departments along with management adopt it universally. The advantages of chef supervisors investing in and applying Deming's quality principles will not only produce satisfied customers and the practical abolition of their complaints, but will also transform the role of the chef supervisor, the team, and the work environment in the kitchen.

Total quality management will reduce waste, build teamwork, increase the motivational environment, and improve employee retention. It will develop institutional pride and increase and expand the technical culinary knowledge of other chefs. Chef supervisors who are proactive will recognize that it is necessary in today's foodservice industry to be more than an excellent cook with first-class culinary skills; they also must be first-class supervisors with great team-building skills. Great culinarians cannot cook all the meals; they need help. It is the help and their disposition toward the organization and the chef supervisor that ultimately will determine the success or failure of the foodservice establishment.

The concepts of TQM, along with the role the chef supervisor has to play in it, are the glue that holds together all the elements vital to success. Future chefs will need to understand and embrace the tenets of TQM if they are to play an important and valuable role in the overall development of themselves and of the foodservice industry. Total quality management will help gain that competitive edge over other establishments. Adopted through Deming's quality principles, TQM changes the kitchen team's relationship with customers, suppliers, and employers through greater focus on meeting and exceeding customer expectations.

Continuous improvement must become the norm; supervising or managing the status quo is no longer an option in an increasingly competitive and uncertain foodservice industry.

In general quality terms within the kitchen, continuous improvements can be considered in relation to:

- Improving external customer satisfaction
- Improving and developing closer supplier partnerships
- Improving communications within the kitchen
- Reducing waste
- Preventing special causes of food preparation variation
- Quantifying quality costs

- Improving food production and service methods
- Improving internal systems
- Providing flexibility and adaptability

Quality is not a procedure, it is a process, and as such is never finished. The culture of quality promotes and sustains change.

Chef Talk: "TQM"

At the Culinary Institute of America we have only one mission: to provide the best culinary education in the world. Naturally, such a lofty goal is much easier to say than it is to do, particularly in this increasingly complicated world. While the Institute has always been successful, in the late 1980s we began to seriously look at how we could accelerate our improvement, further differentiating us from hundreds of new culinary programs that had sprung up in the past decade. While we have always focused on quality we decided to initiate an Institute-wide total quality management (TQM) program. We spent the first phase of our effort entirely on "planning the work." After several months we were ready to "work the plan."

The second phase of our effort called for the training of every full-time employee, from the president down, in the philosophy, techniques, and tools of TQM. We organized these sessions with no regard to position or department so that employees from all levels and functional areas would have a chance to learn about and work with each other. This helped to break down some of the traditional barriers that stifle cross-departmental communication and coordination. The magnitude of our training and the involvement of all organizational levels signaled our deep commitment to TQM.

The next (and ongoing) phase of our plan called for the identification of improvement opportunities and the use of TQM tools and techniques by staff members to make the improvements. Our employee-led quality action teams (QATs) have tackled a wide range of issues, from improving our 96 percent student retention rate to reducing overproduction of student meals. (The recommendations yielded considerable dollar saving!)

The bottom line is that TQM has worked for us in virtually every facet of our institution: administratively, in the classrooms, in the kitchen, for large issues and for small. Our staff feels more empowered and has been trained in how to act on their empowerment. We are measuring quality in ways we never dreamed of before. In short, TQM works.

L. Timothy Ryan, CMC, AAC, Senior Vice President, The Culinary Institute of America, Hyde Park, NY

Total quality management will not go away. It is not the latest quick-fix solution for ailing businesses. It is not a passing fad used for downsizing or rationalization. Implementing TQM in kitchen operations is the beginning of a journey of discovery and the breaking down of barriers. It is the creation of a work climate where team building is possible and where people will enjoy coming to work.

The main aim of the Deming philosophy is empowerment of the individual. The lesson is that we have to empower all our people with dignity, knowledge, and skills so that they may contribute. They have to feel secure, be trained so that they can do the work properly, and be encouraged so that the organization can develop and grow (10).

PHILOSOPHIES, CONCEPTS, AND STRATEGIES OF MANAGEMENT

In recent years there have been many theories, philosophies, strategies, and concepts developed and put forward to assist business organizations, managers, and supervisors to restructure, refocus, and plan for change. All of these contain within them the elements of change, customer focus, quality, and leadership. Many of these theories have their roots in manufacturing industry.

Foodservice organizations and chef supervisors are not immune to the actions and effects of these business strategies and philosophies. The main thrust of this book is toward supervisory management for chefs rather than business management; nevertheless, many of these philosophies, strategies, and theories contain elements that directly impact the chef supervisor's job. One way or another, as we look to the future, chefs will be required not only to cook, but also to know, understand, and apply these theories and philosophies.

The following section identifies some of these common principles associated with change and leadership. Many of them have within them slogans that have become synonymous with quality, customer focus, and leadership. They are not listed in order of importance and include only those relevant to the chef supervisor's role.

SCIENTIFIC MANAGEMENT: A HISTORICAL PERSPECTIVE

Discussion of this topic revolves around time-and-motion studies. The principles of scientific management were put forward by industrial engineer Frederick Winslow Taylor around the turn of the century. Taylor held that human performance could be defined and controlled through work standards and rules. He advocated the use of time-and-motion studies to reduce jobs to simple, separate steps to be performed over and over again.

Scientific management evolved during an era of mass immigration. The workplace was being flooded with unskilled, uneducated workers, and it was efficient to employ them in large numbers. This was also a period of labor strife, and Taylor believed that his system would reduce conflict and eliminate the arbitrary use of power because so little discretion would be left to either workers or supervisors. The methods used included careful selection of workers who were deemed to be competent, conforming, and obedient and a constant oversight of work. This system caused much bitterness between unions and management. It is from Taylor's period that the phrase a "fair day's work" came.

Scientific management gave to employers a system that increased productivity and reduced the number of workers. It was also rule bound, hierarchical, and top heavy with corporate structure. This began the era of standardization that many today believe contributed to the slow recognition of the changing nature of employees and the methods of managing them.

MANAGEMENT BY OBJECTIVES

Management by objectives (MBO) is a philosophy of management first introduced by Peter Drucker in 1954. It seeks to judge the performance of employees on the basis of their success in the achievement of set objectives established through consultation with managers and supervisors. Performance improvement efforts under MBO are focused upon goals to be achieved by employees rather than upon the activities performed or the methods by which employees achieve these goals.

Management by objectives is part of a systemwide set of organizational goals that begins with setting the organization's common goals and objectives and returns to that point. The system acts as a goal-setting process whereby goals are set for the organization, individual departments, individual managers, supervisors, and employees. A feature of MBO is a broad statement of employee responsibilities prepared by the supervisor, reviewed and jointly modified until both are satisfied with them. The goals are accompanied by a detailed account of the actions the employee proposes to take in order to reach the goals. Periodic review assesses the progress that the employee has made. At the end of the review period the employee does a self-appraisal of whether the previously set goals have been achieved.

Management by objectives enabled managers and supervisors to plan and measure their own performance as well as that of the employees. It shifted the emphasis from appraisal to self-analysis. The major criticisms of MBO included the methods by which individuals achieved their goals. Factors such as cooperation, adaptability, and concern were not included as part of MBO rationale. Another criticism of MBO was that employee-rated success is tied to issues that ultimately are not directed toward customer satisfaction. Another problem with MBO is its link to employee evaluation and rewards, which causes conflict between the supervisor's roles as judge and leader.

Deming was particularly critical of MBO. He believed MBO is management by fear (11) and does not have a place in the quality movement because of its reliance on performance evaluations. He also believed that MBO discourages risk taking, builds fear, and undermines team work. In a team, it is difficult to tell who does what. Under MBO people work for themselves, not the organization.

THE EXCELLENCE MOVEMENT

If it ain't broke, fix it anyway (12). About the same time that Deming's quality principles were being rediscovered, the "excellence" movement began: by Peters and Waterman in 1982, with their book *In Search of Excellence*; by Peters and Austin in 1985, in *Passion for Excellence*; and by Peters in 1988, in *Thriving on Chaos*. These books and their strategies blended perfectly into what was happening in the world of business as the pace of change gathered momentum. The basic business and management philosophies put forward by these authors were to make excellence in the management of product, people, and service a first priority. These works proposed many innovative approaches to management. They focused attention on the customer revolution and the need to gain a competitive advantage, to become more effective: "We must end excuse making and look for new organizational models fit for the new world. New survivors will welcome change rather than resist it, and realize that people power, not robot power is our only choice" (13). Central to the "excellence" and *Thriving on Chaos* philosophy is that for organizations to survive and grow, they must have:

- A bias toward action
- A simple form and a lean staff
- Continued contact with customers
- Productivity improvement via people
- Operational autonomy to encourage entrepreneurship
- One key business value
- Emphasis on doing what they know best
- Simultaneous loose and tight controls

Organizations must also see people as a prime source of "value added" and realize that they can never be trained or involved too much. Additionally, in the excellence movement the structure of organizations is flattened, layers of middle management are reduced, and the functional barriers are broken. Peters believes that "front-line supervisors as we know them give way to self-managed teams. Middle managers become facilitators rather than turf guardians. Leaders become levers of change and preachers of vision" (14).

Peters also believes that strategies, ideas, and concepts come from the bottom up. Staff functions support the line rather than the other way around.

Sales and service personnel become heroes with customer relationships. Success in the health care, food, or computer industry will go to those who add value by developing customized products or services that create new market niches.

Clearly, the foodservice world has changed and will continue to change. In order to meet this change, chefs will need to be more than just "cooks." Each team member has a part to play; the operational employee, whether in manufacturing industry or foodservice, is a thing of the past.

Each person has a valuable role in this empowered, motivated, decision-making, innovative well-led kitchen team.

In *management by walking around* (MBWA) chefs are active people, and food production is activity oriented. Good chef supervisors walk around and visit each person's work station.

Ed Carlson, upon taking over at United Airlines, realized it was a service business that had lost sight of the customer. He introduced MBWA. He instilled a hands-on customer focus. He said, "In a service business, you can't have a rigid set of rules. You can have some guidelines, but you must allow people the freedom to make a different interpretation" (15).

REENGINEERING

The newest management philosophy is reengineering. If adopted across the board by foodservice organizations, it will probably have the greatest impact on executive chefs of large multi-unit hotels, casinos, or similarly sized operations. Reengineering essentially calls for a radical rethinking of the ways in which organizations do business. Business reengineering means putting aside much of the received wisdom of 200 years of industrial management (16). It has been described as "an approach to planning and controlling change" (17).

In reengineering, work units change from functional departments to process teams, jobs change from simple tasks to multidimensional work, and people's roles change from controlled to empowered. The focus of performance measures and compensation shifts from activity to results. Values change from protective to productive. Organizational structures change from hierarchical to flat. The role of executives changes from scorekeepers to leaders (18).

Part of the reengineering process is also about positioning within different markets. This planned positioning determines what should be reengineered.

Reengineering involves integrating tasks into processes and reorganizing the company around them. What results, in contrast to the old system of organization by different departments, is a collection of people united in their common purpose of effort, reducing the need for continuous checking and controls. Conceivably in this scenario, chefs could become restaurant or unit managers responsible not only for supervisory functions but also for complete

Chef Talk: "Reengineering"

The word *reengineering* was certainly not found in any of my cook books or apprenticeship texts, and in order for me to understand this word's concept, I had to look elsewhere. My training as a chef over the past 25 years has been purely classical. Along the way I managed to learn not only new cooking methods but also how to manage and motivate people in the kitchen environment.

I now have a much clearer understanding of the vision of the future for our industry. Reengineering is a tool to make this vision come true, and in many cases we have no choice but to go forward, accepting the changes that come toward us no matter how big or small they may seem.

In my case, reengineering came as somewhat of a surprise when I found out that many of my colleagues in the company were without a job and that executive chefs were no longer needed. After looking at this situation a little closer I found out that this reengineering concept was really not as bad as it seemed.

Reengineering gave me the opportunity to look at my organization with a totally different set of eyes, and it made me realize that things can be done differently and in the long run these changes would be beneficial to the customer and the company.

Once I was able to let go of the past, I was willing to accept the challenges of the future. With this new attitude I was able to move forward and develop the necessary plan to put reengineering to work in my culinary world. This meant dismantling the current organizational structures, putting new concepts into place, such as individual business unit leaders, elimination of departments, and redesigning job descriptions. During each of these steps new questions and answers came up and I changed or adapted to them as they came along.

Many already well-defined systems had to be changed, eliminated, or even completely redesigned in order to move forward. Throughout this process many roadblocks had to be removed, only to show up again around the corner. Many personal egos had to be eliminated, and in some cases the people had to go along with them.

We were told by our corporate leaders that only the best would survive, and this was a problem for some. Those who were not willing to change found themselves struggling more and more. They were either terminated or quit during the process. Those who stepped up to the plate and started swinging at the ball made more progress than they even imagined.

We as culinarians should understand that if we don't change the way we do business, we will lose sight of our primary goal, which is customer satisfaction. It is the customer who steers in the direction we must go, and that is into the future.

Bernhard Gotz, CEC, Sheraton Hotel, New Orleans, LA

management of a foodservice operation. Additionally, titles and individual lines of demarcation would disappear.

CHANGE

Studies have shown that people do not basically resist change; they resist being changed, and participation empowers change (19). A major factor to be considered by chef supervisors when changing the foodservice operation is the people affected by the change. Resistance to change within any organization is as common as the need to change. After supervisors decide on making changes, they typically meet with employee resistance, usually aimed at preventing the change from occurring. This resistance generally exists because kitchen team members fear some personal loss, such as a reduction in personal prestige, a disturbance of established social and working relationships, and personal failure due to an inability to carry out new job responsibilities as a result of the proposed change.

Since resistance accompanies proposed change, chef supervisors must be able to reduce the effects of this resistance so as to ensure the success of needed quality improvements. People need time to evaluate the proposed change before implementation. Elimination of time to evaluate how proposed changes may affect individual situations usually results in automatic opposition to change. Those kitchen team members who will be affected by change must be kept informed of the type of change being considered and the probability that the change will be adopted. When fear of personal loss related to a proposed change is reduced, opposition to the change is reduced. Individuals should receive information that will help them answer the following change-related questions:

- Will I lose my job?
- Will my old skills become obsolete?
- Am I capable of being effective under the new system?
- Will my power and prestige decline?
- Will I receive more responsibility than I want?
- Will I have to work longer hours?

If the chef supervisor follows some simple guidelines, then implementing change need not be too stressful. The following steps will assist in getting the kitchen team members to "buy into" the change:

- Inform those concerned in advance so that they can think about the implications of the change and its effect on their position within the kitchen team.
- Explain the overall objectives of the change, the reasons for it, and the sequence in which it will occur.

Chef Talk: "Change"

In 1987 I accepted the position of executive chef of a prestigious city club in downtown Pittsburgh. The club was 110 years old and up until that point had employed only three executive chefs. As the only "outsider" ever to hold this position, I knew my work would be cut out for me. The policy at the club had always been to promote from within. My relatively young age proved to be both an advantage and a disadvantage. On the positive side I brought new ideas and plenty of energy to the position. Additionally I didn't have any long-term friendships in the club influencing my decisions. On the negative side, however, I found myself having to manage people much older than I and some had problems accepting direction from "the kid." Employees were buying into pools betting on how long I would last.

I immediately began working on the menu in an effort to inject more contemporary selections. I developed recipes and worked with kitchen employees at their particular stations on preparation and execution of "new" menu items.

After reviewing the preparation with the cooks, I continued to the next station. This was repeated with each station. I felt much like a fireman running from place to place trying to "extinguish" problems everywhere. I finally realized that without the entire kitchen staff behind me participating in changes there was little chance to succeed. I switched my philosophy; rather than working on the menu I decided the best investment of my time would be first with the people and second with the facility. I felt strongly that if these two items were handled properly the changes in menu and improving quality would fall in line. The foundation and building blocks were the people and facility. If these were strong, the rest would be easy.

I invested in my team. I developed a comprehensive training program that included expense-paid training courses at local colleges. We also developed exchange programs with other prominent clubs across the country. For example, an employee from the bakeshop would have the opportunity to work with a Certified Master Pastry Chef, one of the most talented pastry chefs in the country. We enlisted the services of speakers to present programs to the employees on different topics such as basic skills (cooking), motivation, job safety, health, stress management, food handling, sanitation, wine, spirits, and tableside cooking.

Tom Peer, CMC, AAC, Food & Beverage Director, Duquesne Club, Pittsburgh, PA

- Show people how the change will benefit them. Be honest with the team. If they are not to be part of the future plans of the kitchen objectives, tell them and provide support and ample time for them to secure new positions.
- Invite those affected by the change to participate at all stages of the process.
- Allow time and demonstrate patience as the team adapts to new work or quality-driven changes.
- Provide for constant communication and feedback during the changes.
- Demonstrate constant commitment and loyalty to the change. Indicate confidence in the team and each individual's ability to implement the change.

The most powerful tool for reducing resistance to change is open display by the chef supervisor of a positive attitude toward the derived benefits of quality improvements for the organization as a whole and the individual kitchen team member. As with all change, time should be taken for evaluation, to examine what needs to be modified and what can be added to increase the effectiveness of kitchen operations. Evaluation of change often involves watching for symptoms that further change is necessary, particularly if team members are more oriented toward the past than the future or if they are more concerned with their own "pecking order" than with meeting the challenges of quality.

Often individuals treat change with different responses. Statements that "kill off" creative ideas and change include the following:

- Don't be ridiculous.
- We tried that before.
- It costs too much.
- You must be crazy.
- That's beyond our responsibility.
- It's too radical a change.
- We don't have the time.
- We've never done it before.
- Let's get back to reality.
- We're not ready for that.
- We'd be laughed at.
- We did all right without it.
- Let's shelve it for the time being.
- Let's form a committee.
- It's not practical for an organization like ours.
- It's too hard to get accepted.
- It won't work in our kitchen.

Chef supervisors should listen carefully for these types of remarks and monitor the dissent within the group. This dissent should be met with a positive approach and the benefits of the new ideas pointed out.

Change is the common link in TQM, between all its elements, along with emphasis on leadership qualities, empowerment, training, and inviting the kitchen team to be decision makers by giving them *real* authority and by trusting them. Invest in the kitchen team; embrace the team members' strengths, weaknesses, and *diversity*.

One of the first steps in adopting TQM as part of the kitchen operation is the establishment of focus groups from within all foodservice departments to meet, review, and identify quality gaps or minimum levels of quality performance. A detailed quality action plan should be prepared by the chef supervisor or a designated quality leader, quality objectives identified, and a timetable set for their implementation. This should not be confused with developing goals and performance evaluation strategies for employees. Total quality management focuses very clearly on the end user, the customer.

When these customer satisfaction goals are identified, the next obvious and simple step of quality kitchen management is to give the customers the type of meals they want. Quality cannot be achieved by tight controls over kitchen employees, but quality kitchen team meetings frequently will achieve it. The focus of the team meeting is then on proactive quality issues of consistent improvement and innovation. The key difference between performance objectives and total quality kitchen supervision is that TQM is devoted to getting it right the first time through a motivated, well-trained, empowered kitchen team rather than by developing rigid performance criteria for each kitchen employee. Fundamental to all future kitchen TQM and supervision is a recognition that MBO and other management theories that rely on statements and objectives projected into the future do not directly address the flexibility and ability required to change instantly to meet the needs of customers. As a philosophy TQM fits neatly into the modern requirement of supervising a kitchen team by insisting that chef supervisors be less reliant on authority and more disposed to leadership.

CONCLUSIONS

This brief overview of some of the major historical issues concerned with people management is intended only to give the chef supervisor a glimpse of what has shaped different directions in supervision and management. Each theory has had its own champions at various times. What has happened is the subtle yet vitally important shift of designation from "personnel managers" to "human resources managers" and the greater emphasis placed on developing people. This shift clearly underlines the philosophy that people must be led, not managed. This overview provides insight and understanding of change and the TQM movement. It also shows that workers have changed; they *can* be more than mindless, uninterested employees who need constant control and supervision. Supervision in the kitchen is evolving and changing. Chef supervisors must shift from old traditional "autocratic" rulers to coaches. Chefs who come to realize that not all change is bad will succeed in the future foodservice industry.

SUMMARY

To be successful supervisors, chefs must have an understanding and knowledge of the business and management forces that propel a quality management philosophy. Among these quality attributes is the need for chef supervisors with strong people, culinary, and customer focus skills.

W. E. Deming, along with other quality "gurus" such as Joseph M. Duran and Philip Crosby, provided strategies and philosophies directed toward continuous improvements in all aspects of production. These strategies may be applied in the foodservice industry. Deming's 14 quality principles can be applied in a culinary operation by trained and knowledgeable chef supervisors.

Change is a constant. Chef supervisors must reduce the effects of resistance to change within the kitchen. Understanding the elements of change and the fear with which people approach change is key to moving toward a customer quality focus.

DISCUSSION QUESTIONS

1. How does total quality management impact the chef supervisor's job relative to team members, upper management, and customers?
2. Quality in terms of the kitchen operation may be considered in relation to what areas?
3. What are the various foodservice industry categories in which a chef supervisor operates?
4. What were the main contributions of Frederick Taylor's scientific management?
5. What is the rationale for Deming's 14 principles of quality management?
6. In what way does empowerment contribute to continuous improvements in the kitchen?
7. What are main differences between management by objective, the excellence movement, and reengineering?
8. What are the elements that contribute to people's resistance to change?
9. Who sets the pace for most change in the foodservice industry?

NOTES

1. Mary Walton, *The Deming Management Method*, Putnam, New York, 1986, p. 51.
2. Philip Crosby, *Quality Is Free*, McGraw-Hill, New York, 1978, p. 20.
3. Adapted from *Quality Without Tears*, by Philip B. Crosby, McGraw-Hill, New York, 1984, p. 132–139.

4. Rafael Aguayo, *Dr. Deming*, Carol, New York, 1991, p. 35.
5. Mary Walton, *The Deming Management Method*, Putnam, New York, 1986, p. 27.
6. Deming's 14 points are from *Out of Crisis*, by Dr. Edwards Deming, MIT Center for Advanced Engineering Study, Cambridge, MA, 1989, p. 111.
7. Bill Eacho, "Quality Service Through Strategic Foodservice Partnerships," *Hosteur*, Vol. 3 No. 1, Spring 1993, p. 22.
8. Tom Wood, "Total Quality Management," *Hosteur*, Vol. 3 No. 1 Spring 1993, p. 15.
9. Mary Walton, *The Deming Management Method*, Putnam, New York, 1986, p. 34.
10. Ibid., p. 91.
11. Rafael Aguayo, *Dr. Deming*, Carol, New York, 1991, p. 243.
12. Tom Peters, *Thriving on Chaos: Handbook for a Management Revolution*, Harper & Row, New York, 1988, p. 3.
13. Ibid., p. 357.
14. Ibid., p. 358.
15. Tom Peters, "Putting Excellence into Management," *Managing Behavior in Organizations*, McGraw-Hill, New York, 1983, p. 603.
16. Michael Hammer and James Champy, *Reengineering the Corporation: A Manifesto For Business Revolution*, HarperCollins, New York, 1993, p. 2.
17. Daniel Morris and Joel Brandon, *Re-Engineering Your Business*, McGraw-Hill, New York, 1993, p. 13.
18. Michael Hammer and James Champy, *Reengineering the Corporation: A Manifesto For Business Revolution*, HarperCollins, New York, 1993, p. 79.
19. James A. Belasco, *Teaching the Elephant To Dance*, Crown, New York, 1990, p. 49.

3

Motivation, Morale, and Strokes

Outline

- Introduction
- Defining motivation
- Theories and motivational philosophies
- Morale
- Strokes
- Positive strokes
- Feedback
- Negative strokes
- Conclusions
- Summary
- Discussion questions

Objectives

When you complete this chapter you should be able to:

1. Define motivation within the context of the chef supervisor's job.
2. List the major theories and philosophies of motivation.

3. Explain the elements that contribute to a motivated kitchen team.
4. Describe factors that are the ingredients of morale within the kitchen.
5. Understand the elements of positive stroking.
6. Explain why feedback is an important element of morale.
7. Describe the elements and effects of negative stroking.

INTRODUCTION

An important function performed by the chef supervisor is the creation of a positive motivational environment, one in which great kitchen team morale is present. This can be achieved by providing strokes, for example, praise wrapped in units of attention.

It is the chef supervisor's job not only to structure and arrange work but also to motivate and build morale of the kitchen team so as to achieve the quality objectives that have been established. Part of this process is to determine how well the objectives and goals are being achieved and if there are motivational barriers to the accomplishment of these goals.

DEFINING MOTIVATION

Motivation, as distinct from morale and strokes, requires definition. Motivation contributes to morale and stroking is part of morale. Without all three working together it is almost impossible to create a kitchen work environment in which team building, productivity, and continuous quality improvements can take place.

Motivation is an individual's inner state which causes behavior in a way that ensures the successful accomplishment of goals and objectives. Motivation explains why people behave the way they do. The term *motivation* was originally derived from the Latin word *movere*, which literally means to move (1). While a number of definitions exist, no one definition describes it adequately. What is known, however, is that motivation is concerned with three factors: what energizes behavior, what channels such behavior, and the conditions under which this behavior is maintained. The triggers and drivers of motivation are the same for all individuals. What is clear is that the characteristics of the job environment, in this instance the kitchen, and the characteristics of the chef supervisor (the particular disposition and leadership style) will affect the elements of motivation. The more the chef supervisor understands the kitchen team member's behavior, the better he or she should be able to influence that behavior and make it more consistent with the goals of the foodservice organization. Since quality and productivity are central to the success of the chef supervisor, the creation of the appropriate motivational environment in the kitchen is key to this success.

Each person sees the world from an individual viewpoint. An individual's perception of the world is determined by his or her background and personal experiences, among other variables. The kitchen and the world generally are viewed through this personal and individual lens. Therefore, a chef supervisor should attempt to learn how each team member is likely to respond to different events and understand the diverse cultural issues that occur in the foodservice department. Each kitchen team member perceives and interprets instructions, actions, and communications in a unique way.

A team member's values and culture are a strong determinant of behavior. A value is any object, activity, or orientation that individuals consider very important to their way of life. Culture, on the other hand, refers to the team member's beliefs, practices, traditions, ideologies, and lifestyles. Values and culture have been shown to be related to decision making, motivation, communication, and supervisory success. Values are influenced largely by the culture in which we live and work.

As we look toward the next century the make-up of the work force in the American foodservice industry will change dramatically. In the late 1980s, 47 percent of the work force were native white males. By the year 2000 that figure will drop by 15 percent. The U.S. Department of Labor estimates that by the year 2000, 85 percent of the individuals entering the work force will be minorities and women and many of these new workers will enter the foodservice industry through the kitchen (2).

Humans function in an integrated manner, not in individual parts. It is the total kitchen team member we are interacting with. While it is useful at times to focus our attention on certain segments of personality in order to have a better understanding of the person, in the final analysis the team member should be viewed holistically, as a unified and integrated person.

Chef supervisors must come to recognize that they cannot know the nature of many of the forces influencing the behavior of individual team members, for team members often do not reveal what they are currently experiencing in their lives away from the job. What happens to team members at home, or through other activities, will affect how they feel about their work and other aspects of their lives. What happens away from work also influences how well they perform at work and the degree to which they want their feelings known to others.

Remember, it is impossible to have TQM unless there is total quality respect (TQR) for people, their differences, and the strengths this diversity brings to the kitchen motivational environment.

THEORIES AND MOTIVATIONAL PHILOSOPHIES

Probably the most widely accepted description of human needs is the hierarchy of needs concept put forward by Abraham Maslow. Maslow states that we as humans possess five basic needs: (1) physiological, (2) security, (3) social, (4) esteem, and (5) self-actualization needs. Maslow arranged these needs in a hierarchy of order or importance in which individuals generally strive to satisfy them (3) as follows (see Figure 1).

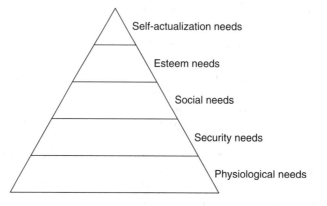

Figure 1   Maslow's hierarchy of needs.

Physiological needs   These relate to the normal functioning of the body and include the need for food, water, air, rest, and sex. Until these needs are met, a significant portion of an individual's behavior is aimed at satisfying them. If these needs are satisfied, behavior is aimed at the next level, the security needs.

Security or safety needs   These are the needs individuals require to keep themselves free from bodily and economic disaster. The foodservice organization can best help employees to satisfy their security needs through good and fair salaries, since it is with these salaries that employees can buy items such as food and housing. As security needs are satisfied, behavior tends to be aimed at satisfying social needs.

Social needs   These include an individual's desire for love, companionship, and friendship. Overall these needs reflect a person's desire to be accepted by others. As these needs are satisfied, behavior shifts to satisfying esteem needs.

Esteem needs   These are an individual's desire for respect and are generally divided into two categories: self-respect and respect for others. Once esteem needs are satisfied, an individual emphasizes satisfying self-actualization needs.

Self actualization   This is the desire to maximize whatever potential an individual possesses. For example, a motivated kitchen team member who seeks to satisfy self-actualization or self-realization might strive to become the leader or supervisor of the kitchen team. Self-actualization needs are at the highest level of Maslow's hierarchy.

These needs are the same for everyone. They apply when team members are at work, at which time there may be problems of *how well* they work.

Maslow's need hierarchy theory is consistent with the reasons people work. However, individuals move from one level to another and are *not* at any one level in life. The motivational and self-realization environment in the kitchen is present only when these basic needs are met.

Herzberg's Two-Factor Theory

Frederick Herzberg put forward the *motivator-hygiene theory*. This theory emphasizes the roles of motivator factors and hygiene factors. Proposed in 1959 by Herzberg, it is also known as the *two-factor theory* of work motivation. The factors that produce job satisfaction are called motivator factors because they satisfy a team member's need for self-realization. According to the theory, hygiene factors are important, but they are *not* motivators.

Herzberg's Hygiene Factors and Motivators

Dissatisfaction: hygiene factors

1. Company policy and administration
2. Supervision
3. Relationship with supervisor
4. Relationship with peers
5. Working conditions
6. Salary
7. Relationship with subordinates

Satisfaction: motivation factors

1. Opportunity for achievement
2. Opportunity for recognition
3. Work itself
4. Responsibility
5. Advancement
6. Personal growth

When hygiene factors (also known as maintenance factors) deteriorate to a level below what a team member considers acceptable, then dissatisfaction is present. However, removing the causes of dissatisfaction does not create satisfaction and will not motivate performance. If kitchen team members are required to work in an environment that is unpleasant, unsafe, and hostile, then a motivational climate cannot be created until such time as the hygiene or maintenance factors are of an acceptable level. When the hygiene factors of policy, supervision, kitchen working conditions, relationships, and pay are good and adequate, the stage is then set for the motivating factors (4). These motivational factors help create job satisfaction, which in and of itself is the primary motivating factor. In Herzberg's theory the opportunity for kitchen team members to advance will require them to seek recognition, assume responsibility, and achieve success through the job. Recognition is the most important factor, more important than pay or any other element of the hygiene factors. If the job or position of a kitchen team member can be enriched to include more motivators, then the opportunity exists to have a motivated, participative member fully committed to the principles of success through TQM.

Herzberg is the person associated with the notions of job enrichment. In 1968 he stressed that "the only way to motivate employees is through challenging work in which they can assume responsibility" (5). This he proposed as a reaction to what he called the KITA (kick-in-the-ass) methods used widely by most managers and supervisors. Central to these proposals is the idea that strategies that modify jobs can offer a more meaningful role for employees and can give them the opportunity for recognition and ultimately greater responsibility.

Theory X–Theory Y

Another motivational theory involves chef supervisors' assumptions about employees and the nature of people. Douglas McGregor, a Massachusetts Institute of Technology professor, identified two sets of these contradicting assumptions. Theory X involves assumptions that McGregor feels supervisors often use as the basis for dealing with people while theory Y represents the assumptions that McGregor feels supervisors should strive to use (6).

Theory X   According to McGregor, theory X assumes that the average person has an inherent dislike of work and will avoid it if possible.

Because of this human characteristic of dislike of work, most people must be coerced, controlled, directed, and threatened with punishment to get them to put forth adequate effort toward the achievement of organizational objectives.

The average person prefers to be directed, wishes to avoid responsibility, has relatively little ambition, and wants security above all.

This view clearly dictates that motivation will primarily be through fear and that supervisors will be required to keep tight observations and control over their subordinates. In the theory X assumption supervisors must protect the employees from their own shortcomings and act out the heavyhanded control and coercion approach.

Theory Y   This approach assumes that the expenditure of physical and mental effort in work is as natural as play or rest. People will exercise self-direction and self-control in the service of objectives to which they are committed. Commitment to objectives is a function of the rewards associated with achievement.

Under proper conditions the average person learns not only to accept but to seek responsibility. The capacity to exercise a relatively high degree of imagination, ingenuity, and creativity in the solution of organizational problems is widely and normally distributed in the population (7).

In contrast to theory X, theory Y emphasizes supervisory leadership through participative management and permits subordinates to experience personal satisfaction as they contribute to the achievement of objectives.

On the other hand, theory X has a part to play in situations that require a firm but necessary position of authority. It has no part to play in team building or the creation of a kitchen team where each player is expected to contribute to the overall success of the team. Empowerment, which is fundamental to TQM success, is most certainly not a part of theory X. The successful kitchen team will fall into McGregor's category of theory Y, which relies on the assumption that people are naturally primed and ready to contribute; the only missing pieces are great leadership and a motivated environment.

Victor Vroom's expectancy model   This model is based on the premise that felt needs cause human behavior. The model addresses the issue of motivation strength. Motivation strength is an individual's degree of desire to perform a behavior. As this desire increases or decreases, motivation strength is said to fluctuate correspondingly (8).

Motivation strength = perceived value of result × perceived probability
of successful completion

According to this model, motivation strength is determined by (1) the perceived value of the result of performing a behavior and (2) the perceived probability that the behavior performed will cause the result to materialize. As both of these factors increase, an individual's motivation strength and desire to perform also increase. In general, individuals tend to perform those behaviors that maximize personal rewards over the long run.

An illustration of expectancy theory applied to kitchen operations might be: A team member believes that if he or she produces meals that satisfy the foodservice establishment's standards and meet the needs of the customer consistently, then the perceived value of utilizing quality standards will produce for the individual a perceived probability of further reward and success.

The Pygmalion effect   The Pygmalion effect states that the expectations the kitchen team have of themselves will determine how well they perform. If you expect great things, great things will happen. If you expect mediocre performance, mediocre performance is what you will get. This is also known as the *self-fulling prophecy*. If you emphasize the positive and what your team can do, team members will begin to believe strongly in themselves. The more the chef supervisor tells the team how successful they can become, the more competent the team will be. When high performance and quality standards are set and team members are told they can rise to the occasion, the self-fulfilling prophecy determines that they will. Positive expectations equal positive results (9).

MORALE

Morale is defined in Webster's dictionary as the "condition with respect to courage, discipline, confidence, enthusiasm, willingness to endure hardship within a group or individual." So far in this chapter we have examined the different motivational theories pertaining to motivating people in the workplace. These are important; they provide insight into what makes some individuals perform well and why some others do not. Motivation contributes to morale. We cannot have great "kitchen morale" without the application of motivational tools by the chef supervisor. The kitchen is often a pressure-filled place of work during busy meal periods. A team spirit with good morale can reduce this pressure and increase the confidence, ability, and harmony of the team and help them to deal with busy service periods.

What then is morale and how can it contribute to the TQM of the kitchen? The first and most important element of morale is the leadership style of the chef supervisor, a leadership style that continuously demonstrates respect and a caring attitude toward the team.

The chef supervisor who will make the greatest impact on morale is the one who believes in people and is sensitive to their difficulties in achieving the kitchen team's goals and one who is sympathetic and approachable. The following elements contribute to morale within the kitchen team. These elements include leadership attributes and a chef supervisor who can:

Create

- A happy relaxed atmosphere in which everyone is clear on *what* to do, *when* to do it, and *how* to do it
- A supervisory leadership style that challenges each team member to contribute the best, a healthy competition, a passion and a pride in being the best, and a team morale that provides a sense of belonging
- An atmosphere in which individuals are encouraged to share opinions and ideas

Show

- A caring awareness of individuals' problems
- A sensitivity and understanding of ethnic diversity and the special problems of integration that may exist within the team
- Respect for individual team members' dignity
- A sense of humor

Chef Talk: "Management by Thought"

Management historians no doubt will recognize the prominent philosophies of the past 15 years: *management by objective, theory X and theory Y*, the *one-minute manager*, and *pursuit of excellence*. At various times, these philosophies taught those who were responsible for the workplace actions of others to develop a management style around thought bytes.

Today, the supervisor's charge is straightforward: Convert suboptimized employees into ones who are fully optimized or (better yet) highly optimized.

In Ogunquit, Maine there is a millionaire who spends sunny mornings picking cigarette butts out of the gutter. The man is William Tower, Jr. The gutter is in front of his restaurant. The restaurant is called Barnacle Billy's. Customers love Barnacle Billy's for many reasons, among them the fact that the restaurant is spanking clean.

The restaurant would be just as clean if someone besides Billy Tower picked the cigarette butts out of the gutter. But Billy might not be as successful. Here's why: All employees begin their workday with the image of Billy Tower cleaning, polishing, washing, and policing fixed in their minds.

It's a powerful message to embed in the fabric of a business. It's a powerful memory for a 16-year-old busboy. That busboy was me. It was my first restaurant job. I thought all foodservice establishments were run that way. I was wrong.

The best bosses I've seen manage by humble example. Unfortunately, they've never been rewarded with the knowledge that they are at the front of a pop management rage. Maybe that will change someday. If it does, allow me to suggest a name: *management by picking up little bits of trash*. Has a nice ring to it, don't you think?

Scott Almendinger, President and Publisher, Journal Publications, Rockland, ME.

- Consistency of behavior in dealing with each member of the team
- Fairness at all times
- Displeasure for poor performance when appropriate

Give

- Praise when it is merited
- Reasons for uncompromising high-quality standards

Be

- An active listener
- A coach and a team builder

Morale is also about empowering and trusting team members to make the right decisions and gives a sense of real involvement to individuals. Once empowerment is in place:

- Give the team members important work to do.
- Allow individual team members to do their work in their own way.
- Give them the resources to do the work.
- Make them feel their decisions are part of the overall plan.
- Actively encourage teamwork.
- Be tolerant with failure.
- Celebrate successes.

The chef supervisor must scrupulously avoid the appearance of favoring one person over another. This may be the most difficult challenge, as no human being is totally objective in dealing with another. We all have biases. Since we cannot be totally objective, we must recognize our subjectivities and compensate for them. To build morale, each individual team member must be treated fairly.

Empowerment contributes to the *esprit de corps* of the kitchen team. Trusting people is a great way to build morale.

Communication is also critical to morale. Team members need to know what is expected of them. Without good, constant dialogue, standards of quality, goals, and objectives for the team and the individual cannot be communicated. Be honest with the team; they want to have confidence in your leadership. They will be more inclined to feel confident when a participative involvement is demonstrated. Be available for discussion, walk around the kitchen, be visible. Make each team member's job more interesting and challenging, get to know each individual, have a sense of their social needs and set a good example.

Another important element of morale consistent with Maslow's needs hierarchy theory is the team members' security. Therefore, a stable, non-threatening environment must be created, one in which unpredictable supervisor mood swings are not present.

As we have observed from different approaches to motivation, employees generally perform at their best when they feel useful and needed, in an environment where they are contributing and valuable team players, where they enjoy a sense of belonging, are involved in decision making, and are trusted and not oversupervised. These elements make up individual and team morale. The creation and maintenance of this morale is part of the chef supervisor's

Chef Talk: "Mood Checks"

Unfortunately not everyone is born with a great attitude toward life and especially toward work. I don't believe I can teach someone to have a good attitude because it truly comes from within and only the individual can have control over it.

However, one can be motivated to feel better about oneself. Therefore, an attitude may take a turn toward the positive rather than the negative things in life.

Motivating my "cast members" has been and always will be fun and is the most creative part of my job. Before I even think about motivating my cast, I take a close look at myself. Each morning I perform my own attitude check. I exercise for 1 hour and then I am ready for the day. I put a positive goal in my mind and I am ready to go to work. After greeting cast members by name, a quick conversation about the previous day's performance, and telling them to "make it a good day," I change into my chef's uniform.

The first item on the day's agenda is the cast members' briefing, which is usually held at 8 a.m. in the main kitchen. The agenda is as follows: 5 to 10 minutes of stretching exercises led by a different cast member each day. The next item is to go over the previous day's financial numbers and any menus and announcements. We talk about the previous day's successes and any challenges we may have run into. We discuss methods of fixing the problems and ways to eliminate them in the future. This gets the momentum going for the day.

One nice addition to our morning briefing is a quick attitude check. This is usually initiated by one of my cast members. It is interesting to see how some of the cast members pull along the others and demand more participation from them, which ultimately leads to better teamwork. I truly believe that if one shows concern for fellow cast members and coaches them in the right direction, positive attitudes and motivation become natural. Remember, you will always win over more employees with praise, good listening skills, and leading by example than with policy and procedures, criticisms, and ridicule. Trust me, no one comes to work in the morning or afternoon saying to themselves: "I'm going to do a lousy job today." You can be the first positive influence for them each and every day.

Bernhard Gotz, CEC, Sheraton Hotel, New Orleans, LA

job. It is very easy to determine when there is poor team morale or no morale at all present in the kitchen; it is difficult to tell if morale is just average; but it is very obvious when good morale is present. It is reflected in low employee turnover and a kitchen that is well led and productive, where team members show pride in producing high-quality customer-focused meals.

STROKES

Strokes are units of attention; they contribute to motivation and morale. Stroking may be in the form of positive strokes, which are strong motivating contributors to morale and come in the form of praise or rewards. Negative strokes may be reprimands or put-downs and are considered demotivators. Strokes can be physical, verbal, nonverbal, or combinations of all three. Most of the strokes we get as adults are verbal and nonverbal as opposed to the physical ones we received as children. Routine stroking is used to describe different aspects and factors that when applied to individual kitchen team members are motivators and builders of morale. Negative stroking in the form of put-downs, insensitivity, insults, sarcasm, poor working conditions, and poor leadership are considered demotivators; they can damage relationships and destroy morale.

Positive Strokes

Positive strokes are necessary in the kitchen to satisfy the esteem and ego needs of individuals. At its simplest, a positive stroke may be a smile from the chef supervisor or a nod of recognition. Other examples of nonverbal strokes include:

- Making eye contact
- Giving listening signals
- Handshakes
- Waving

Verbal strokes include:

- Using a person's name
- Checking for understanding
- Making reference to past experiences
- Praising
- Greeting
- Thanking
- Farewells

Positive stroking is also about catching team members doing a good job. The greatest example and the highest level of stroking is to receive praise in front of the team and other department employees.

Total quality management stroking involves bringing each team member into the decision-making process and the creation of a vision for the foodservice organization. Part of this strategy is identifying quality gaps and planning improvements to fill these gaps on a continuous basis. The chef supervisor can take advantage of this brainpower by involving team members in:

- Setting quality targets
- Setting production goals
- Responding to customer requests
- Evaluating methods of production
- Designing new dishes
- Planning new menus
- Food purchasing: quality and methods
- Improving efficiency
- Promoting certain menu items
- Recruiting new employees
- Improving interdepartmental communication
- Evaluating safety and sanitation

When a climate of cooperation and communication is established through organized sensible stroking, individuals become team participative. This is a challenge for the chef supervisor and the kitchen team, but the potential rewards for the foodservice establishment are great.

Benefits   These are very important motivators, but not the most important. The prospect of earning more money does not motivate as much as recognition, responsibility, and the prospect of advancement. However, incentives and benefits can be used as methods of positive stroking. Organizations that provide health care and insurance benefits usually are ones that invest in people, that care, and that have a low employee turnover. The costs of getting sick and staying healthy are high for most people, especially lower paid employees. The benefits of group programs of health care, insurance, and wellness schemes include reduced stress and increased motivation and morale.

Incentives and awards   These are positive strokes and team reinforcements. Small rewards may be more effective than the large ones. The small rewards may become a cause for positive celebration. Awards, prizes, and ceremonies are important to kitchen team members. What Tom Peters refers to as "little things with high impact" (10) can include:

- Keep a calendar of team members' birthdays and recognize them with a cake, flowers, or a card or by simply wishing them a happy birthday.
- Celebrate happy family events with team members.
- Have a special meal with the kitchen team to celebrate achieving a particular goal.
- Create a player of the week or month program.
- Dine with team members on a regular basis.
- Send out thank you notes regularly.

- Create incentives to address gaps or needs in quality and production.
- Provide opportunities for team members to attend food shows or culinary arts related seminars.

Ensure that all team members are included and are eligible to participate in the program.

Negative Strokes

Examples of negative strokes are reprimanding or putting down of a team member. These are also known as demotivators. If these are in widespread use in the

Chef Talk: "Building Morale"

To build morale at our club we initiated several strategies that worked in creating a sense of family. One of these was the creation of an in-club newsletter through which all of the kitchen team could share their knowledge and different training experiences. The newsletter also acknowledged special awards employees had received as a result of their culinary skills. Special events such as birthdays, new babies, and marriages were included to add a personal touch. This type of employee recognition worked wonders for morale and team spirit.

I began to cross train all employees for all positions in the kitchen. Rather than having one person on a station for years, cross training provided an opportunity for employees to learn new skills and develop a better understanding of problems in areas with which they had previously been unfamiliar. Switching positions exposed both sides of "the fence" and helped to develop problem-solving skills. These programs served as a catalyst for a strong commitment to excellence. It demonstrated a willingness to develop new traditions and not to simply blindly imitate the past.

By providing these opportunities, we were able to attract enthusiastic young culinarians with great potential. This provided the shot in the arm we needed, and it inspired others to seek professional development and certification and to improve performance. The combination of all these changes helped to create improved conditions and build a terrific team spirit in the kitchen. It proved to us that a chain is only as strong as its weakest link. This experience also taught me that without people behind you, bonded by a common thread, nothing can be accomplished. This type of morale results in a strong team spirit and a staff that is dedicated and committed to culinary excellence.

Tom Peer, CMC, AAC, Food & Beverage Director, Duquesne Club, Pittsburgh, PA kitchen, then morale is nonexistent and the leader is probably operating in a theory X mode—the supervisor who leads through fear. If there are no positive strokes available to team members, then they will work for negative strokes rather than suffer the least acceptable situation—no strokes at all. Examples of common negative strokes or demotivators that should be avoided are:

- Inconsistent behavior by the chef supervisor
- Abusive or abrasive behavior
- Poor working conditions
- Fear of supervisor, loss of job, or change
- No team atmosphere
- Lack of recognition
- Poor supervisory leadership
- Lack of incentives, ambitions, or goals for the kitchen team
- Use of ridicule or sarcasm
- Oversupervision and lack of trust
- Unfair job allocations
- Deciding for the team without consultation
- Lack of communication
- Lack of respect for persons of different age, ethnicity, gender, physical abilities and qualities, and sexual preference

When people are unhappy at work, absenteeism increases, productivity goes down, the quality of the meals produced is lower, and employee turnover increases, which all adds up to a failing business. Negative strokes contribute to low morale.

Chef supervisors are required to supervise, which from time to time will require some negative stroking, but this can be equally balanced by pointing to positive stroking on good performance.

Strokes are part of morale building, which together make up the motivational climate. As has been pointed out, motivation comes from within each individual. Simply removing negative stroking and demotivators does not really motivate kitchen team members; it simply brings them to average satisfaction. Therefore, a chef supervisor's leadership qualities and supervisory style will exert a great influence over the team and will determine if individual team members motivate themselves.

FEEDBACK

Feedback is not only a useful method of providing information to the team member on performance but also an excellent method of giving reinforcement and positive strokes. When feedback is given to team members on performance, it should be given only if:

- It is intended to help the person.
- It is given directly to the person (face to face).
- It actually describes what the team member is doing and the effects the actions are having.
- It is a description of a person's actions, not a type of person.
- It is specific, rather than general, with good, clear, recent examples.
- It is given at a time when the team member appears ready to accept it and as soon after the event as possible.
- It is given in private where other team members cannot overhear.
- It includes only those things that the team member can reasonably be expected to do something about.
- It does not cover more than the team member can handle at any one time.
- It is always given when asked for.

The purpose of giving feedback is to reinforce the team member's commitment and abilities. It should be given when requested by a team member. Feedback should be given on two positive levels, described as *needs improvement* or *is doing well.*

Excellent morale within the kitchen is instilled by a chef supervisor who believes that most team members want to do a good job and in most instances will do a good job. The achievement and success of the team are the results of each employee at all levels of the team.

As Daryl Hartley Leonard, CEO of Hyatt Hotel Corporation, states: "If there is anything I have learned in my 27 years in the service industry, it is this, 99% of all employees want to do a good job. How they perform is simply a reflection of the one for whom they work" (11).

CONCLUSIONS

What motivates? As we have learned, each person requires different things. The expression "different strokes for different folks" is perhaps the best way of summing up motivation, morale, and strokes. In the kitchen, people want to join in a group or pursue quality objectives that will enable them to realize their value and potential. They need to see that what they're doing is not wasted effort but is making a contribution to the kitchen team's goals. They must see value in what they are doing. Motivation comes not only from activity but also from the desire to become participative members of the team.

As the TQM of the kitchen develops and gains momentum, the team will support what they create. Being part of the quality objective setting process is motivating; it allows people to feel needed and that their contributions *are* making a difference. When kitchen employees are given the opportunity to have input, they have a stake in the issue. Seeing objectives reached and becoming a reality along with helping to shape the future are fulfilling. Participation in setting objectives and being empowered to make decisions builds team spirit; it enhances morale and allows each team member to feel important.

Stroking and recognition of kitchen employees for the accomplishment of particular tasks also contribute to team morale. Team members want credit for personal achievements and appreciation for their participation in the overall kitchen team objectives. Often giving team members recognition is another way of saying thanks. Kitchen employees are motivated when they know exactly what is expected of them and will then have the confidence to do it successfully. No one wants to assume a task that is vague. Give clear instructions, make the unknown known.

Motivation rises in the kitchen when the objective goals and individual responsibilities are made clear by the chef supervisor. Don't discourage individual team members' growth. Encourage the team to stretch; give them opportunities to try new things and acquire new skills. Chef supervisors should not feel threatened by the achievements and successes of individuals but should be supportive of their success.

Allow the team members to fail as well as succeed. Build a team spirit and *esprit de corps*, which says to each member of the team, "If you grow, we all benefit." Chef supervisors can establish morale through trust, direction, high standards of conduct, encouraging innovation, providing adequate training, treating each team member with dignity, and being a servant of the team.

SUMMARY

Chef supervisors cannot motivate individuals, but they can create a kitchen environment in which individuals can motivate themselves. Each person sees the world from a different and individual viewpoint. Chef supervisors should therefore learn how each kitchen team member is likely to respond to different events.

Motivational theories have demonstrated that most individuals are highly motivated when they can see their value to the goals of the foodservice organization. Among these theories are Maslow's needs hierarchy theory, Herzberg's two-factor theory, Douglas McGregor's theory X, theory Y, Victor Vroom's expectancy theory, and the Pygmalion effect.

Morale within the kitchen is closely related to the leadership ability of the chef supervisor, who can create a happy atmosphere, show respect for individuals, seek their opinions, and build a team environment.

Strokes are units of attention that contribute to motivation and morale. Negative strokes such as put-downs, insensitivity, insults, sarcasm, and poor working conditions are considered demotivators, which damage relationships and destroy morale within the kitchen. Positive strokes are necessary to satisfy the esteem needs of individual kitchen team members. Feedback is an important element of giving strokes.

DISCUSSION QUESTIONS

1. What is the definition of motivation and how can the chef supervisor create the motivational environment within the kitchen?
2. What are the elements of Maslow's hierarchy of needs theory?
3. What methods can a chef supervisor implement to motivate the kitchen team?
4. What are the differences between intrinsic and extrinsic motivators?
5. What are the elements of Herzberg's two-factor theory?
6. What are theory X and theory Y as motivational concepts?
7. What factors contribute to developing morale within the kitchen?
8. What are the effects of the use of positive stroking?
9. Why is feedback important to morale within the kitchen work environment?
10. What effects do negative strokes have on motivation and morale?

NOTES

1. Arthur Sherman, George Bohlander, and Herbert Crudden, *Managing Human Resources*, 8th ed., South-Western, Cincinnati, OH, 1988, p. 290.
2. Mary L. Tanke, *Human Resources Management for the Hospitality Industry*, Delmar, Albany, NY, 1990, p. 45.
3. Abraham Maslow, *Motivation and Personality*, 2nd ed., Harper & Row, New York, 1970.
4. Frederick Herzberg, *Work and the Nature of Man*, World, Cleveland, OH, 1966.
5. Frederick Herzberg, "One More Time: How Do You Motivate Employees," *Harvard Business Review*, Vol. 46, No. 1, 1968, 55.
6. Douglas McGregor, *The Human Side of Enterprise*, McGraw-Hill, New York, 1960.
7. Ibid.
8. Victor H. Vroom, *Work and Motivation*, John Wiley, New York, 1964.
9. Mary L. Tanke, *Human Resources Management for the Hospitality Industry*, Delmar Publishing, Albany, NY, 1990, p. 204.
10. Tom Peters, *Thriving On Chaos*, Harper & Row, New York, 1988, p. 371.
11. Daryl Hartley Leonard, "Perspectives," *Newsweek*, August 24, 1987, p. 19.

4

Developing a Positive Work Climate in the Kitchen

Objectives

When you complete this chapter, you should be able to:

1. Define the elements and characteristics conducive to making the kitchen a great place to work.

2. Describe the barriers within the kitchen that prevent the creation of a positive work environment.
3. Describe the benefits of developing a vision for the kitchen team.
4. Design policies that lead to team building.
5. Identify the steps required to set realistic goals for the kitchen team.
6. Explain the significance of teamwork.

A GREAT PLACE TO WORK

Why would kitchen team members want to say this? Is it because the atmosphere is so relaxed, nobody bothers you, people come and go as they please, the chef supervisor is a "pushover," or there is no harsh discipline and the pay isn't too bad either? No, it's got nothing in common with this scenario. One reason that kitchen team members might believe where they work is a great place to work is because it is well led by a caring, sharing chef supervisor who believes in challenging the other team members to participate in the running of the kitchen, delegates responsibility and empowers the team, and is sensitive to the team's attitudes and feelings. This chef supervisor believes in building morale and a team spirit, and creates a place where people are treated with dignity.

A great place to work is characterized by employees who are proud of their work and organization, who are loyal, and who produce high-quality meals that meet and satisfy customer needs; where *they* encourage the chef supervisor; where high ethical standards are practiced; and where a shared purpose and appreciation exist among all team members. These items come first; pay and working conditions are part of "a great place to work," but they are not the most important ones. John Maxwell, in his book *Developing the Leader Within You*, states, "I know that no amount of money, attention, privileges and promises will motivate a staff member who really does not want to be on the team" (1). If a positive work environment is created in the kitchen and there is no intimidation or anxiety, then the motivational, training, and communication environment is also created.

BREAKING DOWN BARRIERS

Every organization has a certain climate or culture: "That climate can be one that is positive, warm and supportive . . . believe it or not, it can even be a climate in which people have fun and a desire to come to work" (2). In order to create the best possible kitchen work environment, a number of barriers need to be defined, addressed, and overcome. Many of the issues that create barriers are often not even noticed. Some chef supervisors fail to anticipate or recognize potential barriers because of a lack of training, perhaps even insensitivity, and the notion that their supervisory style is okay, because "I treat my team members in a much better way than I was treated." This type of thinking is irrelevant. The chef supervisor who adopts this type of thinking is one who usually fails to recognize the changing nature of the workplace and kitchen employees. Ted Balestreri and Bert Cutino, founders of the award-winning The Sardine Factory in Monterey, California, state (3):

> We thought we had to do everything ourselves in the beginning. We realize however, that there are people who can do things as well, if not better than we can. . . . By bringing talent to the kitchen, giving them the tools, the authority, and the incentive, we found we have moved a lot quicker than we ever thought possible.

According to Jan Carlzon in *Moments Of Truth*, "Everyone wants to be treated as an individual, everyone needs to know and feel that they are needed" (4). Since the main objective of TQM in the kitchen is directed toward customer satisfaction, removing and overcoming barriers are the first steps in that process. The next action is to identify what constitutes a positive work environment in the kitchen and apply it fairly.

DEVELOPING A TEAM VISION

Almost all successful organizations, whether at the corporate level, individual level, or department level, have a "shared vision" that becomes the mission statement of that organization (5). Webster's *New World Dictionary* (1988) defines vision as "the ability to perceive something not actually visible," to see the future, what could be (6). This vision should be a collaborative effort developed by the shared input of the entire kitchen team. The kitchen vision may be the achievement of a target level of measured customer satisfaction: a high rating by a prestigious body, the creation and adoption of a particular type and style of "cuisine," the winning of awards for quality foodservice, or simply to be the best in a particular category. The vision should be a short, simple statement outlining what distinguishes your food style and service in the minds of everybody: customers, kitchen team members, and suppliers. It should also contain clear, inspiring, and empowering criteria.

Through the application of TQM, the effective chef supervisor will therefore have a vision of what the kitchen team can accomplish. That vision will become the energy behind every effort and the force that pushes through all the problems. With vision the kitchen team will accept the direction of the supervisor and a contagious spirit will develop and grow. All great teams possess two things: They know where they are going and they know how to get there. There have perhaps been more inspiring statements written on the subject of vision than any other element of human endeavor. Almost all great leaders and great organizations have shared these great visions. John Maxwell, in *Developing the Leader Within You*, writes (7):

> There are two reasons [for developing a vision]. . . . First, vision becomes the distinctive rallying cry of the organization. It is a clear statement in a competitive

market that you have an important niche. . . . Second, vision becomes the new control tool, replacing the 1,000 page manual . . . the vision is the key that keeps everyone focused.

Tom Peters similarly states: "The vision must support the rule book and the policy manual" (8). Effective visions are also about empowering all kitchen team members by giving them authority to decide. Each team member must contribute to the development of the vision. The process by which the vision is uncovered is part of team building and is also part of identifying barriers to a positive kitchen work climate: "The single thread that runs through all success stories . . . is the involvement of large numbers of individuals in drafting the vision and empowering people to support the vision" (9). Kitchen team members can only be empowered by a vision they understand, and understanding is enhanced by participation. Remember, before the vision is adopted, ensure that it is understood by all team members. The successful chef supervisor along with the kitchen team will always seek to develop the vision and food philosophy and not wait to have it handed down.

In their book *The Leadership Challenge*, Kouzes and Posner discovered that managers who effectively communicated their vision reported significantly higher levels of (10):

- Job satisfaction
- Commitment
- Loyalty
- *Esprit de corps*
- Clarity about the organization's values
- Pride in the organization
- Organizational productivity
- Encouragement to be productive

Clearly, involving the team in your vision produces powerful results.

The following are two examples of vision statements from the book *Teaching the Elephant to Dance*. While these are not from the foodservice industry, they have applications and themes that are certainly most suitable.

Tandem Computers

1. All people are good.
2. People, workers, management, and company are all the same.
3. Every single person in the company must understand the essence of the business.
4. Every employee must benefit from the company's success.
5. You must create an environment where all the above can happen.

U.K. Software Firm (11)

1. Grow partners, employees, customers, and suppliers
2. Best quality and service
3. Market leader in design productivity
4. Constant improvement

The Ford Motor Company The following mission statement was adopted by the Ford Motor Co. and is based on Deming's vision (12):

1. People: Our people are the source of our strength. They provide our corporate intelligence and determine our reputation and vitality. Involvement and teamwork are our core values.
2. Products: Our products are the end result of our efforts, and they should be the best in serving customers worldwide. As our products are viewed, so we are viewed.
3. Quality comes first: To achieve customer satisfaction, the quality of our products and services must be our number one priority. Customers are the focus of everything we do. . . . Continuous improvement is essential to our success. Employee involvement is our way of life. We are a team. We must treat each other with trust and respect.

Vision statements are not just about top, "white tablecloth" restaurants. They are equally relevant to cafeterias, school lunch rooms, hospitals, institutions, industrial and military foodservice organizations, fast-food restaurants, and popular food outlets.

Develop your own vision for your kitchen, get everybody on the kitchen team involved, ask for input. Get a "real" vision of what your goals, food philosophies, and objectives should be. The kitchen should have a particular food philosophy and the type of team and leadership to execute it. Don't just write it down; live it with other team members every day and with every meal served. It takes courage and toughness to create a vision. Vision comes from having a sense of purpose. Vision often has the appearance of being opposed to the mundane aspects of the foodservice organization's goals. Do not put it aside, even when things are not going well.

TEAM BUILDING

Max De Pree stated, "What is it that most of us want from work? We would like to find the most effective, most rewarding, most productive, way of working together" (13). Team building involves getting the members to feel a sense of belonging and ownership in what they are doing as a group: "There is no other business that requires such teamwork . . . with a team effort, with every-

Chef Talk: "Trusting Your Kitchen Team"

I learned some valuable lessons with regard to my co-workers during my time with the U.S. Culinary Olympic Team. When someone is trying out for the team, it is initially an individual effort. Later, when the team is formed, it becomes necessary to retrain oneself for the team effort. What makes a good chef supervisor in this case is one who is able to balance the many commitments. The demands from the U.S. Culinary Team may easily take more time than one's job or personal life. In my case, when the time arrived for tryouts, I had to make sure that my employer would agree to let me take the time off and to help financially.

Fortunately, I was able to build a strong team of chefs in my kitchen. This assured consistency in the quality of the foodservice operation while I was away. This requires placing a great deal of trust in the kitchen team and the chef supervisor.

Later when I started my own restaurant I used the time away from the restaurant in a positive way. Each time I had to go to a team practice, I made sure my guests knew about it, and when I returned, I cooked special Olympic meals and made them aware of what I was doing. My own local support group cheered me every step of the way. My kitchen team also benefited from the experience by seeing the new items prepared and from the projects I was working on. Being involved with the U.S. Culinary Team provided me with sufficient publicity to assure me of being able to find many qualified professionals who wished to work with me at the restaurant.

The important lesson I learned was that I could trust my team and leave my sous chef in charge. While that was a hectic time professionally, it proved to be a very rewarding time, when I, as captain, led our team to a Gold Medal victory. I could not have had any of this success without my kitchen team behind me. It also proved that by treating people with respect and demonstrating trust, they will always rise to the occasion.

Klaus Friedenreich, CMC, AAC, Director, The Culinary Art Institute of Fort Lauderdale, Fort Lauderdale, FL

---

one helping each other the job is so remarkably easy that few could imagine how it could be done any other way" (14).

When the concept of team building is adopted it becomes easier to apply TQM philosophies. It also provides encouragement for team members to work together to develop a team spirit. It helps people to get to know each other so that they in turn can learn to trust, respect, and appreciate individual talents and abilities.

Chef Talk: "Team Building"

Sometimes I think I'm spoiled because I work in a very controlled atmosphere. The Balsams Grand Resort Hotel is the only structure of any significance in Dixville Notch, New Hampshire. One third of my kitchen staff are chef apprentices. They work, eat, and live there, and many of them play there. It's not surprising, therefore, that there is a sense of family, and what makes it so is a strong team spirit.

Teamwork is very important at the Balsams. For me, it's vital for professionalism in the foodservice industry. I coach our apprentices on the importance of team spirit and the value of helping and supporting one another within the kitchen team. Team building is part of developing our young chefs. In addition to cooking skills, they also learn how to interact with each other, to respect each member of the hotel team and the contribution each makes toward ensuring that our guests have a wonderful experience at the Balsams. They appreciate the standards our team sets, particularly in the area of sanitation and professional courtesy, and most importantly they learn to respect themselves.

The nature of our work at the Balsams is both physically and mentally demanding. We work most weekends and public holidays and are here early in the morning and late at night. Therefore, constant coaching is necessary to keep our kitchen team inspired and motivated. Team building, I find, requires a conscious effort. I ask the team for their input every day. We have a 5-minute meeting each night at which time we discuss and assess the events of the day. Our apprentices are inspired by the different distinguished visiting chefs who visit the Balsams as part of our visiting chefs lecture series. We also encourage our apprentices to enter food shows. This is a great tool for developing teamwork. All the apprentices support the competition entry, which produces a great team spirit.

At the beginning of each "season" we come together as a group and brainstorm. We discuss ways to improve menus and production methods and we try to identify new food trends. I seek the opinions of our chefs on new dishes and have them critique these dishes. Together we establish goals for the forthcoming year. This involves the apprentices identifying what they see as priorities in their professional development.

Each day we sit down together and eat as a group. Building a team is not an easy task; without teamwork we would not be successful. We have a warm, caring environment at the Balsams, and team building contributes to this success. Our kitchen employees are a team. They have a sense of pride in their profession with respect for firm, fair, and friendly leadership; they have a strong loyalty to the hotel.

Charles Carroll, CEC, Executive Chef, Balsams Grand Resort Hotel, Dixville Notch, NH

The chef supervisor should empathize with the individual and cultivate a climate of trust and mutual respect. Coaching as a tool of kitchen team building has two important elements: setting specific goals and holding frequent quality progress meetings. Approaches to team building include:

- Developing a shared vision and philosophy of food style and creating long- and short-term goals and plans
- Clarifying individual roles, authority, and accountability
- Clarifying and sorting through interpersonal conflicts
- Setting aside time to learn and apply quality improvement methods and reviewing work methods that affect team performance and the quality of the food served
- Arranging individual and team training needs and listening and reacting to team input

Good coaches are enablers and facilitators; they provide the framework and encouragement for individuals to grow beyond their self-imposed limits and do things they never thought possible: "Before a team can win, they first have to want to win. Second, they have to make the commitment to doing what it takes to win" (15). The chef supervisor needs to believe in the abilities of the team. Also, a positive self-image will be transferred to the team: "Traditional bosses design and allocate work . . . teams consisting of one person or many, don't need bosses; they need coaches. Teams ask coaches for advice. Coaches help teams solve problems" (16). Although the coach appears to be the most important element of team building, the coach is actually dependent on every team member for success. The kitchen team is a unit within a larger team. If the kitchen team produces the best possible meals but customers are served by indifferent, grumpy "wait-staff," then obviously the organizational team has lost. In TQM, for coaching and team building to have meaning within a shared vision, all teams must play to win: "The difference between playing to win and playing not to lose is the difference between success and mediocrity" (17).

GOAL SETTING

An essential component of good coaching is goal setting. Without goals that support the shared vision of the kitchen team, the team does not have the tools or direction to fulfill its vision. Goal setting in the kitchen is more than just menu planning or scheduling. It is part of the application of a TQM plan that meets the needs of the customer and the kitchen team. Goal setting answers the *what*, *when*, and *how* part of TQM. It is part of the nuts and bolts of the vision, the map that will effect on-going improvements.

The first step in goal setting is to establish the "what." *What is to be done?* This spells out the goals for the entire team. Nothing can be more demotivating than uncertainty about what has to be done. "Where are we going, how do I get there, what will I use to get there, and how will I know when I've arrived?" Make the unknown known. Team members' motivation is directly tied to the accomplishment of certain tasks. When these assigned tasks are not accomplished, job satisfaction declines. Goals should only represent improvements in performance, knowledge, or skill, rather than any form of personality change in the individual team member.

The second step in establishing team goals is the "when": Most people will agree that chef supervisors need to be flexible in a coaching and goal-setting capacity. It is easy to set a vague or unrealistic time frame for meeting goals. Time frames should be realistic and definite, yet flexible. Often within the kitchen situations will arise that could not have been anticipated when the goals were originally set.

Third, we must establish how the goals are to be reached. This is where great coaching and training skills are necessary. The individual team members' other priorities must be considered in order to avoid conflicts later on. The how part requires the greatest investment in the kitchen team and its members by the chef supervisor and is based on a comprehensive communication and training effort. Every individual is receptive to new knowledge, and as a result of the training investment, they will be supportive of the supervisor.

(*Note*: See Part II on training.)

Goal setting is particularly important to the delegation process: "Setting concrete, measurable, attainable goals is the basis for authority, accountability, and responsibility. Without clear goals, it is unreasonable, useless, and impossible to transfer these things to an employee" (18).

Make the goals challenging for the kitchen team, ones that inspire thinking; stretch their capabilities. However, make the goals realistic; do not set goals for which you have not provided the resources for the team member to succeed. This may be simple verbal reinforcement, encouragement, or a training session or the physical tools and environment to successfully achieve the set goals. When team members are successful, it builds their self-confidence. It is important also to outline who else is part of the achievement of the goals. (In the foodservice industry it's impossible for the kitchen team to effect the TQM of the kitchen product without the direct participation and involvement of the dining-room or service element of food.) Explain the following team concept: *If one wins, we all win; if one fails, we all fail.* Failure usually results in a poor kitchen work climate that in turn results in poor food preparation and dissatisfied customers.

CONCLUSIONS

Kitchen team members will stay motivated when they see the value to them of the things they are asked to do. Kitchens *are* good places to work. However, like all work places some thought and effort needs to be put into making them a "great place to work." Most people want to do a good job, to give of their best. By creating a positive work climate in the kitchen, the stage is set for implementing in a real way the tenets of TQM. The kitchen as a workplace is no different than any other unit in the foodservice organization. It requires all the correct elements of team building, vision development, coaching, and a nonthreatening environment in order for team members to give their best. The chef supervisor is the vital ingredient in creating this environment.

A concerted effort to provide this environment results in a creative culinary atmosphere. Research supports the notion that most people work and perform at their best when they feel they are part of a team and are asked for their input and opinions. Once the basics of reward in terms of pay and benefits are met, most people work for the intrinsic value of work. Their level of job performance is directly related to a work environment that is mutually supportive. Studies have shown that organizations that provide the best possible working conditions have a smaller turnover in personnel. High employee turnover has been a feature of the foodservice industry for many years. These turnover numbers have fluctuated between 12 and 300 percent, unacceptable levels by any measure.

SUMMARY

Developing a positive work climate in the kitchen is necessary to building a team atmosphere in which each team member is committed to the fulfillment of the culinary operations goals. Barriers to team-building success must be removed along with fear in the workplace. Each person must be valued and treated with dignity and respect by the chef supervisor.

To support on-going quality improvements, a team vision should be developed. With vision, the kitchen team will accept the direction of the chef supervisor, and a contagious spirit will grow that will enhance a positive work climate.

When the concept of team building is adopted by chef supervisors, it becomes easier to apply TQM philosophies.

An essential component of coaching and team building is goal setting. Motivation in the kitchen is directly tied to the accomplishment of goals. When the achievement of certain things is missing, then job satisfaction declines.

DISCUSSION QUESTIONS

1. What are the steps a chef supervisor can initiate to create a "great place to work"?
2. What barriers may inhibit team members from reaching their goals?
3. Why is it important for team members to participate in developing the "team vision"?
4. What are the links between TQM and "vision" development?

5. In team building what do the terms *enablers* and *facilitators* mean?
6. Coaching is critical to team building. How should chef supervisors coach?
7. How are goal setting and delegation linked?
8. What is the value of setting goals within the kitchen? Describe.
9. What are the benefits of developing a concerted effort in team-building and vision development?
10. How does employee turnover relate to a positive work environment?

NOTES

1. John C. Maxwell, *Developing the Leader Within You*, Nelson, Nashville, TN, 1993, p. 165.
2. Wolf J. Rinke, *The Winning Foodservice Manager: Strategies for Doing More with Less*, 2nd ed., Achievement, Rockville MD, 1992, p. 206.
3. T. Balestreri, "Nobody's Perfect," *Lessons in Leadership*, Van Nostrand Reinhold, New York, 1991, p. 18.
4. Jan Carlzon, *Moments of Truth*, Ballinger, Harper & Row, Cambridge, MA, 1987, p. 5.
5. James A. Belasco, *Teaching the Elephant to Dance*, Crown, New York, 1990, p. 98.
6. *Webster's New World Dictionary*, 3rd College ed., Simon & Schuster, New York, 1988.
7. John C. Maxwell, *Developing the Leader Within You*, Nelson, Nashville, TN, 1993, p. 126.
8. Tom Peters, *Thriving On Chaos*, Harper & Row, New York, 1988, p. 486.
9. James A. Belasco, *Teaching the Elephant to Dance*, Crown, New York, 1990, p. 99.
10. James M. Kouzes and Barry Z. Posner, *The Leadership Challenge*, Jossey-Bass Inc., San Francisco, 1988, p. 109.
11. James A. Belasco, *Teaching the Elephant to Dance*, Crown, New York, 1990, p. 111.
12. Mary Walton, *The Deming Management Method*, Putnam, New York, 1986, p. 136.
13. Max De Pree, *Leadership Is an Art*, Dell, New York, 1989, p. 23.
14. Jim L. Peterson,"Self-Esteem Is Essential to Building a Team," *Lessons in Leadership*, Van Nostrand Reinhold, New York, 1991, p. 68.
15. Mary L. Tanke, *Human Resources Management for the Hospitality Industry*, Delmar, Albany, NY, 1990, p. 210.
16. Michael Hammer and James Champy, *Reengineering the Corporation: A Manifesto for Business Revolution*, Harper Collins, New York, 1993, p. 77.
17. John C. Maxwell, *Developing the Leader Within You*, Nelson, Nashville, TN, 1993, p. 166.
18. Andrew E. Schwartz, *Delegating Authority*, Barron's, New York, 1992, p. 29.

5

Total Quality Respect

Objectives

When you complete this chapter, you should be able to:

1. Describe issues and elements that create fear within the kitchen work environment.
2. List the steps that contribute to encouraging team members to give feedback.
3. Describe the changing nature of the kitchen work environment relative to a diversified work force.
4. Define the elements of diversity and capitalize on diversity as an advantage.

5. Reduce potential conflict among kitchen members resulting from cultural misunderstandings.

6. State the elements that make up sexual harassment and describe the legal responsibilities of the chef supervisor in this area.

INTRODUCTION

Point 8 of Deming's 14 points is "driving out fear, so that everyone may work effectively for the company." In the foodservice industry, and the kitchen in particular, this directive is important. The use of fear as a tool of control prevents people from thinking: "It robs them of pride and joy in their work and kills all forms of intrinsic motivation. The thinking and creative potential of the workers are stopped cold" (1). Most chef supervisors who rely on fear believe those working under them are incapable of thinking, and this concept becomes a self-fulfilling prophesy. Fear is harmful to the foodservice organization and to the individual kitchen team member. Chef supervisors may *not* be able to eliminate all fear from the lives of all the kitchen team members, but they can eliminate the sources of fear built into the management structures. Ferdinand Metz, President of the Culinary Institute of America, recommends: "Build a team that will work towards a common objective. Lead by example. Always be willing to do what you ask others to do. They will respect you for this" (2).

Aspects that enable chef supervisors to drive fear out of the kitchen include being:

- Sensitive to issues and interests of team members
- Respectful of differences in people
- Open and participative in problem solving
- Anxious to use the power of their position to serve the team well
- Fair and equitable in the distribution of work
- Constant in their efforts to find solutions that are both technically and politically sound
- Constant in seeking individual team member input on decisions
- Willing to put the welfare of the team before private interests
- Never "better" than other team members
- Honest and willing to consider retaliation a sign of serious weakness

According to Ryan and Oestreich in *Driving Fear Out of the Work Place* (3), supervisors who use threatening and abusive behavior "immediately destroy trust and end communication. They create a thick wall of antagonism and resentment." No one respects a supervisor who repeatedly puts others down or loses control of his or her temper. Among the elements of threatening or abusive actions or behaviors that demean, humiliate, isolate, insult, and threaten team members are:

- Silence and glaring eye contact
- Snubbing or ignoring people
- Insults or put-downs
- Blaming, discrediting
- Aggressive, controlling manner
- Threats about the job
- Yelling and shouting
- Angry outbursts or loss of control
- Physical threats
- Racial, ethnic, or gender slurs
- Blatant or discriminatory comments

There are times when the chef supervisor must criticize a team member's performance, but if correctly and sensitively handled, criticizing is less likely to give offense. The following are guidelines to giving negative feedback in a positive manner:

- *Limit the comments to the team member's behavior*. Don't label the person as always stubborn, difficult or easy-going. Do not criticize the *person*; focus on the *activity*, not on the type of individual he or she is. Be specific and don't generalize about a particular behavior.
- *Criticize as quickly as possible following the problem*. The problem is fresh in the mind of the team member, so you will probably get a more accurate response.
- *Listen carefully to what individual team members have to say*. Get their opinion, let them tell you what went wrong. Ask what they think the problem is. Do not prejudge an answer. Keep an open mind to what you hear.
- *Be considerate*. Get your point across without being loud, rude, or abrupt. Losing control will put the other person on the defensive and probably won't help you solve the problem or determine its cause.
- *Don't present criticism with praise*. This sends a confusing message. Often there is a tendency to want to say something nice to soften the blow. It rarely works; it may blunt the criticism, but the praise means nothing. The team member only hears the bad news.
- *Don't trap or humiliate kitchen team members*. If a complaint is received from a customer, the chef supervisor should be straightforward in talking with the person about the complaint.
- *Don't blame the entire kitchen department for a problem*. Mistakes happen. It may be someone's fault, but as a supervisor, you should not generalize and accuse the entire kitchen team of acting poorly.

Verbal criticism is usually less severe than written criticism. Unintended results may occur as a consequence of written criticism. It can be far more severe than verbal criticism, and it becomes part of the individual's record, which could affect promotions and layoffs. The kitchen team member may not have had an opportunity to respond or explain what occurred. Written criticism remains an issue for an extended period of time and comments made may lack clear meaning because the tone of voice or any further explanation is not available to the reader. Criticism should also be communicated in private. Choose a time that will facilitate solving the problem. Generally, the best time to criticize is early in the day so that the team member can get on with the job.

Encourage the kitchen team to give you feedback. Encouragement communicates trust, respect, and a belief in someone else. Discouragement results in lowered self-esteem and alienation from others. A discouraging chef supervisor is one who:

- Constantly criticizes and points out mistakes
- Has unrealistic expectations of others and does not allow for mistakes

An encouraging supervisor will use words such as:

- "What did you learn from that mistake?"
- "You did a good job."
- "Keep trying; you will succeed."
- "Great improvement."
- "If you need any help, let me know."

The difference between the best kitchen team members and the average ones often depends on the leadership style and ability of the chef supervisor. A good chef supervisor can turn some average team members into outstanding performers. It is what the chef supervisor does that influences performance. Sincerity is of the utmost importance. If team members are treated with total quality respect, then they are their own best source of motivation.

DIVERSITY

The foodservice industry has always had higher numbers of minorities and women than most other industries in the United States. However, it has not always enjoyed the best of reputations in its handling of women and minorities. All analyses and indicators show that 65 percent of the new jobs created during the 1990s will be filled by women. By the year 2000, nearly one-half of the civilian work force will be women and by the year 2050, one-half of the U.S. population will be composed of African Americans, Hispanic Americans, Native Americans, and Asian Americans (4). There's probably more diversity in the foodservice industry—more women, more minorities—than in any other industry (5).

As we look toward the next century, the foodservice industry is faced with issues of supervising not only greater numbers of people, but also a more diverse work force. Supervision within the kitchen will require a greater awareness of TQM and TQR for the values and cultures of all kitchen team members. An establishment that values diversity is one in which kitchen team members learn to appreciate individuality and avoid prejudging people. An encouraged awareness of diversity will facilitate the discussion of assumptions each team member may hold regarding certain groups of people. "Understanding and accepting diversity enables us to see that each of us is needed: recognizing diversity helps us to understand the need we have for opportunity, equity and identity in the workplace" (6).

According to R. Roosevelt Thomas Jr., total quality and diversity are similar in perspective and intent. As stated in his book *Beyond Race and Gender*, "practioners may argue about the scope of total quality, but they generally agree on what it is. Total quality's skills and techniques are more advanced than those of managing diversity. Yet their commonalities are more significant" (7).

Generally, until human beings have the opportunity to learn otherwise, they assume that other people look at the world as they do, everyone having similar values and motivated by the same things.

Acceptance of diversity by chef supervisors can mean getting used to different accents or languages or people who dress differently. It means feeling comfortable with team members whose skin is a different color. Diversity in a team refers to the following physical and cultural dimensions that separate and distinguish us as individuals and groups: age, gender, physical abilities, ethnicity, race, and sexual preference. Miller et al. state: "Failure to understand and to respect the diversity of your employees can result in misunderstandings, tension, poor performance, poor employee morale, and higher rates of absenteeism and turnover . . . when diversity is respected, the working environment is richer" (8).

The first step in improving respect for diversity is communication. Establish a climate that encourages a free exchange of ideas. Explore how all team members come to the kitchen with a unique combination of backgrounds and influences. Start with yourself and your own background. Get to know your team members. Don't make ethnic- or gender-oriented jokes, and don't tolerate even good-natured jokes in this area. Encourage diversity and an awareness of different cultures through events such as special days in the cafeteria devoted to ethnic foods.

If individuals are having difficulty with English, be patient and encouraging. Ask them for their input. The fact that some people may not say anything does not mean they have nothing to say. Persons changing from one culture to another may experience culture shock, which may be manifested as fear. Encourage the rest of the team to understand and respect differences in people. As a chef supervisor, believing and showing that you respect team members who come from different backgrounds is very important. The self-esteem of diverse team members remains intact if they believe their backgrounds are accepted and respected.

Chef Talk: "Women in the Kitchen"

Diversity in the foodservice industry has far-reaching effects on the integrity of the workplace. Kitchens are places where sensitivity and tolerance are commodities in short supply as they pertain to diversity.

As a female chef, I can attest to the importance of management's concerted efforts in creating a challenging, yet satisfying environment for all employees, including women. Working in this industry has only reinforced in my mind the impact of the statistical ratio of males to females in the professional kitchens of America and the different treatment each population receives.

When I sought employment at one of Boston's oldest and most prestigious hotels, little did I know the extent of experience and knowledge I would be gaining. Unlike my experiences in the small restaurant and catering scene, working at this hotel opened my eyes to the biases that occur in favor of Caucasian males within the foodservice industry.

After working for three months at this hotel, I approached the Executive Chef, expressing an interest in cross-training in another department. The chef was very receptive and expressed his approval and support for my wishes. However, five months passed before my transfer occurred. In the meantime, I saw two male cooks who had been in the hotel a shorter time than I transfer out of my department, and six male cooks were also transferred to other departments. Through networking with other female African American and Spanish cooks in the kitchen, I began to identify a pattern. Four other cooks had experienced similar treatment. As the fifth month since my initial talk with the Executive Chef ticked by, my job satisfaction dropped significantly. The transfer eventually occurred, but by that time the damage to my morale was done and my perception of the organization was altered considerably. It was apparent to me that my numerous requests had been handled with less urgency than those of male chefs.

In industries throughout this country the number of working women is beginning to outnumber men. Women bring a new dynamic element to the workplace that stretches beyond education; it includes skills, dedication, and attention to detail. Because of their traditional societal role as caregivers, they also possess superior communication and interpersonal skills. It is up to the modern foodservice supervisor to maximize these skills, which in turn will benefit the organization.

Christine Stamm-Griffin, Johnson & Wales University, Providence, RI

Chef Talk: "That Was Then"

The years 1958–1960 ushered into the U.S. mainstream a new respect for quite a few things. It was also around this time that I began my career in culinary arts. It was during this era that most restaurant kitchens were manned by a staff comprised of an executive chef, a sous chef, and a kitchen manager (all Caucasian); the "grunt" crew was composed mostly of African Americans. *Respect* was a word seldom used in kitchens at that time. Fear was the order of the day, and authoritarian rule produced an atmosphere of fear and resentment. I am African American, and despite these intimidating conditions, I learned to love cooking. I also developed a resolve to be successful.

Today, I am happy to say that I have been successful in spite of the awful conditions that existed for African Americans in those pre–equal rights times. I am a chef supervisor as well as Chief Executive Officer of my own company. My background has conditioned me to be more sensitive to those that I am called upon to supervise. I constantly check my performance to ensure that I am not subconsciously reenacting the role of my earlier supervisors.

It is crucial that chef supervisors prepare themselves for a changing work environment in the kitchen. Minorities have proved that they are as capable and as competent as any other workers in the foodservice industry. When a chef supervisor understands that there are no "big I's" and "little you's," only an engine and the rest of the train, he or she can celebrate total quality respect in the kitchen.

Clayton Sherrod, CEC, AAC, Birmingham, AL

The following is abstracted from a job notice that appeared in an advertisement in the *Boston Globe*, October 7, 1990. It demonstrates a comprehensive understanding of "valuing differences":

In every aspect of life there is diversity. Accept this and you open yourself to endless possibilities. Close your mind to diversity and you are confined in isolation. Where one may see a problem, two may find a solution.

We value and encourage the contributions of all. We recognize that while each one of us sees our own level of achievement, acceptance, and recognition, together we can attain higher goals. We can contribute to the well-being of our community by building strong bonds and implementing new ideas. This is our team—a group of people working together for the common good, while accepting the views, support and uniqueness of each individual.

A kitchen work environment filled with ethnic diversity has the potential for conflict based on differences. This conflict may be based on misconceptions or stereotyping by chef supervisors and other kitchen team members about different ethnic groups, languages, or cultures. Each side can misinterpret or dismiss the viewpoint of the other by failing to understand the framework in which the other operates.

HARASSMENT

In recent times harassment in the workplace has become mostly synonymous with sexual harassment. There are many forms of harassment in the foodservice industry: of people who are different; of gay people, minorities, and physically or mentally impaired people. Federal laws, executive orders, court cases, and state and local statutes provide a broad legal framework that protects these categories of employees.

The Equal Employment Opportunity Commission (EEOC) issued guidelines on sexual harassment in 1980, indicating that it is a form of discrimination under Title VII of the 1964 Civil Rights Act. The EEOC states that sexual harassment consists of "unwelcome advances, requests for sexual favors, and other verbal or physical conduct of a sexual nature." The conduct is illegal when it interferes with an employee's work performance or creates an "intimidating, hostile, or offensive working environment." The *Uniform Guidelines* holds employers strictly accountable for preventing the sexual harassment of female or male employees. The EEOC also considers an employer guilty of sexual harassment when the employer knew about or should have known about the unlawful conduct and failed to remedy it. Employers are also guilty of sexual harassment when they allow nonemployees (guests or salespersons) to sexually harass employees. Where sexual complaints or charges have been proved, the EEOC has imposed severe penalties that include back pay, reinstatement, payment of lost benefits, interest charges, and attorney's fees. Sexual harassment can result in criminal charges if it involves physical contact. Damages are assessed against both the offender and the employer. Studies and surveys indicate that as many as 88 percent of all working women and as many as 15 percent of men have experienced some form of sexual harassment (9).

Increasingly, foodservice organizations are becoming more proactive in the area of sexual harassment. According to figures released by the EEOC in 1993, "sexual harassment actions against eating and drinking establishments are trending at a 27 percent increase" (10). There is a fine line between harassment, teamwork, and camaraderie. While certain working conditions in the foodservice industry may contribute toward sexual harassment, it is people who commit the offenses. The majority of sexual harassment situations involve harassing women; the occurrence of women harassing men is also on the increase. In both instances not acting to prevent sexual harassment is the same as condoning it.

Chef supervisors have a responsibility to recognize and prevent sexual harassment in the kitchen. Every organization must have a clearly defined policy on sexual harassment. It should be clearly communicated to every team

Chef Talk: "Pioneer Apprentice"

In 1978 Elizabeth Tobin became the first female apprentice in my kitchen. Up until that time options for female chefs were confined to working as "cooks," usually in hospitals or other institutions or as assistants in the pastry shop. The title "chef" was reserved for males only. From the first day, I insisted that Elizabeth break from the traditional mold set for women in the kitchen. At that time women did not even wear the traditional chef's uniform. It was difficult for Elizabeth; she was battling 100 years of male dominance in the culinary world of the Gresham Hotel. She encountered many difficulties, not least among them the idea that women could not handle the stress and tension of service time in a busy kitchen or the often "rich" language used in kitchens.

Elizabeth was a pioneer female apprentice back then. Not only was she an excellent chef, but she turned out to be a great role model for aspiring young female chefs. She rotated through all the departments and graduated with flying colors.

The purpose of this insight into the first female apprentice in my kitchen (which was also the first time the trade union recognized female chefs) is to outline the progression in thinking from 1978 to the present time. As I reflect back on that time, it seems almost inconceivable that culinary arts or the kitchen in general were male-only preserves.

Noel C. Cullen, Ed.D., CMC, AAC, Boston University, Boston, MA

member. The best cure for workplace sexual harassment is a policy and an educational program designed to prevent it. Policy statements should be in writing and stress that harassment will not be tolerated.

The following are the fundamental elements of an effective sexual harassment policy:

- A systemwide comprehensive policy on sexual harassment should be developed. Experts in the area of sexual harassment should be involved in its preparation. This policy should be part of all new employee induction and orientation training programs. Current employees should be made aware what the policy is, and a strong organizational statement condemning sexual harassment should be issued by management.
- Chef supervisors should receive training in how to prevent sexual harassment in the kitchen.
- Procedures for dealing with complaints in this area should be established.

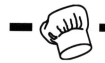

Chef Talk: "Managing Diversity"

The demands of managing a multicultural work force are particularly important in the foodservice industry. Any of us who spend our working hours in and around kitchens, whether they be in hotels or in hospitals, know that our staff represents a multiplicity of national origins, ethnicities, religions and languages. Even within groups that appear to be homogeneous from the outside, there are important differences to be considered. It is this diversity that we need to first acknowledge, then learn to respect and value, in order to incorporate this sensitivity into our management endeavors.

Many chefs might be delighted to experiment with and proudly serve Thai-inspired entrees or develop regional twists on Tex-Mex recipes but then slur an immigrant worker who grew up on the cuisine they are trying so hard to perfect. The same curiosity and creativity we apply to exploring culinary diversity seems to get lost in dealing with "different" people. We need to examine more closely the "ingredients" of our staffs, get to know their characteristics and the richness of their textures, how they mix together, what treatment they can and cannot tolerate before "spoilage," and then develop the best management "recipe" we can to make our operations as productive and positive as possible.

In our operation, we have over 250 people representing 30 countries of origin and even more cultures. To effectively motivate people and to choose appropriate means of communication so that we understand each other better, we initiated a "Valuing Differences" program. Its purpose was to promote increased tolerance, acceptance, and hopefully appreciation of the many backgrounds we represent.

We started a "Who We Are" map. All employees, from sanitation worker to cooks and cashiers to director, are photographed on the job and interviewed with regard to their backgrounds and their favorite foods. Each photograph is placed on a world map with the employee's interview information. Thus the program acknowledges each person individually and the group as a whole—it's fun and educational. We of course are striving for more efficiency and better teamwork, but we are also seeking to measure our success on a more human level, more smiles, increased courtesy, and a better tolerance of our unique differences.

Recognizing our quality as individuals is a basic recipe that can only result in improved quality output and services, no matter what one is cooking.

Rudolf Gautschi, CEC, Director, Food Services, Brigham and Women's Hospital, Boston, MA

- Action should be taken immediately to investigate complaints of harassment.
- Offenders should be disciplined and in serious cases dismissed instantly. The policy should be equally and fairly applied to all team members.

CONCLUSIONS

While many management philosophies exhort employees to greater attention to detail in terms of providing quality food and service, there also needs to be a similar commitment and effort to managing all the elements of multiculturalism. Sadly, the foodservice industry has not always enjoyed the best reputation in this area. As the make-up of employees continues to change, a greater understanding and tolerance of diversity must occur. Many studies have shown that when there is a culture of respect in the workplace, productivity increases. Total quality respect for all our team members will build TQM. Without TQM we are managing people as a cost, not as a resource upon which continuous improvements can be based.

SUMMARY

Total quality respect is linked closely to valuing the differences among individuals. It is about driving fear out of the kitchen and adopting a sense of tolerance toward all ethnic and gender differences.

Criticism of individuals within the kitchen team must be conducted with sensitivity. Negative feedback can be given in a positive manner.

Understanding and valuing diversity will enable the chef supervisor to see that each team member has a special contribution to make. The self-esteem of diverse team members will stay intact if they believe their backgrounds are accepted and respected.

Chef supervisors are required to be aware of all forms of sexual harassment and they have a responsibility for recognizing and preventing it.

DISCUSSION QUESTIONS

1. Point 8 of Deming's 14 principles concerns driving fear out of the workplace. How is this linked to total quality management?
2. What are the steps that can contribute to creating fear within the kitchen work environment?
3. What factors contribute to alienating team members within the kitchen?
4. What are the phrases a chef supervisor uses to encourage the kitchen team?
5. Women and minorities are often lumped together as a single class. What do these two groups have in common? What are the major differences between them?
6. How could a foodservice operation use diversity as a competitive advantage?

7. Why is management of diversity vital? Is this a temporary or long-term phenomenon?
8. When is sexual harassment illegal? What are the consequences of these illegal actions?
9. Why do chef supervisors have a responsibility to prevent sexual harassment?
10. Why is it that total quality management is not possible without total quality respect?

NOTES

1. Rafael Aruayo, *Dr. Deming*, Carol, New York, 1991, p. 184.
2. Ferdinand Metz, "Success Has a Future Perspective," *Lessons in Leadership*, Van Nostrand Reinhold, New York, 1991, p. 36.
3. Kathleen Ryan and Daniel K. Oestreich, *Driving Fear Out of the Workplace*, Jossey-Bass, San Francisco, 1991, p. 75.
4. John P. Fernandez, *Managing a Diverse Work Force: Regaining the Competitive Edge*, Heath and Co., Lexington, MA, 1991, p. 5.
5. Ted Balestreri, *Nation's Restaurant News*, September 20, 1993.
6. Max De Pree, *Leadership Is an Art*, Dell, New York, 1989, p. 9.
7. Thomas R. Roosevelt, Jr., *Beyond Race and Gender*, AMACOM, New York, 1991, p. 163.
8. Jack E. Miller, Mary Porter, and Karen E. Drummond, *Supervision in the Hospitality Industry*, 2nd ed., John Wiley, New York, 1992, p. 92.
9. Susan L. Webb, *Step Forward: Sexual Harassment in the Workplace*, Master Media, New York, 1991, p. 87.
10. Theresa Howard, "Sexual Harassment in Foodservice," *Nation's Restaurant News*, August 23, 1993.

6

Dealing with Conflict and Complaints

Objectives

When you complete this chapter, you should be able to:

1. Identify the issues that contribute to team member frustration.
2. Describe steps to deal effectively with team member complaints.

3. Define the connections between motivation and job satisfaction.
4. Outline the basic steps in health, safety, and accident prevention in the kitchen.
5. State the advantages and disadvantages of counseling and know when to intervene or refer team members for outside help.
6. Identify the benefits of employee assistance programs and their impact on team member wellness.

INTRODUCTION

Complaints are an indication of discontent among the kitchen team. The chef supervisor is the key to addressing complaints before they develop into something they are not and become even more difficult to resolve. Speedy resolution of grievances and complaints is part of a positive, well-led kitchen work environment. Wise handling of complaints affords the greatest opportunity to win kitchen team members' respect and to gain their confidence.

Most interpersonal conflicts in the foodservice industry have been between dining-room and kitchen team members. A traditional animosity has always existed between these two groups. Chefs view themselves as the skills-oriented aristocrats of the foodservice organization. Service personnel are viewed by chefs as the lesser participants in the big scheme of things. Ironically, and this may come as a big surprise to many chefs, dining-room team members also view themselves as aristocrats and the most important people in the organization. They have similarly low opinions of chefs. Of course, although both positions are ridiculous, they are a great source of conflict. In the TQM environment, departments that conflict or fail to focus on the objective of customer satisfaction will doom the entire foodservice organization to failure. Every member of the organization must be a committed team player totally focused on continuous improvements that facilitate the provision of high-quality food and service; both are inextricably intertwined.

FRUSTRATION

When examined, the working day of a kitchen team member will reveal that all needs are *not* satisfied fully. They may be prevented from reaching a particular goal or objective or there may be conflicting goals. Either condition will produce a state of dissatisfaction and tension that may prevent a harmonious team spirit in the kitchen. Chef supervisors should understand the forces and factors that contribute to tension and dissatisfaction. Barriers to achieving individual goals produce a frustrating condition. Typical sources of frustration are:

- Hostile chef supervisors
- Monotonous tasks

- Unpleasant working conditions
- Economic insecurity
- Unfair work assignments
- Abuse of established working procedures
- Lack of orientation training
- Being ignored

A frustrated individual may respond by engaging in disruptive behavior. The distance between frustration and aggression is a short one. Aggression typically involves verbal or physical attacks against the person or persons perceived to be the cause of the frustration. Chef supervisors have a responsibility to be sensitive to the warning signs in this area. Not all sources of frustration are under the direct control of the supervisor. However, an awareness of potential areas of frustration and a sincere effort to handle them effectively through better organization, planning, and communication can help to remove many of the conditions that cause frustration.

When individuals sense that they are in danger, they may experience a feeling of anxiety. In contrast to fear, anxiety results when the source of danger cannot be identified. The physical symptoms of anxiety are similar to those associated with fear: nausea, trembling, a pounding heart, and dryness in the throat. This anxiety is a form of stress that is emotionally and physically harmful. Anxiety may account for various kitchen team members' behaviors that are often misunderstood or misinterpreted, particularly in individuals of different backgrounds and cultures. Anxiety is also frequently caused by the prospect of change. This activity can often be misinterpreted by supervisors as team members being difficult rather than simply anxious or frightened.

COMPLAINTS

Complaints from team members concerning other team members will come to the forefront very quickly. Most people don't hesitate to complain about each other. It is a normal human phenomenon. Complaints about other people can be presented in a highly emotional way or in a cool, calculating manner. But usually this is done with a great deal of emotion, which colors the facts involved. Therefore, very often the real problem is not obvious. What is important is that the issue be dealt with as soon as possible. The longer the complaint remains unresolved, the more other people get involved and the more the quality of the work is affected. This impacts immediately on customer satisfaction. If the chef supervisor has difficulty in resolving the complaint, then it is appropriate to seek further help from senior management. The main point is that there should be some avenue by which the complaining kitchen team member can obtain a full and fair hearing, particularly if he or she is dissatisfied with the decision of the chef supervisor.

The "ideal" resolution of complaints is to bring the situation around from where one loses and one wins. The best possible result is a "win-win" situation. This is achieved through participation by the team member with the chef supervisor in resolving the issue. One of the most useful approaches is the application of a systematic approach to resolving complaints. The following steps can lead to a satisfactory resolution and investigation of the complaint:

- Check out fully the team member's record. Look for evidence of tardiness or absenteeism. Get the facts. Perhaps there are hidden reasons for seeking attention by complaining.
- Attempt to understand why the team member has made the complaint and what his or her feelings are. Allow the individual to "vent." Let him or her communicate freely and without interruption. Watch for body language and observe facial expressions.
- When other persons are involved, check for accuracy of information.
- Avoid an argumentative disposition when hearing the complaint.
- Keep senior management informed.
- Admit a supervisory mistake. Do not try to conceal it if you have caused the complaint.
- Record the formal complaint; do not depend on memory. Be specific; include day, date, time, place, those involved, the type of complaint, and any other relevant facts.
- Prepare a written statement that includes the resulting decision and the rationale for this decision.
- Together with the team member, establish facts and a definition of the complaint. Seek solutions, exhausting all avenues. Finally, bring the resolution to a mutually agreeable set of terms that includes steps for avoiding future problems in the area of the complaint.

Complaints are sometimes ways which kitchen team members use to draw attention and also to send messages regarding unfair wage scales, poor working conditions, and discriminatory actions against team members on the basis of ethnic origin, gender, or sexual preference. The individual making the complaint is entitled to a fair hearing. Complaints that are not handled promptly and decisively can lead to problems of arbitration with labor unions. By bringing the complaint or problem to a win-win situation the chef supervisor is dealing with the immediate problem. However, win-win solutions can involve a promise to solve the complaint through higher authority. What is important in dealing with complaints is that the chef supervisor recognize that the old-style theory Y type supervisor is replaced with a theory X type, which in some instances represents a major shift in attitude for the chef supervisor. It replaces the notion that complaining kitchen team members are adversaries and it focuses on solutions, assuming that both parties are aiming for the same goals. The win-win approach is consistent with the basic tenets of TQM at its best: directed to continuous improvement of product and service. In the foodservice industry, positive, motivated, happy team members are critical to success.

JOB SATISFACTION

Like motivation, job satisfaction means different things to different people. At its highest level, it is the kitchen team member who derives happiness in the knowledge that the foodservice customer had an outstanding dining experience. Generally, the satisfaction individuals receive is dependent upon the extent to which the job and everything associated with it meets their needs and wants. The "wants" are items the individual feels will deliver satisfaction. Typically, "needs" represent tangible rewards such as pay and benefits. The wants are perceived differently within the team and are based on differences in age, educational level, sex, health, family relationships, personality, and other factors. They are very often of an intrinsic nature.

Job satisfaction has been shown to be closely linked to turnover and absenteeism. The higher an individual's satisfaction, the less likely it is that he or she will leave the organization. According to Lendal Kotechevar, in his book *Management By Menu*, turnover in the foodservice industry varies between 12 and 300 percent (1). This represents an unacceptable level by any set of measurements. The link between turnover and satisfaction in the foodservice industry (and presumably kitchen employees reflect similar numbers) indicates that many employees are unhappy. Is it pay or working conditions? Clearly, to implement and maintain a TQM program in the kitchen, the first requisite is a team that is stable and satisfied. Apart from the team-building and visionary aspects which are crucial to TQM, replacing a kitchen team member can be time consuming and expensive. It is far better and more cost effective to invest in current team members rather than constantly hiring and training new people.

Replacement costs cover three areas: separation costs for the departing employee, recruiting and hiring a replacement, and the time and training costs of the new hire. Total replacement costs are two to three times the monthly salary of the departing team member. The intangibles of a dissatisfied kitchen team member are potentially more costly. This includes the effect on morale within the team and its impact on customer satisfaction and the missed opportunities to utilize the team member's talent and potential to grow.

Job satisfaction is affected by all of the elements discussed in this chapter. Chef supervisors should invest in the kitchen team through excellent supervisory skills and by providing conditions within the kitchen that provide the basis for job satisfaction. Mentally challenging work with which each individual can cope successfully is of primary importance. Ideally each member should love food and have a strong sense of culinary professionalism. The atmosphere in the kitchen should be open and non-threatening, led by a firm but friendly supervisor who seeks input and support from the team, and in which each team member is valued. Satisfaction is not about winning popularity contests; rather it is about the creation of a team and an environment where the individual is respected. Most studies in the area of job satisfaction conclude that a link exists between satisfaction and performance. The role the chef supervisor plays in this link is crucial.

Chef Talk: "Satisfaction and Growth"

A very wise man once said, "as one looks at life's challenges, there are things that are optional and things that are certain." Growth in one's life, be it personal or professional, is optional, but change is certain.

I experienced a tremendous amount of change in my 30 years as a chef, and many times I chose to grow with it, but at times I refused to grow. I found that whenever I chose to grow with change, positive things happened, in contrast to when I refused to grow, when negative things happened.

I started my career in the old world of the culinary profession. Learning, motivation, and communication were dealt with in medieval methods: intimidation, ridicule, and even occasional beatings were common practice. For example, the chef under whom I did my apprenticeship used a braising fork as a motivational tool. He would actually poke anyone he thought was working too slowly or otherwise doing things the wrong way. Recipes were never shared, and one had to learn by secretly watching the chefs.

This is pretty hard to believe in today's world of modern education, but that is the way it was. Obviously, these methods greatly influenced my thinking. For many years, I used the same method (except the beatings and the braising fork). The results, as one might suspect, were the problems most chefs experienced then; there were no days off, long hours, and lots of stress. Since I motivated others only from the outside through fear and intimidation and I never shared my skills with anyone, I had to physically be there to assure that everything was taken care of all the time. I had no loyalty from my employees, frustration was high, and so was the turnover, which in turn resulted in lack of consistency and quality.

Over the years, I saw the changes. Formal educational systems were introduced in our kitchens, old methods became obsolete, and a new way of thinking entered. It was "discovered" that cooks, chefs, waiters, etc., were human beings and wanted to be treated as such. It was also discovered that there were tremendous resources and a great deal of potential within every single person working in our industry.

Carl Guggenmos, CEC, Director of Culinary Education, Johnson & Wales University, Charleston, SC

HEALTH AND SAFETY IN THE KITCHEN

Foodservice employers are required by law to provide working conditions that do not impair the safety or health of kitchen employees or indeed any other unit or department member. Therefore, they must provide an environment that protects employees from physical hazards, unhealthy conditions, and unsafe or dangerous practices by other kitchen team members. Effective health and safety practices promote a positive work climate in the kitchen by providing for the physical and emotional well-being of all team members as well as enhancing their economic security.

Safety hazards in the foodservice industry range from the use of knives, power-driven equipment, slippery floors, and chemical cleaning materials. These hazards can produce accidents resulting in individuals falling, cutting themselves, burning themselves, receiving an electric shock, scalding themselves, or worse. These accidents occur because of ignorance of safety procedures and carelessness.

In the late 1960s, Congress became increasingly concerned that each year job-related accidents accounted for more than 14,000 deaths and nearly 2.5 million disabilities (2). Eventually, these concerns led to the passage of the Occupational Safety and Health Act (OSHA) in 1970. The Act was designed to "assure so far as possible every working man and woman in the nation safe and healthful working conditions and to preserve our human resources." One of the responsibilities of OSHA is to develop and enforce mandatory job safety and health standards. These standards cover workplace issues of machinery and equipment, materials, power sources, processing, protective clothing, first aid, and administrative requirements. OSHA also requires that supervisors train and inform employees of any known safety hazard in the kitchen. In 1988 OSHA issued the Hazard Communication Standard (HCS), which requires employers to inform employees what chemicals they are working with and to detail their risks and what can be done to limit these risks. HCS is achieved through training programs and detailed labeling on or near chemical containers. Material Safety Data Sheets (MSDS) are part of this standard. A system of priorities for workplace inspections (which includes kitchens) has been established by OSHA (3):

- Inspection of imminent danger situations
- Investigation of catastrophes, fatalities, and accidents resulting in hospitalization of five or more employees
- Investigation of valid employee complaints of alleged violation of standards or of unsafe or unhealthful working conditions
- Follow-up inspections to determine if previously cited violations have been corrected

OSHA provides a free on-site consultation service that helps employers identify hazardous conditions and corrective measures. The penalties for violations were raised in 1990. According to the new law, a minimum fine of $5000 is mandatory for intentional violations with a maximum fine of $70,000 for intentional or repeat violations. A maximum fine of $7000 applies for all other violations, including failure by an employer to post the required OSHA notice (4).

One of the best methods for identifying potential hazards in the kitchen is to simply consult the team. Have them develop a list of accident prevention measures. They see hazards in and around the kitchen every day.

Chef supervisors may unintentionally reinforce unsafe acts by not correcting them when they are first observed. Through mandatory and proper supervision, unsafe work practices can be corrected. The nature of food production requires that many items of equipment be sharp or hot. The most common types of kitchen accident injuries are directly related to these two areas as well as to the presence of wet or greasy floors and the element of human error. The most common type of injuries and their causes in the kitchen include the following.

1. *Lacerations*. These are caused by improper use of chef's knives, slicers, choppers, broken ware, or glass.

2. *Power-driven equipment*. When used improperly, blenders, mixers, slicers, grinders, or buffalo choppers can cause accidents. The chef supervisor is responsible for ensuring that each kitchen team member is fully trained in the safe use of all power-driven equipment.

3. *Glass and dishware*. Glasses, bowls, cups, and plates are sources of injury. Broken glass in dishwashers or sinks causes accidents. Glasses and dishes should be stored separately to avoid crushing.

4. *Burns*. Common injuries in the kitchen, burns and scalds of varying degree can result from contact with the hot surfaces of grills, ovens, stove burners, steam tables, fryers, and any other heating equipment that might be in use (5).

5. *Slips and falls*. Falls in the kitchen are typically caused by wet or greasy floors left unattended. The danger from greasy or wet floors is compounded by team members rushing about during busy periods. The kitchen team should be made aware by the supervisor of the necessity to keep floor surfaces safe. Kitchen team members should wear shoes with rubber soles or ones made from neoprene to prevent slipping. Leather-soled shoes should never be worn in the kitchen. Safety shoes that have strong uppers without openings should be worn, as these help prevent cuts or crushing injuries.

6. *Fires*. Because most kitchens usually have open flames of some type, potential fire hazards are obvious. More fires occur in foodservice establishments than in any other type of business operation. Chef supervisors should check these potential fire hazards regularly. Special fire protection equipment should be provided in all areas where fires are likely to occur. These include hoods, grills, deep fryers, ovens, and stove tops. Direction in the use of fire extinguishers and evacuation procedures for guests and employees should be part of every new kitchen member's induction and orientation training.

Since training alone will not assure continual adherence to safety, chef supervisors should observe team members at work and show approval for safe work practice. When unsafe actions are observed, immediate corrective action should be taken.

Make work interesting. Fatigue and stress can contribute to the cause of accidents. Simple changes can often be made in the kitchen to make tasks more meaningful.

Establish a safety committee composed of kitchen team members and other dependent department supervisors and managers. The safety committee provides a means of getting team members directly involved in the operation of the safety program. The duties of the committee include inspecting, observing work practices, investigating accidents, and making recommendations. The committee should meet regularly, at least once a month, and attendance should be mandatory.

Other helpful items that promote safety include:

- Publishing safety statistics. Monthly accident reports should be posted. Ideas and suggestions should be solicited as to how these accidents can be avoided.
- Using bulletin boards and menu wall display areas throughout the kitchen to display posters, pictures, sketches, and cartoons depicting safety situations.
- Setting high expectations for safety. Encourage the kitchen team to recognize positive safety actions and acknowledge those who contribute to safety improvements.

Employee health   Until recent times safety and accident prevention received far more attention than did employee health. However, this has changed. Statistics show that occupational diseases may cost industry as much as or more than occupational accidents (6). Many foodservice organizations now not only have attempted to remove health hazards from the work place, but also have initiated programs to improve employee health.

COUNSELING

Counseling is used by kitchen team builders to ensure good relations and to generate a team spirit. Team members may have problems of a personal nature that demand the chef supervisor's attention. These problems may or may not be job related. Changes in an individual's behavior, such as excessive absenteeism, tardiness, hostility, moodiness, withdrawal, and a decline in job performance, should be monitored. Good coaches interact with their team on a constant basis and are usually in the best position to identify and observe these changes.

There are advantages and disadvantages to the chef supervisor assuming the role of counselor. The primary advantage is that the chef has the opportunity to become well acquainted with the individual. They can learn the team member's pattern of judging, valuing, thinking, and understanding and can predict an individual team member's behavior. However, the disadvantage to assuming the role of counselor within the team is that the chef supervisor may not be adequately trained to deal with complex human problems. It is then advisable to refer the team member to a specialist. Needless to say, the act of referring a team member for assistance requires considerable tact and skill.

Within emotional and personal crises, alcoholism and drug abuse are considered to be personal matters. They also become the chef supervisor's problem when they affect the team member's ability to perform satisfactorily in the workplace.

Typically in large organizations Employee Assistance Programs (EAPs) exist. These programs are in place to help employees overcome problems, and they provide guidance and referrals to outside professional help.

The most prevalent problems among individuals are personal crisis situations involving mental, family, financial, or legal matters. These are problems that can be brought to a chef supervisor's attention. Depending on the type or difficulty of the problem, in-house counseling or referral to an outside agency may be necessary.

Chef supervisors should be aware that the behavior of some team members may be adversely affected by some elements of the "physical" kitchen environment, which may necessitate reassigning or rotating individuals to different sections of the kitchen.

It is estimated that 1 out of every 16 workers in the United States is affected by alcohol (7). This results in lost work time, declining productivity, and increased absenteeism. Alcohol abuse has been a problem for the hospitality industry in general and the kitchen employee in particular. Many theories for its prevalence have been put forward, from the notion that its accessibility contributes to the problem to the idea that the hot kitchen environment encourages the use of alcohol.

The approach to handling alcoholism is to monitor all kitchen team members regularly and systematically. Evidence of declining performance on the job should be carefully documented, so that the individual can be confronted with unequivocal proof that his or her work is suffering. Offers of help should be made available without any penalty to the individual. Mention of alcoholism should be avoided. The team member should be allowed to seek aid as for any other health problem.

Drug abuse among employees is one of the wider societal issues confronting industry. While alcohol is the most abused substance, marijuana, cocaine, heroin, crack, and varieties of abused prescription drugs are found to be in use in the foodservice industry. Various approaches are used to assist individuals with a dependency. They range from out-patient treatment for an extended period to in-patient treatment. A recent survey by the federal government estimates that one in every four Americans uses drugs and between 10 and 23 percent of Americans use drugs while on the job.

It has been estimated that substance abuse costs U.S. employers over $100 million annually. At any given time, approximately 25 percent of all employees in the work force are troubled by a personal problem serious enough to impact job performance. Related accidents cost industry over $32 billion annually in disability programs, workers' compensation, lost productivity, and poor morale. Employees who use drugs claim disability 5 times more often, have 4 times as many accidents, and are 16 times more likely to be absent from work (8).

In recent years few workplace issues have received as much attention as AIDS (acquired immune deficiency syndrome). This is particularly important for the foodservice industry from the standpoint of transmission of the virus. There is no evidence that AIDS can be transmitted through casual contact or through food preparation. However, one of the major problems employers face is educating team members and customers on this issue. Since no cure or vaccine for AIDS presently exists, many foodservice organizations are turning to education as the most viable means of combating both the medical and social dilemmas posed by AIDS. The potential benefits of an AIDS education program for kitchen team members are:

- Prevention of new infections among individuals by helping everyone understand how human immunodeficiency virus (HIV) is and is *not* transmitted (HIV is the first stage of AIDS)
- Alerting managers and chef supervisors to the legal issues raised by HIV infection in the workplace
- Helping to prevent discrimination by fearful or misinformed employees, which can decimate productivity. Through education, the same employees are equally capable of creating a humane, supportive, and therefore healthy working environment.
- "Raising morale through AIDS education training" (9)

Employees who test HIV positive are protected under the Americans with Disabilities Act (ADA). This act provides comprehensive civil rights protection to individuals with AIDS. It bans discrimination against people on the basis of their disability. Employers are prohibited from dismissing or transferring infected team members from food-handling duties simply because they have AIDS or have tested HIV positive. Management has a responsibility to maintain confidentiality of any employees who report they have AIDS or any other illness.

Unfortunately, all indicators are that the AIDS epidemic will continue to spread. It is important for chef supervisors to understand that these issues are present among the kitchen team. It is also important for chef supervisors to recognize their limitations as counselors. However, through their roles as coaches and educators much can be done to make it known that help is available.

STRESS

Stress comes from two basic sources: physical activity and mental or emotional activity. The physical reaction of the body to both is the same. The kitchen can be a stressful environment, particularly at busy service periods. However, not all stress is harmful. Positive stress is a feeling of exhilaration and achievement. This can be associated with a successful busy service period during which everything went well in the kitchen. Team members performed well as a group, record numbers were served, and 100 percent customer satisfaction was achieved.

Negative stress may cause people to become ill. Kitchen-induced stress can be caused by:

- Conflicting expectations between chef supervisor and team member
- Uncertainty over team member's expected contribution to the team effort
- An unpleasant kitchen environment
- Poor preparation for the job
- Threats and hostility
- Performance evaluations
- Lack of social interaction
- High noise levels in the work environment
- Tasks that do not fully utilize team members' skills
- High temperature levels
- Long and irregular hours
- Personality conflicts
- Working during public holidays
- Group pressures
- Insensitive supervision

Arguments with supervisors or fellow team members are a common cause of stress. Feeling trapped in a job to which a person is ill-suited can be equally painful. Other strains include lack of communication on the job and lack of recognition for a job well done. Stress has been linked to many things. It manifests itself in several ways: increased absenteeism, job turnover, lower productivity, and mistakes on the job. Stress-related disorders include tension, high blood pressure, muscle tightness in the chest, ulcers, and others requiring medical attention. Burnout is considered to be the most severe form of stress. Career burnout usually occurs when work is no longer meaningful to the individual team member. The factors that cause burnout are those that cause stress; in fact burnout and stress have been viewed as interconnected issues.

Wellness programs   These are becoming a common feature in foodservice organizations. Although these types of programs have been in existence for many years in other industries, they are relatively new to the foodservice sector. Essentially, wellness programs are designed to prevent illness and enhance the well-being of each individual. They include periodic medical exams, stop smoking clinics, improved dietary practices, weight control, exercise and fitness, stress management, immunizations, and cardiopulmonary resuscitation (CPR) training. Documented results from these types of programs have shown a reduction in employee sick days and lower major medical costs. It is expected that as health care costs continue to increase, wellness programs will grow.

CONCLUSIONS

Supervising people in what can at times be an unpleasant environment at a busy service time (hot, noisy, steamy, stressful) requires a great deal of skill. In addition to knowing how to cook and understanding the principles of heat transfer, the chef who can also build a team and tap into their collective culinary resources will succeed. There are no good reasons why kitchens should be unpleasant places, even during busy service. Poor physical working conditions can be overcome.

Considering the team member in a holistic way, with all that entails, is now considered to be a worthwhile investment. Needless to say, when frustration on the job is dealt with effectively and a safe and healthy work environment exists in the kitchen, job satisfaction is possible. What is more difficult to overcome is the breaking of the stereotypical animated image of temperamental chefs. The modern chef, as the literal translation of the word means, is a leader as well as a first-class culinarian.

SUMMARY

Most conflicts in the foodservice industry are interpersonal, between kitchen team members and other departments.

Frustration is a common contributor to conflicts, complaints, and grievances. Most frustration is caused by hostility, unpleasant working conditions, lack of training, insecurity, and being ignored on the job.

Complaints within the kitchen should be dealt with as soon as possible after they are made. The longer the complaint remains unresolved, the more other people get involved. Work quality suffers immediately, which impacts on customer satisfaction. The ideal resolution of complaints is a situation in which all feel they have won.

Job satisfaction has been shown to be linked to turnover and absenteeism. The greater the individual's job satisfaction level, the more productive he or she becomes. Job satisfaction revolves around the creation of a team environment where each person is valued and respected.

Chef supervisors have a responsibility to ensure that a safe work environment exists, a place free from physical hazards, unhealthy conditions, and unsafe or dangerous practices. Effective health and safety practices promote a positive work climate.

Chef supervisors should be aware of the counseling role they may be asked to play with regard to team members' personal problems. They should know their limitations in this area and know how and when to seek professional help.

As with all other considerations for a safe kitchen environment, stress and stressful situations must be recognized and avoided.

DISCUSSION QUESTIONS

1. How does team member frustration impact total quality management? How can these elements of frustration be removed from the kitchen?
2. What are the steps chef supervisors should follow in dealing with team member complaints?
3. What does the term "win-win" mean?
4. What are the differences between "needs" and "wants" in the area of job satisfaction?
5. What, if any, are the links between job satisfaction and team member turnover?
6. What propelled the passing of the Occupational Safety and Health Act in 1970?
7. What are the advantages and disadvantages of chef supervisors engaging in counseling?
8. What are the elements that contribute to stress in the kitchen?
9. Wellness programs within the kitchen can contribute to reducing costs. How is this achieved?
10. What can be done to reduce interpersonal conflicts within the kitchen?

NOTES

1. Lendal H. Kotschevar, *Management By Menu*, Wm. C. Brown, East Lansing, MI, 1987.
2. Arthur Sherman, George Bohlander, and Herbert Crudden, *Managing Human Resources*, 8th ed., South-Western, Cincinnati, OH, 1988, p. 576.
3. Jack E. Miller, Mary Porter, and Karen Eich Drummond, *Supervision in the Hospitality Industry*, 2nd ed., John Wiley, New York, 1992, p. 98.
4. *Applied Foodservice Sanitation*, 4th ed., Educational Foundation of the National Restaurant Association, East Lansing, MI, 1992, p. 258.
5. Ibid., p. 259.
6. Lloyd L. Bryars and Leslie W. Rue, *Human Resources Management*, 4th ed., Irwin, Boston, 1994, p. 499.
7. Arthur Sherman, George Bohlander, and Herbert Crudden, *Managing Human Resources*, 8th ed., South-Western, Cincinnati, OH, 1988, p. 592.
8. Joseph L. Picogna, *Total Quality Leadership: A Training Approach*, International Information Associates Inc., Morrissville, PA, 1993, p. 312.
9. Lloyd L. Bryars and Leslie W. Rue, *Human Resources Management*, 4th ed., Irwin, Boston, 1994, p. 507.

7

The Chef as Communicator

Outline

- Introduction
- Elements of communication
- Barriers to communication
- Nonverbal communication
- Listening
- Ways to improve listening skills
- Giving directions
- Leading a TQM meeting
- Written communication
- Communication via the grapevine
- Conclusions
- Summary
- Discussion questions

Objectives

When you complete this chapter, you should be able to:

1. Describe the elements of effective communication.
2. Identify barriers to good communication.
3. Describe aspects of nonverbal communication.
4. Define the elements of effective listening and describe ways to improve listening.
5. Outline the steps for leading and managing kitchen team meetings.
6. Identify methods of giving directions to kitchen team members so as to ensure satisfactory and timely completion of tasks.
7. Effectively communicate in written form.
8. Identify the positive and negative aspects of communication via the grapevine.

INTRODUCTION

A chef supervisor uses communication to gather, process, and transmit information essential to the well-being of the organization. Since this communication moves in many directions, the needs of peers, superiors, and fellow team members need to be given careful consideration. Communication is a crucial element of the supervisory process. Chef supervisors often run into problems because of their inability to communicate effectively. As much as 85 percent of a chef supervisor's day is spent in some form of communication, most of it speaking and listening to others (1).

Communication involves a sender and a receiver and the transfer of information from a source to a destination. Effective supervision—delegating, coaching, team building, and information transfer—depends on understanding all the elements of communication. It is the most exacting of all supervisory skills and the one the chef supervisor is called upon most frequently to use. Communication is the basis for understanding, cooperation, and action within the kitchen. An open well-developed communication system will result in a higher standard of quality food production and service through a two-way flow of ideas, opinions, and decisions.

Communication grows and develops in a positive kitchen work environment in which the elements of trust and understanding are adopted. The purpose of communication in the foodservice establishment and particularly the kitchen is to ensure that all individuals understand the vision, goals, objectives, policies, and procedures of the organization. Kitchen team members who are confused, unhappy, and *uninformed* may become discontented. Communication is much more than talking, speaking, and reading. If successful, the sender will direct or communicate a message that is clear and accurately understood by the receiver in a way that the sender intends. Most problems with effective communication lie in the middle portion of communication, which is known as the "noise" or the elements that cause misunderstanding.

Communication between sender and receiver passes through filters of culture, age, gender, education, and our different fields of past experiences, which cause noise in the understanding of messages (2). This often leads to misperceptions, misinterpretations, and misevaluations. It is therefore necessary to recognize these differences and develop a communication style that helps each individual to understand. Words and gestures often mean different things to different people. Understanding these differences is an important skill for a chef supervisor.

Communication must flow in many directions—upward from supervisors to higher management, downward to subordinates, and laterally to team members. Effective upward communication can help team members contribute to the organization and can provide an opportunity for the chef supervisor to get to know and understand each team member better. The more avenues are created to facilitate communication within the kitchen, the better the work environment.

The chef supervisor should set an example of being open and honest. The more feedback and ideas provided to the kitchen team, the more comfortable they will feel about sharing *their* ideas and feelings. To encourage open communication, the chef supervisor should reward rather than punish open expressions of feelings, opinions, or problems. Openness should be rewarded by showing appreciation for team members who share negative or sensitive messages.

Some chef supervisors may feel threatened by ideas from creative individuals within the kitchen. This need not be so. In some cases supervisors may talk down to individuals, thus causing feelings of anger and hurt. If messages are understood as intended, only then can effective coaching be a reality. Misinterpretations can cause many problems in the kitchen among the team and between different departments. For example, if a customer's meal order is misunderstood, not only is this costly in wasted food and time, but also it contributes to customer annoyance and delays and exasperation on the part of the wait-person.

Since often foodservice employees do not speak English, it is important to understand the barriers to communication based on different cultural attitudes, values, and beliefs. In some cultural groups people say "yes" when they do not mean "yes" (3). In addition to the difficulty in understanding English, nonnative speakers may have difficulty interpreting body language. These signals may have different meanings for different groups and thus cause communication problems. Good communication within the kitchen is essential for successful implementation of goals and objectives. It also ensures a safe work environment. Communication consists of many parts and has different elements, which are discussed in the following sections.

Communication, what went wrong?

This is the story of four people: Everybody, Somebody, Anybody and Nobody.

There was an important job to be done and Everybody was sure that Somebody would do it.

Anybody could have done it but Nobody did it.

Somebody got angry because it was Everybody's job.

Everybody thought that Somebody would do it.

But Nobody asked Anybody.

It ended up that the job wasn't done, and Everybody blamed Somebody, when actually Nobody asked Anybody.

Anonymous

ELEMENTS OF COMMUNICATION

The communication activities of a chef supervisor involve interpersonal communication. To be complete, the interpersonal communication process within the foodservice industry must contain the following three basic elements:

$$\text{Source/sender} \leftarrow \text{signal/message} \rightarrow \text{destination/receiver}$$

- The *source/sender* is the person who originates and encodes the message he or she wishes to share with other members in the foodservice operation. Encoding is the process of putting information in some form that can be received, decoded, and understood by others. Using menus to convey ideas and thoughts is one such encoded message.
- The *signal/encoded information* that the source (sender) intends to share is a message. A message that has been transferred from one team member to another is called a signal.
- The *destination/receiver* is the person who receives the message and with whom the sender is attempting to share information. The team member receives this information and decodes or interprets the message for its meaning. Communication, therefore, is an interpretive transaction between individuals. The sender of the message encodes it according to his or her knowledge (field of experience) and the receiver decodes it according to his or her field of experience.

What is important to effective, clear, and accurate understanding of information in the kitchen is the skill in encoding the message by the chef supervisor so that the message means the same thing to those receiving it. Within the kitchen, team members come from many different backgrounds. Each will interpret a message differently based on his or her background (field of experience).

Often, jargon or French culinary technical terms are used to describe skills and culinary principles. Assuming that each individual has a clear understanding of these terms may frequently cause communication gaps. It should not be assumed information has been transferred and interpreted in the way intended.

Assuming each team member has understood can cause confusion and frustration for both parties. Check for understanding; not doing so may cause operational problems. The aim of good communication is to ensure that the sender and the receiver both have the same picture of the message in their minds. To increase the probability that communication will be successful, the message must be encoded by the sender (chef supervisor) to ensure the way in which the signal is decoded is equivalent to the receiver's experience of the way it should be decoded. Simply put, it should mean the same thing to both the sender and the receiver.

Overlapping fields of experiences ensure successful communication (4). Communication guidelines for the sender include:

- Keeping the message focused on its original purpose. This makes communication clearer and easier to follow for all team members.
- Checking for understanding. Ask questions and request feedback.
- Using open questions beginning with *who, what, when, where,* and *how.* This demonstrates interest and encourages clarity of interpretation.
- Communicating ideas at the proper time and place. Try to catch team members at a time when their frame of mind is receptive to information. Use nonverbal signals. This shows you are interested in what is being said.
- Complimenting the team member. This will enhance the receiver's self-confidence and encourage communication.
- Including the receiver's name whenever possible. This demonstrates respect and acknowledgment.
- Using care in tone of voice, facial expressions, words, body language, and appearance. All of these factors affect the reception of the message.
- Being sure that the message is clear in your mind before communicating. The more systematically the chef supervisor analyzes the problem or idea to be communicated, the clearer it becomes. Planning is essential to good communication. Consideration of the attitudes and emotions of the receiver who will be affected must be factored into the communication plan.

Chef Talk: "Open Communication"

Often we are faced with the delicate issue of communication or imaginary communication, or simply miscommunication, on a daily basis in the kitchen.

Each week I work out the employee duty roster. It is always difficult to satisfy requests for time off, but one has to continuously try. One instance of scheduling that caused a major morale problem in the kitchen was based on a particular set of requests. Three people in the kitchen had requested the same day off, a white male-female couple and an African American chef. My policy was to facilitate these requests on a first-come, first-served basis. Based on this policy, I agreed to the white couple's request and denied the other one. I was not prepared for what happened next. I was accused of being a racist and favoring the white couple.

Our kitchen team is an ethnically diverse group, and generally we all work well and harmoniously together. Being accused of racial bias came as a major hurtful blow to me. I had always prided myself on my fairness, tolerance, and sensitivity to each team member's needs and wants.

The source of my problem was a lack of communication. I knew the scheduling policy, but I had failed to communicate it clearly to any other member of the kitchen team. I had not written it anywhere, it was not stated in any company policy manual, I had not announced it at any kitchen team meeting, so how could employees possibly know that I considered scheduling requests on a first-come, first-served basis?

What eventually solved our dispute and the problem of morale was open communication. I initiated a program of 10-minute meetings each morning, at which time each employee outlined five good things and five bad things about the previous day's work. This system also allowed me to make any announcements or to share any necessary information. The effect of this communication awareness meeting was to greatly facilitate morale building and to develop a family spirit. By implementing this system, many problems were solved before they became problems. I had learned my lesson. Just because I say I have open communication does not mean there is open communication. For communication to be real and meaningful, we have to live it every day in the kitchen.

Helmut Holzer, CMC, Executive Chef, Renaissance Hotel, Atlanta, GA

Communication guidelines for the receiver include:

- Summarize by paraphrasing or restating the core of the message.
- Ask questions when unsure. A lot of confusion may be avoided by asking the sender to repeat or rephrase the message.
- Respond to nonverbal cues. This clarifies the meaning of a bodily reaction. It will ensure that behaviors and words convey the same message and also demonstrates understanding.
- Sincerity and *insincerity* in communicating will become apparent if careful thought is not part of the reception of ideas and opinions. In any communication there must be feedback from the receiver to the sender. The receiver should be made to feel free to respond fully.
- Seek not only to be understood, but also to understand.
- Be a good listener. When we are talking, we are often not listening. Listen for the full meaning of the sender's message.
- Analyze body language, eye contact, and the verbal message in order to reach meaningful conclusions about the information.

BARRIERS TO COMMUNICATION

Factors and issues that decrease effective communication within the foodservice operation are called communication barriers. One of these barriers is language. A high proportion of foodservice workers do not speak English, and this can pose many problems that need to be overcome. When dealing with team members whose native tongue is not English, it becomes important to be familiar with not only their language but also their culture. Barriers to effective communication become obvious during the first few minutes of interaction when attention span is at its highest, the eye and ear focus on the sender, and the brain receives what it sees and hears. People tend to focus on what they see first.

The following gives individuals the information needed to assess others:

- Skin color
- Gender
- Age
- Appearance
- Facial expressions
- Eye contact
- Movement
- Personal space
- Touch

It only takes 2 to 4 minutes to create a positive or negative impression (5). Success as a communicator is measured by the impressions created in

Chef Talk: "Total Quality Communication"

Total quality communication (TQC) is an initiative developed as an extension of the Johnson & Wales policy that students come first. Not to be confused with a program, which has a distinct beginning and end, TQC is intended to become a part of the culture of our organization, to permeate all written and oral communication. TQC is a style, it is a tone, it is an attitude, not just a set of rules that govern our written and oral communication. TQC will set us apart from other educational institutions and will say to our students and to the world that we care about people, that we respect our students, and that no matter how large we become, we will never lose sight of the human aspect that is the core of a "business" education.

TQC is reactive when responding to complaints or problems (which in TQC are called "concerns"). But TQC is proactive when it is used consistently in all of our daily jobs, whether answering a telephone call with a smile, sending a form letter that has been revised to include a positive and professional closing, or writing an "attaboy/girl" memo or note to a fellow employee who has excelled in his or her job or contributed to the university above and beyond the expected. The benefits to be gained when TQC is proactive are incalculable. The more we, as chefs and managers, practice quality communications as part of our daily lives, the fewer concerns there will be. When an individual has a favorable impression of us at the beginning of an encounter rather than frustration bred by previous unpleasant experiences, our lives will become easier and more enjoyable.

Quality communication means having pride in our work. Understanding customers' needs is our top priority. Approaching each situation with an optimistic and confident attitude projects professionalism. Listening before speaking and thinking before writing demonstrates our commitment to effective communication. Involving others in TQC promotes a positive professional image. Taking responsibility for improving all communication fosters personal and professional growth. Ensuring the success of TQC is up to *you*.

Thomas L. Wright, Vice President, College of Culinary Arts, Johnson & Wales University, Providence, RI

the kitchen. Four key questions need to be addressed to overcome perception barriers:

- How am I perceived by others?
- How do I "sound" to others?

- What do I say to others?
- How well do I listen to others?

Depending on the field of experience of the receiver, significance may be applied to a part of you that has little to do with the skills of the chef supervisor, for example, the nonverbal messages sent by body language, how quickly you speak, your handshake, and how well you maintain eye contact.

What you sound like tells a lot about your personality, attitude, and anxiety level. Being aware of how you sound can help to correct and improve your communication skills. It is possible to learn to recognize signs of tension and stress in your voice and the voices of others. Verbal skills should support and balance the nonverbal and verbal messages sent. What you say is reflected by how you say it. Balance between language and delivery is critical in removing barriers. Trust and success are built on consistency and balance of interpersonal communications.

Since the kitchen team will be diversified, agreement on meanings will vary. There will be variations on what is a "pinch" of salt, a "dash" of pepper, or a "big" steak or what "seasoned to taste" means. Assumptions and expectations distort the intended communication. Clarify and explain each piece of the message. Clearly, a skillful chef supervisor does more than just relay the message. The problem is that many barriers muddle the process and hinder clear communication.

It should not be assumed that just because the chef supervisor "gave the message" the receivers "got it." One of the biggest problems of communicating in a tension-laden kitchen environment is the emotions of people who are sending and receiving messages. If something is said in anger, then it is the anger that comes across and not the message. Tempers flare, the receiver is likely to hear things that were not said, and the sender is likely to say things that were not intended. When we are criticized, we often become emotional and excited. Defensive reactions to feedback on job performances are common.

The fundamental communication barrier between people stems from differences in backgrounds, personalities, beliefs, education, religion, life experiences, and professional outlook. Our ability to receive messages is limited by our tendency to hear only what we want or expect to hear. It is a normal human phenomenon that the mind resists what it does not expect or want to perceive. We have a natural tendency to judge or evaluate statements and to reach hasty conclusions. We evaluate messages from our own frame of reference instead of understanding the sender's point of view. This does not add up to effective communication. Instead, two ideas are being advanced without an exchange of information. A closed mind hinders communication.

Limits on time impede communication. Chef supervisors are busy people and tend to give hurried instructions and then move on to the next task. The receiver can be confused or frustrated by these incomplete messages. Additionally, chef supervisors should pay particular attention to the problem of stereotyping. Stereotypes are attitudes favoring or rejecting certain groups without examining individual circumstances or traits. The need to understand numerous tasks forces the mind to arrange things into easily identifiable groups. Another barrier that often surfaces in the kitchen is the tendency to see everything in black and white, which distorts reality and oversimplifies situations.

In the kitchen a great deal of jargon is used. The use of French culinary terms is quite common. This jargon is familiar to those within the chef profession but is usually unintelligible to outsiders. Care should be taken when using terms such as *mise-en-place*, *sauté*, *garde manger*, *sous chef*, *chinois*, *rechaud*, and *a la carte* and the names of various dishes in different languages. This use tends not only to alienate team members, but also adds to confusion. Because many words have several meanings, word meanings can easily become confused in conversation. They often convey meaning to a receiver quite different from the meaning intended by the sender. Nonverbal signals, such as tone of voice, gestures, and appearance, are the most important factors in determining how a message is received and understood.

NONVERBAL COMMUNICATION

In general, senders are consciously attentive only to the spoken word. Individuals often communicate without using words. This is referred to as nonverbal communication or body language. Elements of nonverbal communication include gestures such as nodding of the head, use of hands, and facial expressions. All of these send messages. Smiling and frowning convey emotion, as does voice intonation or loudness. Ideally, the right nonverbal cues accompany the verbal communication. Nonverbal communication may influence the impact of a message more than verbal communication alone.

The meanings of gestures and movements vary from culture to culture. Communication scholars agree that nonverbal communication is most successful between people of similar cultural characteristics. When these characteristics differ, communication barriers occur (6). Nonverbal gestures that would not be considered offensive in some cultures may be insulting to team members from other cultures. Following are some common gestures and what they mean:

- Leaning forward is a positive gesture. The person is listening and wishes to hear what is said. This also suggests acceptance and willingness to take action.
- Direct eye contact is a positive gesture in Euro-American cultures. Lack of eye contact despite sincere words is interpreted as untrustworthiness. However, many Oriental societies find direct eye contact rude.
- Open hands may be a sign of agreement and careful listening, while crossed arms and legs or leaning backward may be considered defensive, resisting, and rejecting.

- Arms folded over the chest with fists clenched is usually a sign that the person is not listening. This is indicative of a person who is nervous, anxious, uptight, and holding in emotions.
- Leaning away from you in a chair may indicate disinterest in what you are saying.
- Leaning far forward with defiant expression, hands spread on table, is indicative of a person with a volatile personality who may be frustrated, angry, and explosive.
- Backing away or avoidance is generally a sign of disagreement with what you say.
- To shake a closed fist is a threatening gesture.
- Shoulders hunched forward and down with arms extended and hands overlapped in front of the body will usually indicate shyness.

The chef supervisor should be aware of the gestures and body language used as well as the signals sent with such gestures. Many cues may be picked up from nonverbal body language that will indicate when communication will be most effective. These aspects of nonverbal communication are expressed through facial gestures, posture, orientation, gestures, eye contact, and appearance.

LISTENING

Communication is always a two-way process. One person says something and another person hears what was said. Since each person comes to the listening situation with different fields of experience, there is often a gap between the speaker's intention and the listener's interpretation. Listening is the complex and selective process of receiving, focusing, deciphering, accepting, and storing what we hear. Listening does not occur without these five interrelated, yet distinct, processes (7). Hearing is the absorption of sound. Listening is something quite different. Ineffective listening can be a major communication problem. Chef supervisors who listen carefully to their team will have fewer problems and greater success in implementing TQM. Poor listening habits may result in conflicts, costly errors, and inefficiency.

Becoming an active and effective listener in the kitchen has important benefits:

- The chef supervisor can gain information from sources that may have been previously missed through poor listening.
- Even though the supervisor may not always agree with team members, at least the supervisor would be perceived as being open and fair-minded.

This is achieved by being open and listening to team members' work problems without jumping to conclusions. Maintaining eye contact, an interested facial expression, and a calm voice reflect a posture of good listening. If the chef supervisor is narrow-minded, then active listening is impossible. Understanding the active listening process allows supervisors to target deficiencies in their own listening skills and to better receive messages. In addition, active listening is one of the most powerful means of creating warmth and sensitivity, which contributes to the overall motivational environment in the kitchen.

Types of listening

- *Critical listening*: This involves analyzing a message and judging the message for facts, documentation, logic, relationships, inferences, and personal biases. We use this form of listening whenever people try to persuade us to their point of view.
- *Discriminative listening*: This involves comprehension and recall. It requires listening for details, sequences, and then developing questions and answers, summarizing main points, evaluating ideas, and giving feedback. This is an essential listening skill for a chef supervisor.
- *Therapeutic listening*: This involves listening with an understanding of another person's feelings, beliefs, and values. It requires supportive and sympathetic verbal and nonverbal feedback. It is appropriate when kitchen team members have work-related or personal problems they want to talk out. Nonverbal feedback includes sympathetic gestures—smiles, nods, and leaning toward the speaker. This type of listening creates an atmosphere that lowers the speaker's defenses, allowing him or her to verbalize the problem.
- *Appreciative listening*: This type of listening is generally reserved for relaxation, satisfaction, or gratification. It is for personal enjoyment and can range from listening to music or enjoying the sound of the speaker's accent—the tone, rhythm, or brogue.
- *Courteous listening*: This is conversational and social listening. We use courteous listening to keep interpersonal relationships intact. Courteous listening is used mainly to keep lines of communication open.

WAYS TO IMPROVE LISTENING SKILLS

- Avoid distractions; focus and concentrate. Don't let your mind wander. Most people think at a rate of 500 words per minute. People talk at a rate of 150 words per minute. Stay focused on what is being said, or you will risk missing key points.
- Listen for main ideas. People sometimes formulate ideas as the conversation develops. These ideas and comments may be vague. Individuals may have trouble coming to the point, particularly if it concerns sensi-

tive issues. Restate the other person's main ideas in your own words and ask if you have understood correctly.

- Ask questions. If something is unclear or seems to contradict your personal sense of logic, seek clarity. This encourages the talker and shows that you are listening and are interested in what he or she has to say.

- Suppress your biases. We all have biases, opinions, prejudices. While listening we often allow certain words, ideas, or statements to trigger emotional responses. Give the speaker a chance to make the point. We may not like what is being said, but we should listen.

- Bounce feelings back to the sender. This shows empathy and clarifies the sender's position. However, refrain from interrupting the person speaking until he or she has had a chance to complete the sentence or thought.

- Refrain from fidgeting, squirming, scribbling, twiddling your thumbs, sorting papers, and writing menus. Give the speaker your undivided attention. Most of us can do only one thing well at a time. Looking away during conversation communicates indifference to what the other person is saying. Show the other person the interest and attention that you yourself would like to receive.

- Listen for the rationale behind what the other person is saying. This is important if what they are saying does not make sense to you. A kitchen team member may be making a request on the basis of erroneous information about the organization. Be sensitive and make sure you understand why people say what they do.

- Respond to nonverbal cues. This clarifies the meaning of a reaction. It ensures that behavior and words convey the same message and shows understanding.

- Listen to all messages, not just the interesting ones. If we are poor listeners, our inclination is to stop listening. Don't stop the flow. Too often we allow external or internal distractions to divert us from the speaker's message. Active listening skills are key. Seldom is a message so boring that we can't find reasons to listen.

- Consider the other person's emotions and background. Some people's background and motivations are so different from ours that we tend to ignore their perceptions. Listen to their point of view. You may learn something new.

Listening will help in getting in touch with the feelings of the kitchen team. Chef supervisors who actively listen demonstrate respect, sensitivity, and patience toward the kitchen team. In addition, team members may have suggestions that might improve ways of speeding up production and may suggest new menu items and recipes. But unless the chef supervisor is willing to listen, the ideas are lost, and so are additional team-building opportunities.

People generally like to hear what is consistent with their own belief structures; they usually resist contrary ideas (8). It takes an open mind to be able to listen to criticism. Feedback as an element of communication is closely linked with good listening abilities. Unfortunately, most people do not learn feedback skills and therefore give critical feedback poorly.

Ten commandments for good listening

1. Stop talking! You cannot listen if you are talking.
2. Put the talker at ease. Help the talker feel free to talk. This is often called a permissive environment.
3. Show the talker that you want to listen. Look and act interested. Do not read your mail while he or she talks. Listen to understand rather than to oppose.
4. Remove distractions. Don't doodle, tap, or shuffle papers. Wouldn't it be quieter if you shut the door?
5. Empathize with the talker. Try to put yourself in the talker's place so that you can see his or her point of view.
6. Be patient. Allow plenty of time. Do not interrupt the talker. Don't start for the door or walk away.
7. Hold your temper. An angry person gets the wrong meaning from words.
8. Go easy on argument and criticism. This puts the talker on the defensive. He or she may "clam up" or get angry. Do not argue: Even if you win, you lose.
9. Ask questions. This encourages the talker and shows you are listening. It helps to develop points further.
10. Stop talking. This is the first and last commandment, because all others depend on it. You can't listen well while you are talking. Nature gave us two ears but only one tongue, which is a gentle hint that we should listen more than talk.

GIVING DIRECTIONS

Giving directions to other team members in the kitchen is what gets every task started. The manner used to give directions is as important as the information given. The clarity of directions given, along with tone of voice and facial expressions, will determine how well the direction will be received (9).

Timing is very important. Try to catch team members in a frame of mind to listen. Present one idea at a time. For example, if you are training team members in the preparation of a new dish, break the process into its most basic steps. Present each step separately and ensure each step is understood before proceeding. Keep to the topic. Try to speak clearly. Avoid ambiguities. Moderate the volume and speed of your speech. Maintain eye contact and leave time for questions and answers. Give team members any background information they may need to fully understand the direction. Keep it simple by using basic language with commonly used words. Explain any technical terms and take special care to explain culinary terms. Make it brief. Don't use more words or time than needed. Too much information is as bad as too little. Without making it too obvious, repeat anything that is important for the listener to remember.

Personalize what you are saying and present it to the team member. Avoid generalizing or sounding vague. Eye contact is important. It enables the chef supervisor to gauge reactions. We cannot respond to one another without it. Sounding bored or looking disinterested tells the team member that what you are saying is unimportant. Speak clearly and loudly enough to be heard. Do not mumble or talk fast; a short, sharp growl will ensure that the team member will not accept the direction. Explain carefully; do not assume that the team member knows what you are thinking. Make sure you're understood. If they look confused or don't question your ideas, chances are they have not understood. Encourage the team member to give thoughtful answers. Ask questions about what you have said. This will allow you to check for understanding.

An atmosphere conducive to open communication, cooperation, and trust will bring about a collaborative team that will accept directions as a natural extension of coaching (10). Bringing team members together on issues of mutual interest to generate suggestions is one way to do this. When kitchen team members recognize the benefits of helping one another and realize it is expected, they will work together to achieve common goals. The effectiveness of the chef supervisor's ability to give direction to the kitchen team is directly related to the ability of the team to carry out the workload to the required total quality standard.

LEADING A TQM MEETING

Total quality management requires meetings on an on-going basis. The chef supervisor who can skillfully manage these meetings will provide the basis for improvements through getting the entire kitchen team involved. These meetings should proceed on the basis of what is known to the unknown information. Meetings can be time consuming. The following guidelines facilitate more productive meetings:

- Keep the meeting to under 12 people.
- Start the meeting on time.
- Be informal. Put the team at ease.
- Respect the contribution of each team member. Never belittle or ignore any statement made; every individual has the desire to be recognized. In their minds, whatever they say is worthwhile.
- Avoid arguments.

- Avoid personally disagreeing with a team member in the group. Instead, call on others for their opinions and convey your thinking through their answers.
- Be tactful when correcting statements or opinions.
- Avoid giving too many personal opinions and experiences.
- Help each person in the team share in the discussion. Ask people in the team to speak up. Be sure that any question an individual asks is heard by the entire group. If the question asked is still inaudible, repeat the question before giving the answer. It can be most annoying to the team when an answer is given to a question that most of the group has not heard.
- Help all team members to formulate a statement or to express themselves. If anyone is finding it difficult to put across his or her point or if the statement is being misunderstood, rephrase the comments briefly before any discussion begins.
- Recognize those in the group who are bored or fail to show sufficient interest in the meeting. Direct "opinion" questions to them. Disinterested team members invariably become interested when their opinions are asked.
- Be alert to guide and encourage the nervous or timid members of the team. Avoid asking them fact questions. Draw them into the discussion by asking their opinions, directing "do you agree" questions to them, and complimenting them when they volunteer correct answers, saying, "that's exactly right" or "that's a good point."
- When the meeting gets out of control, direct a question to a specific person in the team or interrupt and summarize the key points under discussion. Conclude with the correct information and begin discussion on another topic.
- To arouse discussion if the team appears disinterested or is slow to offer opinions, direct rapid-fire questions as a review, calling on specific individuals; make a negative remark to arouse a defensive response from the team; or ask debatable questions (such as "Which is a better method . . . " or "Which is more practical. . . . ").
- If you have had a particularly good session compliment the team before you close the meeting.
- Before closing a meeting, develop interest in the next meeting. Briefly give highlights of the next session.

Meetings with productive outcomes are greatly influenced by how well the chef supervisor manages the meeting. Keep the discussion focused. Don't let the team go off on tangents or other issues. Save other issues for future meetings. The goals of a good meeting are action and results. Summarize the meeting and assign key result areas to individual team members with agreed benchmarks for future areas of improvement.

WRITTEN COMMUNICATION

Menus

In the kitchen many instructions are transmitted to the team via written menus. How these menus are written by the chef supervisor determines how well individual team members perform the skills required for high-quality culinary art. Menus that are "posted" may be forthcoming banquets, special functions, or seasonal offerings. While the menu is primarily designed to convey descriptive meaning to customers, it is also the technical written document through which the team receives instructions. How well menus are written will convey not only all the essential dish ingredients but also other information such as portion size and various accompaniments. Therefore, team members need precise instructions regarding the recipes. Along with ingredients and methods of production, particularly with banquet or special occasion menus, the where, when, what, and how must be conveyed.

In the past the menu was merely a listing of what the restaurant offered. The menu in the modern foodservice industry is really a blueprint of the foodservice operation since so many of the operating procedures depend on it. A menu used as a written form of communication and job instruction to kitchen team members should contain the following:

- Full descriptions and recipes for each dish
- How the dish should be prepared: breaded, cutlet, etc.
- Method of cooking: roasted, braised, sauteed, etc.
- Cut of meat: shoulder, loin, rib steak
- Quality of grade: USDA, choice, prime, etc.
- Method of serving: casserole, skewer, etc.
- Explanation of all culinary terms
- Cooking time instructions
- Garnishing information
- Number of portions to be cooked
- Who are to perform tasks

Following these simple yet important steps will provide effective culinary communication and will result in:

- Consistent high quality
- Efficient use of the kitchen team's resources and skills
- Increased team member satisfaction by making the unknown known to each team member
- Forward workload planning for the team

- Input from the team on methods of food preparation and ease of service
- Time saving and simplification of the tasks

A key component of writing menus and utilizing them as methods of communication in the kitchen is the ability to write a recipe. A common fault in recipe writing is the assumption that those preparing and writing the recipe understand culinary terms. The following lists the essentials of writing a clear recipe (include a photograph of the finished dish). Decide the:

- Menu classification: dinner, lunch, breakfast, brunch, banquet, room service, or take-out
- Name of dish
- Yield, number of servings, portions
- Equipment and smallware needed
- Ingredients in order of use
- Quantity of ingredients (allow for cooking shrinkage)
- Complete detailed instructions
- Timing and temperatures to be used and other information for each phase of the preparation and an outline of any special instructions
- Descriptive passages (avoid long ones; use simple instructions)
- Equipment needed for service
- Setting times and temperature for reconstituting prepared items
- Template to assist layout

Audiences

The first thing to do is to establish exactly who the audience is with regard to the written communication. When this is known, it will help in communicating to that audience in a more unambiguous and effective way. It will also help limit the task of getting the message across. Decisions regarding the interpretation of the message will become clearer. How much time is available to your audience to determine their attitude toward the topic and writer? What do they know already? How much do they need to know? How will they use the information?

Business Writing

In addition to menu writing, the chef supervisor is involved in other types of business writing, such as memos to team members, superiors, and other department heads; the preparation of job descriptions, policies, and procedures; and notices to and general business communication with suppliers and vendors.

Before writing a communication the following questions should be addressed:

- Why am I writing this? Is there a better way of getting my message across?
- What am I trying to say?
- What do I want the reader to do?
- How will I approach my subject?
- Who are my readers?
- Why will they be reading what I write?
- What does the reader already know about the subject?
- How will the reader use this document?
- What should I include?
- What should I leave out?
- What should I say first?
- How will I know when I've said enough?
- The bottom line: If the reader forgets everything else, what key point do I want remembered?
- Should I be writing this at this time?
- Should I send this at all? Am I too late?
- Is someone else communicating the same information? Should I check with that person?
- Should I include deadlines?
- Is my method of transmission the best? For example, should I be using electronic mail, traditional mail, or fax?

The Use of Language in Writing

When writing it is necessary to avoid ambiguity, long words, and above all, culinary jargon. Simplify the subject for the reader and be brief.

Where possible use action verbs as opposed to passive verbs. Be direct and to the point at all times. This is essential, particularly when giving written instructions.

Sentences should contain one idea and should normally average 20 words. The correct use of punctuation in sentences is important in order to highlight certain items and not to confuse the reader.

Paragraphs are used to signal the reader and contain a theme. They should be of six to seven lines in length. The first sentence of the first paragraph sets the tone of the communication.

Simple Words and Phrases

Short words are easier to read. Shorter words (or phrases) are easier to understand than longer ones.

Don't write	**Instead, write**
accordingly	so
activate	start, begin
approximately	about
consequently	so
continue	keep up
demonstrate	show
dispatch	send
discontinue	stop
endeavor	try
facilitate	make easier
implement	carry out
nevertheless	but, however
optimum	best
purchase	buy
requirement	need
terminate	end
utilize	use

Don't write	**Instead, write**
assuring you of our best attention	NOTHING! Leave it out!
for the purpose of	for
further to my letter	following my letter, in my letter of
in accordance with	by, under
inasmuch as	since, because
in order that we may	so that we (or I)
make application to	apply
only too pleased to	very glad to
please find enclosed	I enclose
prior to	before
subsequent to	after
trusting this meets	NOTHING. Leave it out!
with your approval	Perhaps use "I hope this is what you wanted."
we would be grateful	please

Memos

Memos are frequently used by chef supervisors to convey information to the kitchen team. These memos may vary in length, although they tend to be short notes. They often serve as permanent records of decisions and plans made during telephone conversations or meetings. The memo might be a reminder, a request, an acknowledgment, or a complaint. It might also convey good or bad news, information, or speculations. Memos may be sent to one team member or other individuals within the foodservice organization. With this broad range of purpose and audience, memos vary considerably in formality.

Letters

Like memos, business letters vary in length and formality. Some are actually brief notes and others extend over a number of pages. Since letters allow chef supervisors to present themselves to outsiders, they can serve as an important public relations tool. The businesslike format of a letter is as important as its clear prose style and coherent organization. The purpose of most letters is to inform, request, or persuade. Unlike a telephone conversation or other oral communication, letters provide written records and often serve as contracts. As in all written communication, revision and rewriting are essential. Write simply; use concrete words and short sentences. Unify paragraphs on a single topic. The first sentence should set the tone and give the reason for the communication. Last, never sign a letter until you are sure it is perfect. Regardless of who processes the letter, if you sign it, you are responsible for its appearance and content.

Is the content worthwhile?

- Is the content relevant to your audience?
- Is the content informative? (material or insight new and significant to the audience)
- Is the content credible? (believable and convincing)
- Have you brainstormed to discover worthwhile content?
- Have you provided enough information for readers to understand your meaning?
- Have you gained your audience's attention and interest?
- Have you answered your readers' probable questions?
- Is your explanation reasoned and reasonable?
- Have you eliminated gaps, foggy areas, or needless details?
- Have you stressed benefits?
- Have you provided details appropriate to your audience's technical knowledge?
- Have you supported your opinions and assertions?
- Have you presented both sides of the issue?
- Are your conclusions and recommendations supported by facts?
- Have you presented all the relevant data and interpreted it impartially?
- Does your explanation show that your decision is based on sound analysis?
- Is your refusal the logical outcome of your analysis?
- Have you explained the desired action sufficiently to make it easy to follow?

Is the organization sensible?

- Have you stated the major point or idea in the first sentence?
- Have you considered a plan for an audience that could be angered, resentful, or disappointed about the content? (explanation given before refusal)
- When presenting bad news, have you begun with a neutral statement that your reader will find agreeable?
- Have you provided enough transitions and connectors to signal relationships?
- Is the material organized for best emphasis?
- Have you used a topic (orienting) sentence to begin each supporting paragraph?
- Are your paragraphs short enough to be readable?
- Does the document have a distinct introduction, body, and conclusion?
- Have you closed positively?

Is the style readable and appropriate?

- Is each sentence clear? (understandable on first reading)
- Is your message concise? (the most information expressed in the fewest words)
- Are your sentences fluent? (sentences varied in construction and length)
- Is the document written in plain English? (words that the audience will understand)
- Is the language precise? (conveys your exact meaning)
- Have you replaced abstractions and generalizations with concrete, specific, exact language?
- Is the tone unbiased and appropriate for your purpose and audience?
- Have you focused on the audience's needs and interests? (*their* perspective)
- Have you addressed your readers directly?
- Have you eliminated sexist language?
- Is your tone informal and conversational? (11)

COMMUNICATION VIA THE GRAPEVINE

The "grapevine" is informal communication, and it typically follows the pattern of personal relationships among kitchen team members. Informal communication networks generally exist because team members have a desire to know information that is not formally communicated. The informal communication, grapevine, or gossip element can be a useful way for the chef supervisor to test a new idea or some proposed change. The grapevine has several distinct characteristics. It springs up and is not controlled by the chef supervisor. It is used largely to serve the self-interests of the members within it.

Chef supervisors should be aware of the potential advantages and disadvantages of the information conveyed via the grapevine. It may be used to test team members' reactions prior to the official "handed-down" information. Obtaining feedback informally from the team can be used to gauge acceptance or compliance with new ideas or change. It is important that the information carried through the grapevine will not harm or frighten team members. Rumors relating to change can cause team members to feel insecure and create fear. If based on false or damaging information, the grapevine can be harmful to the overall foodservice organization. The degree of harm inaccurate information causes is largely dependent upon the work climate prevailing in the kitchen. If morale is low and poor chef supervision exists, the harmful rumors can easily find acceptance.

Some rumors should be dispelled immediately. To do this, the source of the rumor needs to be established. Ask the team members about the rumor and offer to share the facts. Rumors flourish when there is limited communication. By supplying the facts and adequate information in an open, honest, and free atmosphere, rumors can be quashed and the uncertainty upon which they grow removed. Gossip regarding team members' personal dispositions should not be tolerated.

CONCLUSIONS

Communication is a vital element of the chef supervisor's job. Without open, honest, continuous communication, the vision of TQM is lost. Yet it is not unusual to encounter chef supervisors who believe that if they are "removed" and aloof from the rest of the kitchen staff, they are effective leaders. In the past this type of chef supervisor was acceptable. This is no longer true. Team building, coaching, and continuous improvement of the foodservice operation require communication, which is fundamental to supervision. A good chef communicator will be rewarded with a motivated team prepared to give their best and go beyond the norms. Communication, of which listening is such an important element, will also convey sincerity and develop trust among the team. Communication is important. It is the bedrock of TQM. Information is power. When transferred to the team, it *empowers* them to develop, grow in confidence, and make valuable contributions to the growth of the business and the reputation of the foodservice organization.

SUMMARY

As much as 85 percent of the chef supervisor's working day is spent in some form of communication. Effective supervision relies on the ability of the supervisor to transfer information in such a way that it is understood by the receiver in a way that the chef supervisor intended. Open and honest communication is critical to this process.

Interpersonal communication contains three basic elements: the source/sender, the message, and the destination/receiver. Understanding these elements ensures successful communication. Barriers may exist that prohibit effective communication. Communication barriers between people stem from differences in background, personalities, and life experiences.

Nonverbal communication is important. The chef supervisor should be aware of gestures and body language used. Many cues may be picked up from body language.

Listening is an important aspect of good communication. Supervisors who listen carefully to their team have fewer problems and greater success in implementing TQM. Poor listening skills often result in conflicts, errors and inefficiency. Ways to improve listening skills should be understood and practiced.

Giving directions is what gets the job done. The manner and methods used to give these directions are as important as the directions given.

Managing meetings effectively requires skills. Carefully managed and controlled meetings can make major contributions to continuous improvements and TQM. Productive outcomes are greatly influenced by how well the chef supervisor manages the meeting.

Written communications via memos, business letters, and the menu are important methods of transferring information. The language used should be clear and jargon free.

The "grapevine" is also a method of transferring information. Therefore the chef supervisor should have an awareness of the potential advantages and disadvantages of this informal communication method.

DISCUSSION QUESTIONS

1. Communication between sender and receiver passes through filters of culture, age, gender, education, and fields of experience. What are the effects of this process?
2. How do overlapping fields of experience often lead to effective communication?
3. What are the elements of nonverbal communication? How do these differ within various ethnic groups?
4. What are the different types of listening? Give a brief explanation of each.
5. In what five ways can chef supervisors improve their listening skills?
6. Giving directions to other team members is what gets every job started. What are the five steps essential to getting the job done?
7. Meetings can be time consuming! What steps can be taken to decrease meeting time consumption and increase meeting effectiveness?
8. What strategies should be adopted with regard to written communication?
9. How can communication via the grapevine be used to serve the interests of those within it?
10. What is meant by the phrase "Information is power" with reference to the kitchen team?

NOTES

1. Donna Fantetti, *Career Directions*, P.A.R. Inc., Providence, RI, 1987, p. 34.

2. Robert Heinich, Michael Molenda, and James D. Russel, *Instructional Media and the New Technologies of Instruction*, 3rd. ed., Macmillan, New York, 1989, p. 6.

3. Anna Katherine Jernigan, *The Effective Foodservice Supervisor*, Aspen, Rockville, MD, 1989, p. 31.

4. Robert Heinich, Michael Molenda, and James D. Russel, *Instructional Media and the New Technologies of Instruction*, 3rd. ed., Macmillan, New York, 1989, p. 6.

5. Donna Fantetti, *Career Directions*, P.A.R. Inc., Providence, RI, 1987, p. 34.

6. Franklin B. Krohn and Zafur U. Ahmed, "Teaching International Cross-Cultural Diversity to Hospitality & Tourism Students," *Hospitality & Tourism Educator*, Nov. 1991.

7. Raymond Dumont and John M. Lannon, *Business Communications*, 2nd ed., Brown & Co., Boston, 1987, p. 526.

8. Bruce B. Tepper, *The New Supervisor: Skills For Success*, Irwin, New York, 1994, p. 48.

9. Robert B. Maddux, *Team Building: An Exercise in Leadership*, Crisp, CA, 1992, p. 48.

10. Ibid., p. 49.

11. Adapted from *Business Communications*, 2nd. ed., by Raymond A. Dumont and John M. Lannon, Brown & Co., Boston, 1987.

8

The Chef as Leader

Outline

- Leadership defined
- The power of leadership
- Trait theories
- Behavioral theories
- Leadership styles
- The nature of culinary leadership
- Building leadership self-confidence
- Developing culinary leadership
- Humor as a leadership tool
- Conclusions
- Summary
- Discussion questions

Objectives

When you complete this chapter, you should be able to:

1. Distinguish between supervision and leadership.
2. Describe the elements of directive behavior and supportive behavior.

3. Describe desirable leadership behavioral qualities.
4. Explain directing, coaching, supporting, and delegating as they pertain to situational leadership.
5. Outline actions that contribute to leadership self-confidence.
6. Apply steps that are particular to culinary leadership.

LEADERSHIP DEFINED

Leadership is the process of directing the behavior of others toward the accomplishment of some objective. Directing in this sense means causing individuals to act in a certain way or follow a particular course. The central theme of leadership is getting things accomplished through people. Leadership in the kitchen, as part of a TQM process, confers on the chef supervisor the privilege and responsibility to direct the actions of the kitchen team in carrying out the pursuits of the organization and TQM. The distinction between a supervisor and a leader is that the supervisor is an assigned organizational role, whereas the leader is a role that can be assumed by anyone. Therefore, not all supervisors are leaders and not all leaders are supervisors. Leaders play a crucial role in quality. They have to be primary agents for improvement. They work to create an environment where the kitchen team can experience pride. Their efforts are directed to allowing all kitchen team members to perform their jobs to the utmost. Leaders take risks based on the self-knowledge that mistakes are opportunities, not failures. They have the ability to let go of concepts that block new ideas of learning. Leaders balance action against inaction and praise against correction. Competent leaders have sufficient expertise to make good judgments and get things done.

Leading is not the same as supervising, although some chef supervisors are leaders. No single model of leadership behavior can be applied to all situations in the kitchen, where chef supervisors can influence the actions of others.

President Eisenhower summarized leadership as follows: "The one quality that can be developed by studious reflection and practice is the leadership of men" (1). Leadership in the kitchen does not depend on team member incentives or pleasant working conditions. The chef supervisor's ability to motivate people to perform is independent of these factors. Leaders are *made*, not born. Leadership can be learned the way chefs learn culinary skills. Myth associates leadership with superior position. It assumes that when you are on top you are automatically a leader. But leadership is not a place; it is a process. It involves skills and abilities that are useful whether one is in the executive suite or on the front line (2). The one who influences others to follow only is a leader with certain limitations. The one who influences others to lead is a leader without limitation (3).

Bennus and Nanus, in their book *Leaders: The Strategies for Taking Charge*, observed the following myths (4):

Myth 1: "Leadership is a rare skill." Nothing could be further from the truth. While great leaders may be as rare as great runners, great actors, or great painters, everyone has leadership potential. The truth is that leadership opportunities are plentiful and within the reach of most people.

Myth 2: "Leaders are born, not made." Biographies of great leaders sometimes read as if they entered the world with an extraordinary genetic endowment, that somehow their future leadership role was preordained. Don't believe it. Whatever natural endowments we bring to the role of leader can be enhanced.

Myth 3: "Leaders are charismatic." Some are, most aren't. Charisma is the result of effective leadership, not the other way around.

Myth 4: "Leadership exists only at the top of an organization." In fact, the larger the organization, the more leadership roles it is likely to have.

Myth 5: "The leader controls, directs, prods and manipulates." This is perhaps the most damning myth of all. Leadership is not so much the exercise of power as the empowerment of others. Leaders are able to translate intentions into reality by aligning the energies of the organization behind an attractive goal. Once these myths are cleared away, the question becomes one not of how to become a leader but rather of how to improve one's effectiveness at leadership.

Traits that are the basic elements of leadership can be taught. When the desire is present in the chef supervisor to be a good leader, nothing can stop the process. Ninety percent of the leadership traits can be taught through development. The 10 percent who are gifted will succeed only if the development and growth of leadership are pursued.

The terms *management* and *leadership* are often used interchangeably. They can be synonymous but they mean different things. In the past terms such as *people management* were used to indicate authoritarian controls. This people management philosophy has been shown to be folly. As H. Ross Perot states: "People cannot be managed. Inventories can be managed, but people must be led" (5).

The following piece from the *Wall Street Journal* subtly attempts to demonstrate the differences between management and leadership:

"Let's get rid of management"

People don't want to be managed.
They want to be led.
Whoever heard of a world manager?
World leader, yes.

Educational leader.

Political leader.

Scout leader.

Community leader.

Labor leader.

Business leader.

They lead.

They don't manage.

If you want to manage somebody, manage yourself.

Do that well and you'll be ready to stop managing and start leading.

According to Patrick L. O'Malley, Chairman Emeritus of the Canteen Company, leadership in the foodservice industry is about the following (6):

Doing the job at hand with the energy required with all your resources being used efficiently. It means getting the right people in the right place for the job they will be committed to do. It means motivating your colleagues and employees, directing them skillfully, providing adequate training, getting to understand them and communicating with them.

In order to skillfully lead the kitchen team, chef supervisors must master the skills of leadership and have a passion to succeed. They must show the way and lead by example. They must have a clear idea of what they want to do and the strength of purpose to persist in the face of setbacks, even failures. They know where they are going and why.

Calvin Coolidge astutely pointed out that persistence in any endeavor will equal success. Developing leadership skills requires a great deal of persistence:

Nothing in the world can take the place of persistence.

Talent will not; nothing is more common than unsuccessful men with great talent.

Genius will not; unrewarded genius is almost a proverb.

Education will not; the world is full of educated derelicts.

Persistence, determination alone are omnipotent.

Leadership style is something that each chef supervisor will develop individually. Essentially, style is based on two behaviors, known as directive behavior and supportive behavior (7). Directive behavior is the authoritarian behavior, which concentrates on control, structure, and strict supervision. Supportive chef leadership behavior style is about enabling, coaching, facilitating, and praising.

Chef Talk: "The Good Old Days"

I experienced many chef leadership styles. One I particularly remember is the master chef I worked for when I was an apprentice chef in Munich, Germany. His reputation preceded him. According to him, there were only two great chefs: Escoffier and himself. He ruled his kitchen with an authoritarian leadership style. He actually kept a long, thin stick by his side. When the hot food left the kitchen, it was covered with a silver "cloche." If a nosy waiter or chef lifted the lid to have a peek, down across the knuckles came the stick.

In another hotel where I worked, the chef governed his domain with leadership and example. He maintained his own personal herb and flower garden behind the hotel, which was his pride and joy. Every morning he would gather some fresh herbs and flowers for the daily production. He would divide the herbs among the stations, and when the hot food left the kitchen, it was placed on a silver underliner with a folded napkin. He placed a fresh flower on the side of each dish as it passed by him on the way to the dining room. Whenever the menu or a dish changed, the chef would leave a note explaining the preparation and specific garnish on his podium in the kitchen for the chef de partie to pick up. He felt this saved time and would not put the chefs in the awkward position of having to ask. But his true leadership by example came through when one afternoon he had two teeth pulled and showed up for dinner to take his post at the helm of his disciples. He felt he could not leave them by themselves, abandoned, during the peak season dinner hours, expediting with a numb, swollen mouth. In this fashion we toiled, with sweat on our faces, spending the best times of our lives. No matter what one says about the good old days, they helped shape our lives and profession and also gave us leadership direction in the culinary arts.

Klaus Muller, CCE, AAC, Director, Academy of Culinary Arts, Atlantic City, NJ

THE POWER OF LEADERSHIP

Authority is derived in three ways:

- Situations occur that require leadership in the kitchen. Through a general consensus, one individual in the group earns that recognition. The leader assumes control.
- Specific activities in the kitchen require a leader. This is often the chef with the most skill or experience. Skill or experience is frequently a factor in the promotion to the position of supervisor.

- Titles can provide leadership, for example, being addressed as "the chef." However, this does not guarantee that the chef has any leadership skills. If the chef's authority is by virtue of the title alone, it is likely that there will be a lack of team commitment, poor morale, low productivity, and high turnover in the kitchen work force.

Solid chef leadership is established through a combination of these. A true leader is a person people want to follow because they trust and respect that individual.

Leadership development is first a process of self-development. It is facilitated by education, training, mentoring, and experience. Supervisory success for the chef is dependent upon more than the source of authority or having a title thrust upon him or her. The better the chef's leadership skills, the greater the satisfaction and productivity of the kitchen team. These kitchen leadership qualities and skill sets include:

- Creativity
- Confidence in one's abilities
- Good communication skills
- Ability to make decisions
- Trust in the kitchen team to do the job
- A desire to develop skills in others
- A comfort level in giving directions
- An ability to motivate the people
- An ability to take measured risks

These elements of leadership are necessary so that the team may have confidence in the chef as a supervisor and in the knowledge that there is direction and purpose for what they do. Trusting the chef supervisor is vital to leadership in order to have a productive kitchen team environment. Leadership includes open and honest communication and helps to promote loyalty and commitment of the team (8).

TRAIT THEORIES

The trait approach to leadership is based upon early research that seemed to assume that a good leader is born and not made. The reasoning was that if a complete profile of the characteristics (traits) of a successful leader could be summarized, it would be fairly easy to pinpoint those individuals who should (and should not) be placed in leadership positions. This was known as the "Great Man" theory (9). The theory has been abandoned over the years because an evaluation of a number of these trait studies proved to be inconclusive. Over 80 years of study have failed to produce one single personality trait or set of qualities that can be used consistently to separate those who are leaders and those who are not. Chefs of diverse backgrounds, ethnic origins, gender, and personality have been effective leaders. All they needed was the desire to lead. However, studies have also shown that there are some personal characteristics that distinguish effective leaders from ineffective ones.

Research has shown that there are two distinct dimensions of leadership: (1) employee centered and (2) production centered. Therefore, a leader's personal characteristics and behavior do not in themselves guarantee leadership effectiveness. Perception of the kitchen team, the nature of the tasks, the relationship with the team members, and the organizational climate in the kitchen must all come together to provide effective supervisory leadership.

BEHAVIORAL THEORIES

Behavioral theories were directed to the study of leaders, supervisors, and work groups, rather than just focusing on the characteristics of successful leaders. In the past emphasis was placed on studying the behaviors that provided effective interaction between work-group members. Studies have shown that two characteristics arrived at independently of one another were important elements of supervisory behavior (10):

- Elements of *consideration* include behaviors indicating mutual trust, respect, and a certain warmth and rapport between the supervisor and the group.
- *Structure* includes behavior in which supervisors organize and define group activities and their relations to the group.

In their book *The Leadership Challenge* Kouzes and Posner similarly reported that behaviors followers expect from their leaders include honesty, competence, vision, and inspiration (11). Another study by Cichy, Sciarini, and Patton, reported in the *Cornell Quarterly*, discovered 14 desirable leadership behaviors and qualities (12). Individuals with these qualities:

- Provide a compelling message or vision.
- Have a strong personal value or belief system.
- Recognize that the ability to adjust is a necessity.
- Make desired outcomes tangible.
- Encourage and reward risk taking.
- Listen as well as, if not better than, they speak.
- Provide appropriate information, resources, and support to empower employees.
- Are inquisitive.
- Emphasize quality continuously.

- Know personal strengths and nurture them.
- Place a high value on learning.
- Maintain precise desired outcomes.
- Change their minds seldom.
- Have strong family values.

Denis Kinlaw, in studies outlined in *Coaching for Commitment*, uncovered similar behaviors of superior leaders, which he summarizes under six sets of common practices (13):

1. *Establishing a vision*: Superior leaders create expectations for significant and lasting achievement. They give meaning to work by associating even menial tasks with valued goals.
2. *Stimulating people to gain new competencies*: Superior leaders stimulate people to stretch their minds and their wills. They freely share their own expertise and keep people in touch with new resources.
3. *Helping people to overcome obstacles*: Superior leaders help others to overcome obstacles. They help others to find the courage and strength to persevere in the face of even the greatest difficulties.
4. *Helping people to overcome failure*: Superior leaders help people to cope with failure and disappointment. They are quick to offer people who fail new opportunities.
5. *Leading by example*: Superior leaders are models of integrity and hard work. They set the highest expectations for themselves and others.
6. *Including others in their success*: Superior leaders are quick to share the limelight with others. People associated with superior leaders feel as successful as the leaders.

LEADERSHIP STYLES

The emphasis of leadership study has shifted from the trait and behavioral approach to the situational approach. This modern situational approach to leadership is based on the assumption that all instances of successful leadership are different and require a unique combination of leaders, followers, and leadership situations. According to Blanchard, Zigarni, and Zigarni in *One Minute Manager*, the four basic styles of situational leadership are (14):

Style 1: *Directing*—The leader provides specific instructions and closely supervises task accomplishment.

Style 2: *Coaching*—The leader continues to direct and closely supervise task accomplishment but also explains decisions, solicits suggestions, and supports progress.

Style 3: *Supporting*—The leader facilitates and supports subordinates' efforts to task accomplishment and shares responsibility for decision making with them.

Style 4: *Delegating*—The leader turns over responsibility for decision making and problem solving to subordinates.

This has also been summarized as "different strokes for different folks." There is no one best or appropriate style suited to all situations. A leadership style often described as made up of the three F's—firm, fair, and friendly—is a combination of many elements, but at times this style does not work. The three F's presuppose there is a homogeneous kitchen team who will readily react and perform favorably to this chef leadership style.

As a situational leader the chef supervisor will need to analyze the team. Within the group there will be individuals who have high commitment to the team and its goals but without the necessary array of skills. In this situation the chef supervisor uses a detailed set of instructions to lead the team member—a directing style. Other team members may have some culinary skill competence but a low commitment to the team's vision and goals. Here, a coaching and correcting style highly supportive of the team member would be appropriate. A team member who is sometimes committed and has a lot of skills will require a supporting leadership style. Such a team member is capable of working alone with little direction, while team members with well-developed skills and a great deal of team commitment require that tasks be delegated to them in order to feel fulfilled.

Leadership ability is inextricably linked to motivation. As we observed earlier, what motivates one person may not motivate another. Motivation comes from within the individual. The leadership style provides the basis for a motivational environment.

An extreme in leadership style is the strict authoritarian, aloof chef who rules the kitchen with a rod of iron. The advantage of this style is good control and discipline over the team. The disadvantages are resentment, no cooperation, and poor communication with subordinates. These are certainly not the ingredients of a coaching leadership style in a TQM environment.

The other extreme is the chef who tries to be democratic to be accepted by other team members as a complete equal. The democratic style promotes a good atmosphere, good communication, and cooperation. However, the disadvantages can outweigh the advantages because the democrat is taken for granted, has no authority, and will eventually lose control of the team. Somewhere between these two extremes is the ideal leadership style.

The old-fashioned authoritarian, dictator style chef has no place in the complex modern culinary world. Kitchen team members need to be led, not controlled or managed. The best leadership style in the kitchen is one that works for the individual chef supervisor and is based on the make-up of the team, the personal characteristics of the chef supervisor, and the ever-chang-

Chef Talk: "Power and Authority"

When I was appointed Executive Chef at Dublin's celebrated Gresham Hotel I was 26 years old. It was my first "real" executive chef position. My predecessor, fondly referred to as "Macker," had held the position for 36 years before retiring. I inherited responsibility for 31 chefs and cooks and 23 additional kitchen support staff. Many of the chefs were much older than I, and they resented my appointment. I came to the Gresham with a good deal of prepublicity, having gained some notoriety winning gold medals at food shows, becoming a master chef, and being elected President of the local Chef's Association.

The goals set for me by the hotel's management were to improve the food standards, reduce the food cost, reduce the labor cost, and get a high rating for the restaurant (sound familiar?).

My first three months were a disaster. The food cost went up, customer complaints increased, absenteeism increased, and the kitchen staff's resentment of me grew. What was wrong? I had confidence in my goals, objectives, and abilities. Why then would the kitchen staff not "buy into" my plans? After a lot of soul searching, reading many books, talking with other chefs who had similar problems, and taking some supervisory development courses, I began to understand. First, I realized I had confused totally the issues of power, authority, and leadership. I was aloof and distant and my communication was by way of directives, usually written. Not surprisingly, my team worked against me. I reassessed my role and style of leadership and began to involve the other chefs in planning menus, work scheduling, production incentives, and directions in food styles. After a short time things began to improve. In fact, the chefs became more rigorous in the pursuit of our objectives than I was. We were successful, food costs went down, productivity increased, our restaurant was voted one of the top 50 in the world, but more importantly we created a terrific team environment. *They* were responsible for the ensuing success. My part was to recognize that just because I had the power and authority of the position did not necessarily mean that I was a leader and that the kitchen staff would follow. Today, I am happy to say, they make me look good professionally, and our operation is successful. We have become a team, and all of the chefs are my friends.

Noel C. Cullen, Ed.D., CMC, AAC, Boston University, Boston, MA ing daily situations facing the chef supervisor. Situational leadership provides the chef supervisor with a flexible approach to each situation as it arises.

THE NATURE OF CULINARY LEADERSHIP

Few concepts are as difficult to analyze as leadership. Why do some individuals seem to effortlessly succeed and others fail so miserably? Within the culinary world, there exist tremendous opportunities for leadership. As Jerry Hill, former Chairman of the Michigan Restaurant Association, observed (15):

> If you are interested in developing leadership skills and tackling leadership responsibility, you'd be hard pressed to find another field that offers more opportunity than the foodservice industry. Not only are many leadership positions available, but those positions are likely to be true leadership roles. We fortunately have a wealth of culinary leaders to draw analysis from.

But what is the nature of leadership? A good place to start is to look at the principles of leadership listed in the U.S. Army's manual of leadership. The following 10 principles have been adapted from this manual and may be applied to culinary leadership (16):

1. *Know yourself and seek self-improvement.* Identify your strengths and weaknesses. Set goals for each weakness or desired improvement. Develop plans to achieve goals. Evaluate progress toward goals.
2. *Be technically and tactfully proficient.* Be knowledgeable in all aspects of your job. Be able to pass this on to your fellow kitchen team members.
3. *Seek responsibility and take responsibility for your actions.* When you see a problem, initiate actions to solve it. Do not wait for others to tell you what to do, or say "it's not my job." If you have made a mistake, admit your errors, accept your criticism, and promptly correct the matter.
4. *Make sound and timely decisions.* Use problem-solving, decision-making, and planning methods to come to a rapid assessment of the situation and make the most appropriate decision. Indecisiveness causes confusion and a lack of confidence.
5. *Set an example.* As a role model, this is the chef supervisor's most important leadership skill. You should not ask your fellow team members to do anything you would not do yourself. As a leader, you should earn the respect of the team, not demand it.
6. *Know your subordinates and look out for their well-being.* Take the time to learn about your team by listening to them. Know what it takes to motivate each member individually. It is important to recognize their need to be needed. If you take care of your kitchen team, they will take care of you.

7. *Keep your subordinates informed.* Don't give just orders; explain the rationale for the request. Informed persons consider themselves part of the team effort. Your kitchen team cannot grow and perform well if you keep them in the dark.

8. *Develop a sense of responsibility in your subordinates.* Delegation of responsibilities will enhance the development of the team. It will reflect your confidence in them and cause them to seek additional responsibilities. Acknowledging their accomplishments fosters their initiatives.

9. *Ensure that the task is understood, supervised, and accomplished.* Orders and directives should be clearly understood and all team members should know what is expected of them. There is a fine line between undersupervision and oversupervision. Giving the order is 10 percent; the other 90 percent is ensuring it gets done.

10. *Train your personnel as a team.* Team work occurs when all members of the team are proficient in their individual assignments and have the mutual respect and trust of one another. A team must have its own spirit and confidence in its ability to accomplish the culinary and customer satisfaction objectives. Cohesion builds confidence and morale.

These fundamental elements of leadership are common sense. Each one has its own merits and they complement each other. People leadership, unlike "thing management," has a connection with the heart. When chef supervisors resort to logic alone, not only do they risk treating their team members like machines, but also are often unable to motivate and inspire. In addition to being sensitive to the emotional needs of the team, the chef supervisor should encourage and reward risk taking to accomplish the organization's goals.

Culinary leadership is demonstrated by the chef supervisor who:

- Can sacrifice personal glory for the good of the team, has strength of purpose to achieve the goals, cannot be easily discouraged, and does not compromise, but adapts.

- Understands that working through hardship is an experience that builds courage, can deal with adversity and overcome mistakes, and can achieve anything for which he or she is willing to pay the price.

- Does not allow team members' weaknesses to prevail over their strengths and will always set realistic goals for each team member based on his or her abilities.

- Has an open style and believes in a win-win relationship with the team and uses diplomacy based on respect of, trust in, and courtesy to the team.

- Has a clear vision of the possibilities of the team's potential and inspires them through motivation and aims high and goes after things that will make a difference, rather than seeking the safe path of mediocrity.

- Has stamina, high energy levels, tenacity, and a positive attitude. Once committed to the foodservice organization's goals and objectives, he or she helps the team reach these goals, communicates openly with them, shares the risk taking, and leads by example.
- Has a sense of humor, shuns publicity that may be at the expense of the team or the organization, and accepts failure in some things in order to excel in more important ones.
- Focuses on problems as opportunities, is tolerant, and never confuses power with leadership.
- Invests himself or herself in adequate training of the team, adopts a coaching and correcting style, and understands that training the team is the vital ingredient for TQM, supervision, and leadership.

BUILDING LEADERSHIP SELF-CONFIDENCE

Confidence is a matter of style. Chef supervisors should be assertive, not overbearing. Leadership self-confidence can be developed in four action steps. All have to do with one fact—self-confidence—which will increase as leadership tasks are accomplished successfully. In his book *The Art of the Leader*, William Cohen suggests the following action steps to increase leadership self-confidence (17):

1. Become a leader by seeking out situations and volunteering to be a leader whenever you can.
2. Be an unselfish teacher and helper to others. Others will come to you for leadership. Always treat those you lead with respect.
3. Develop your expertise. Expertise is a source of leadership power.
4. Use positive mental energy. Simulations in the mind are rehearsals for success. They are interpreted by the mind as real experiences. So they will boost leadership self-confidence just like the actual experience.

The kitchen team will readily follow a chef supervisor who displays confidence. It demonstrates the right to authority. It also makes the team feel comfortable that there is direction and purpose for what they do.

The way the chef supervisor dresses is also part of developing leadership self-confidence. The chef's professional attire and grooming must always be outstanding. This obviously includes a clean, well-groomed white chef uniform with safe, polished shoes. Personal grooming should be immaculate and reflect the highest standards. The supervisor is the role model. Professional practices and high personal standards in the kitchen set the chef apart as a leader. Involved in this is the practice of a code of professional ethics for culinary art. Great leaders throughout the ages have understood that their number one responsibility was their own discipline and personal growth. If chef supervisors cannot lead themselves and manage their lives, then they surely will be unable to lead others. Leaders can never take other people further than they have gone themselves. Dwight Eisenhower once said: "In order to be a leader, a man must have followers, a man must have their confidence. Hence, the supreme quality for a leader is unquestionably integrity" (18). Training and experience develop a personal assurance with which chefs can meet the challenges of leadership. Those who portray a lack of self-confidence in their abilities to carry out leadership assignments give signs to the team that these duties are beyond their capabilities. They therefore become weak leaders.

William Cohen stated, "The first way to develop self-confidence while you develop your leadership skills is to become an uncrowned leader" (19). There are many opportunities for individual chefs to become leaders. In the kitchen there may be team members who need help. Seizing the opportunity to lead can help these people build the confidence of the chef as a leader. Waiting for management to give direction on team building may stunt a chef's leadership potential. A thinking proactive chef will not wait for direction from above. Instead he or she will begin immediately to take charge and lead the rest of the team to greater total quality culinary heights.

According to Bennus and Nanus, "Being a manager has to do with doing things right. Being a leader has to do with doing the right things" (20). It is therefore unnecessary to have an official sounding title to be a leader. Leadership development is first and foremost a process of self-development.

DEVELOPING CULINARY LEADERSHIP

What is culinary leadership? Is it about winning gold medals at food shows? Is it about being a celebrated TV chef or being highly rated by some agency? Is it about being an executive chef in a large prestigious hotel or restaurant? Well, the answer is, it could be all of these things, but not necessarily. The best rating you can have as a culinary leader is from the customers who come back to your restaurant and a loyal kitchen team that follows the chef leader and is concerned for the success of the foodservice operation. Culinary leadership is all about high standards of culinary practices which satisfy restaurant guests and for which the kitchen team have been motivated and trained. Remember, quality is quality no matter what size or type of foodservice operation.

There are several areas in which leadership within the kitchen may be developed. The following are some suggestions that work and will assist in developing a great team atmosphere and contribute enormously to culinary leadership.

- Develop a particular food philosophy and style. Get each chef team member involved. Set up food tasting/critique sessions. Involve your customers and dining room staff in these sessions. Formulate your menu items based on the results of these critiques. Aggressively put forward innovative culinary philosophies. Become known for a particular style of food.

Chef Talk: "Leadership in A Busy Kitchen"

How do we know if we are good leaders? Simply by asking yourself if people follow you because they have to or because they want to. The leadership skills I like to see in my supervisors are the same attributes I want my subordinates to see in me. Holding management positions in large-scale operations has broadened my horizons on motivating employees in a positive manner. Cultural diversity is a major factor in large-scale operations. How do you get a massive work force made up of many ethnic backgrounds and different age groups to march to the same beat? You don't. The answer is, we deal with every employee in a different way. Each employee must be nurtured to the same finish line. Some of our employees need more encouragement or confidence in their work while others need the reins tightened every now and then. Some need both in the same given day or hour. I strongly believe there is a task for every employee and it is up to the supervisor to find what employee is best suited for each work assignment. Constructive criticism and praise is very important following individual or group work assignments. Manage in a positive manner. Don't tell a cook she cannot work a sauté station on a Saturday night because she is not fast enough or skilled. Tell her that she is the only cook you have who can handle the vegetable station on the busy nights and that you will cross train her on a weekday when business is slower. This second statement is also true, and now the employee feels like an integral part of the team and will produce twice as much for you. Employees will always monitor how fair you are in handling all employees. Treat all employees with the same respect, from the kitchen steward up to the Maitre D' in the dining room. People will notice this and respect you for this alone. Our employees and co-workers are much more sensitive to our actions than we think. Don't confuse your work force. Set straight, simple goals for them to aim toward. Don't change your plan in the middle of a game unless it is absolutely necessary to obtain final objectives. Supervisors who constantly change their game plan appear to be incompetent in their judgment. The crew will then be incompetent in their work. If you realize you made a bad decision, sometimes you should ride it out rather than changing course in the middle of service. Most importantly, never be afraid to admit you've made a mistake.

Alfonso Contrisciani, CEC, Johnson & Wales University, Providence, RI

- Educate yourself. Take development courses. Join a professional chef's organization. Become certified within your profession. Read trade magazines. Study the latest culinary trends. Network with other chefs.

- Involve the team in entering food shows. This is an excellent method of building team morale and esprit de corps. Train your team. Invest continuously in training. Training a kitchen team is a never-ending task.

- Allocate days during the week for each chef team member to have his or her own signature menu item.

- Provide the team with distinctive uniforms.

- Insist on the highest culinary standards. At all levels, give the team the authority and responsibility to solve problems and prepare exceptional menu items.

- Build partnerships with your purveyors. Set specifications on quality with them.

- Seek out ways to constantly develop your team. Enroll them in development courses. Arrange for them to attend chef seminars and conferences.

- Involve the support team in all the chef and food philosophies. They are an integral part of the total quality effort.

- Maintain scrupulous standards of personal hygiene. Insist on high standards of safety and sanitation within the kitchen area.

- Show concern for the welfare of the kitchen team. Treat each member with respect, and trust them to carry out the assigned tasks. Be approachable and sympathetic in the kitchen.

- Visit the dining room. Meet your customers. Encourage feedback from them. Build a strong relationship with the dining room staff. They are vital to achieving culinary success.

- Recognize that empowerment is not a substitute for leadership or a reduction of authority. The more the kitchen team is empowered, the greater the need for culinary leaders who can set goals and define a vision. The paradox of empowerment is that in order to gain power, you must give some of it away.

- Implement the solution through the kitchen team. Solving a problem in the kitchen is not worth much unless you can do this.

- Celebrate your kitchen team and their success, their promotions, awards, birthdays, marriages, reunions, anniversaries, holidays, along with the organization's anniversary, the introduction of new menus, and the articulation of the food service organization's vision. Celebration within the kitchen can build individual self-esteem. Each team member will feel important and empowered. It enhances communication, promotes teamwork, and makes members feel bonded. It makes work fun and creates a positive outlook.

Developing culinary leadership is concerned with encouraging the kitchen team to succeed. To encourage is to inspire others with courage and spirit. Encouragement will help kitchen team members change behaviors and attitudes. It will develop in individuals self-confidence and positive feelings about their own capabilities. Encouragement should be given during times of stress, particularly when failure is looming. It should be given equally and fairly to all team members, emphasizing the positive and not the negative in others. Encouragement will give the kitchen team a sense of belonging, provide positive self-image, and encourage positive attitudes toward the chef supervisor.

When the team is placed first, the highest possible productivity will result in the kitchen as well as total quality relative to culinary practices and customer satisfaction. Profits for the foodservice organization will follow.

HUMOR AS A LEADERSHIP TOOL

Fun relieves tension and improves concentration. It counteracts boredom and reduces the potential for conflict within the kitchen. The enjoyable interaction between team members reduces the need to get social support outside of the kitchen team. A kitchen team enjoying and supporting one another is more productive.

Humor is a powerful tool for enhancing self-confidence and building empathy. Humor can promote positive attitudes within the team, making it easier to hear feedback and new information. Humor also distracts from worry, lightens stress, anxiety, depression, and pain, increases creativity, and offers perspective and balance. It can help express the truth when the truth is feared and repressed. The use of humor decreases discipline problems and pressure on team members to be perfect. It also improves listening and employee retention and creates a comfort level in the kitchen.

The potential of each person can best be utilized in an atmosphere of open communication. Studies have shown that employees who have fun at work are less likely to be late or absent (21). Chef supervisors can cultivate a sense of humor and then use it to motivate and create a positive quality work environment. The following are some tips for putting humor into leadership:

- Maintain a humor file.
- Include appropriate humor in your team meetings.
- Tailor your humor to the tastes and preferences of the kitchen team.
- Look for humor in those little interruptions that occur during meetings or during the service period.
- Don't joke about people's gender, ethnicity, and personal or physical characteristics.
- Keep your humor brief.
- Recognize when humor is not appropriate.

When injecting humor, keep the material short, tell it slowly, and always wait for others to laugh first. Questions of mood, taste, and context should be

Chef Talk: "Chef Leadership"

During the 30 years of my career, I have experienced many forms of leadership, from the very simple and basic in the beginning to the complex and brilliant later. I had the privilege to learn from some of the best not only in a working environment, but also during Culinary Team practices and association activities. In order to develop my own style, I was able to listen to good advice as well as experience some less desirable forms of leadership. For some reason it seems easier to recall the horrors than the positive situations. This may be due to the fact that good leaders seldom resort to extremes to get the job done.

During the early part of my apprenticeship, when I was very young, 15 in fact, a transformation of power was going on that I found interesting to reflect upon later. Being that young, my father was reluctant to give up his control over me. This was apparent by his overly protective interest in what I was doing. I spent most of the day working a split shift. I started at 8:00 a.m. and returned home at 10:00 p.m. with a 3-hour break in the afternoon. My father wanted me to be at home to work during my break. My chef, on the other hand, wanted us to use this time to study and rest because the work load from school was heavy and we worked 6-day weeks. I was not doing well in school and my chef realized that he needed to intervene. He suggested to my father that I should stay with other apprentices in the room at work and go home on my day off. My father agreed reluctantly. My chef spent some time with me studying and I made a remarkable turnaround in school.

Since my chef took an interest in me, I became more confident in my work. Soon I was helping him with his work on shows, and during my last year, in 1960, he took me to Frankfurt to the IKA (Culinary Olympics) for my first exposure to this remarkable show. My chef's leadership style was not very polished. He could have been described as rough and abrasive. He would say, "Let them do hard and dirty work for one year and if they are still there I might remember their name." If you made it, however, it got better in the third year. The kitchen was run by the apprentices on Mondays, two from each year, when the chef and cooks were off. This was our turn to practice leadership by getting the job done. Since we had a daily menu, the third year apprentices could write it and direct the kitchen. Looking back, I noticed that every Monday the crew elected me to be the chef. What made it happen was that I was willing to do the research necessary to write the menu, order the food, make the production charts, and most importantly, take the heat if something went wrong. Not much went wrong on my Mondays because I made sure everything was well planned.

Klaus Friedenreich, CMC, AAC, Director, Art Institute of Fort Lauderdale, Fort Lauderdale, FL considered. Humor can be used to form a connection with all team members. Chefs can humanize themselves as leaders by using self-deprecating humor; it comforts the team to know that leaders share their faults and weaknesses and that they have the ability to laugh at themselves. Laugh with others, not at them. Laugh at yourself; it is the sign of a healthy ego. Take yourself lightly, but take your responsibilities seriously.

Humor can be used in the kitchen to illustrate points and create retention of ideas and scenarios. Team members can view themselves more objectively. Humor increases spontaneity, allowing flexibility of thinking. It facilitates change and helps build rapport and trust among the team. Using humor can be difficult at first, but it pays off in the long run. People respond better to the operational environment of the kitchen when they are in a good mood. It may be one of the most powerful tools the chef has for motivating and stimulating creativity and improving job performance.

CONCLUSIONS

There is no single best style of leadership. The best leadership pattern is the one that works best for *you*. Excellent personal qualities and characteristics help in being a good leader. However, leadership skill sets are learned and are not something that you are born with. The team is the greatest resource the foodservice operation has. How they are led will ultimately determine the total quality success or failure of a restaurant.

A very old leadership tenet states that you should be willing to do everything you ask those you lead to do. Therefore, personal example is very important. Most people do not like to follow leaders who cannot make up their minds or have trouble coming to a decision. Therefore, be a decisive leader. The leader sets the tone. A large component of this tone is a leader's ego. If the leader sets a positive example—one of service, dedication, support, and concern—others will strive toward the same goal. The leader's role is one of service. His or her job is to create structures that allow each team member to achieve the desired quality result. Good chef leaders actively create structures and symbols that remind the team of their concern for the human side of the culinary operation. Items that support this effort are:

- Periodic social get-togethers
- Recognition of individual and team accomplishments; ensuring everybody in the organization (not just the kitchen) knows what the kitchen team does
- Creating an internal kitchen team slogan
- Encouraging mild competitiveness among team members and between department groups
- On a rotating basis, putting up photos of various people in the team

Though such things may seem frivolous, they are important as they help keep a human feeling in the kitchen.

There are only two ways to get others to do what you want. You can compel them to do it or you can persuade them. Persuading requires an understanding of what makes people tick and what motivates them, that is, a knowledge of human nature. Great leaders possess this knowledge. Max De Pree, in *Leadership Is an Art*, sums up what he feels are the traits and behaviors most people resent in leaders (22):

- Superficiality
- A lack of dignity
- Injustice, the flaw that prevents equity
- Arrogance
- Betrayal of principles of quality
- Overuse of jargon, because it confuses rather than clarifies
- Viewing customers as interruptions
- Watching bottom lines without watching behavior
- Never saying thank you to others
- Failure to permit team members to do their best
- Dependence on policies and hierarchy rather than on trust and competence

Many leaders note that the most efficient way to get good performance from others is to treat them like heros. Giving public credit to someone who has earned it is a great leadership technique. Successful leaders often say that if you trust others to do well, they will. If, on the other hand, you believe your team will fail, they will. Good leaders learn to sound and look like winners. Competence will galvanize the team. They will look to you for guidance and direction. When kitchen team members understand the importance of total quality, they will lend their mental strength to all the quality efforts. When they get excited about their work, all team energy is powered into the tasks. The best way for the chef supervisor to generate excitement is to be enthusiastic. It is contagious. Good leaders cannot do it alone. They should delegate. Make the team look good, and the team will make the chef supervisor look good.

SUMMARY

Leadership in the kitchen as part of a TQM process confers on the chef supervisor the privilege and responsibility to direct the actions of the kitchen team in carrying out the goals and objectives of the foodservice organization.

Leadership can be learned in the same way chefs learn culinary skills. Leadership development is a process of self-development. It is facilitated by education, training, mentoring, and experience and is dependent on the chef supervisor's ability to lead people in such a way that team members will want to follow.

The trait approach to leadership was based on early research that assumed that good leaders were born, not made. Behavioral theories are directed to the study of work groups, leaders, and supervisors, rather than focusing solely on the characteristics of successful leaders.

Situational leadership is based on the premise that different situations will require different leadership styles. The four basic situational leadership styles are directing, supporting, coaching, and delegating.

Culinary leadership is as much about respecting and valuing kitchen team members as it is about great culinary creations.

Humor is a valuable leadership tool. Laugh with your kitchen team, not at them.

DISCUSSION QUESTIONS

1. In what way is leadership different from supervision?
2. What are the more significant factors that affect chef supervisors' leadership styles?
3. What are the differences between autocratic and democratic leadership styles?
4. Is there one best leadership style? Explain.
5. What are situations appropriate for the four styles of situational leadership?
6. What are some of the myths associated with leadership?
7. What are the essential differences between the leadership behaviors of "directive" and "supportive"? When and why are they used?
8. The "Great Man" theory relied on profiling a certain set of characteristics. When these were summarized, it was believed it would be easy to pinpoint leaders. Do you agree with this theory? Give reasons for your answers.
9. What are eight characteristics of chef supervisor leaders?
10. The paradox of empowerment states that in order to gain power, you must give some of it away. How does this impact the chef supervisor as a leader?
11. What are the benefits of using humor as a leadership tool?

NOTES

1. Dwight D. Eisenhower, *Great Quotes From Great Leaders*, Ed. Peggy Anderson, Lombard, IL, Great Quotations, 1989, p. 53.
2. James M. Kouzes and Barry Z. Posner, *Credibility: How Leaders Gain and Lose It, Why People Demand It*, Jossey-Bass, San Francisco, 1993.
3. John C. Maxwell, *Developing the Leader Within You*, Nelson, Nashville, TN, 1993, p. 103.
4. Warren Bennus and Burt Nanus, *Leaders: The Strategies for Taking Charge*, Harper-Collins, New York, 1985, p. 222.
5. James M. Kouzes and Barry Z. Posner, *The Leadership Challenge*, Jossey-Bass, San Francisco, 1988, p. xv.

6. Patrick L. O'Malley, "Make Excellence a Habit," *Lessons in Leadership*, Van Nostrand Reinhold, New York, 1991, p. 40.

7. Kenneth Blanchard, Patricia Zigarni, and Drea Zigarni, *Leadership and the One Minute Manager*, Morrow & Co., New York, 1985, p. 31.

8. *Sky Magazine*, Delta Airlines, July 1993.

9. Warren Bennus and Burt Nanus, *Leaders: The Strategies For Taking Charge*, HarperCollins, New York, 1985, p. 5.

10. Arthur Sherman, George Bohlander, and Herbert Crudden, *Managing Human Resources*, 8th ed., South-Western, Cincinnati, OH, 1988, p. 355.

11. James M. Kouzes and Barry Z. Posner, *The Leadership Challenge*, Jossey-Bass, San Francisco, 1988, p. 16.

12. Ronald Cichy Ronald, Martin P, Sciarini, and Mark E. Patton, "Food-Service Leadership: Could Attila Run a Restaurant," *The Cornell Hotel and Restaurant Administration Quarterly*, Feb. 1992.

13. Denis C. Kinlaw, *Coaching For Commitment*, Pfeiffer, San Diego, CA, 1993, p. 122.

14. Kenneth Blanchard, Patricia Zigarni, and Drea Zigarni, *Leadership and the One Minute Manager*, Morrow & Co., New York, 1985.

15. Jerry L. Hill, "Steer Clear of the Minefields" *Lessons in Leadership*, Van Nostrand Reinhold, New York, 1991, p. 135.

16. *Sky Magazine*, Delta Airlines, July 1993, pp. 24–28.

17. William A. Cohen, *The Art of the Leader*, Prentice-Hall, Englewood Cliffs, NJ, 1990, p. 97.

18. Dwight D. Eisenhower, *Great Quotes From Great Leaders*, Ed. Peggy Anderson, Lombard, IL, Great Quotations, 1989, p. 52.

19. William A. Cohen, *The Art of the Leader*, Prentice-Hall, Englewood Cliffs, NJ, 1990, p. 85.

20. Warren Bennus and Burt Nanus, *Leaders: The Strategies for Taking Charge*, HarperCollins, New York, 1985, p. 23.

21. Joseph L. Picogna, *Total Quality Leadership: A Training Approach*, International Information Associates Inc., Morrissville, PA, 1993, p. 348.

22. Max De Pree, *Leadership Is an Art*, Dell, New York, 1989, p. 138.

9

Total Quality and Training in the Kitchen

Outline

- Introduction
- TQM and training
- A systems approach to training
- Types of training
- How people learn
- Adult learning
- Barriers to learning
- Conclusions
- Summary
- Discussion Questions

Objectives

When you complete this chapter, you should be able to:

1. Describe the contribution of training to TQM and relate to the concept of training as an investment in people relative to the cost of quality.

2. Describe a systems approach to training and explain how training interacts with the quality goals of the foodservice organization.

3. Define the types of training models and their strengths and weaknesses and describe situations appropriate for each method.

4. List the major categories of learning, and explain how they influence the rate of learning.

5. Understand the concept of androgogy and outline the challenges in this area for the chef supervisor.

6. Identify factors that inhibit learning.

INTRODUCTION

Training is the basis for TQM success in the kitchen. Without a strong and committed investment in training the kitchen team will not be successful. The principles of total quality are rooted in a trained team approach. Part II of this book is therefore directed toward training and how it affects the success of the foodservice organization, in particular the culinary operation.

Total quality management will not happen within the kitchen unless the team and the chef supervisor do certain things. Quality training requires money and time. Time costs money; therefore, quality has a cost. This cost should be viewed as an investment in the future growth of the foodservice organization. Quality and training can be viewed as investments, rather than as expenditures. Philip Crosby, in his book *Quality is Free*, argues that achieving quality costs nothing. He points out that the real cost of quality is doing things wrong—the cost of waste (1). The ultimate aim of quality in the kitchen is to eliminate waste and not do things wrong at any stage in the culinary process. Therefore, if every stage is done correctly and conforms to the quality standard, then costs are not incurred and real value is accrued. Training, as well as the training skills of the chef supervisor, is the total quality compass that points the way to continuous daily improvements and results in satisfied customers.

TQM AND TRAINING

As previously stated, TQM requires that each function required to produce quality food, ambience, and service within the restaurant be identified and improvements be applied at every stage. Proficiency in TQM skills cannot be achieved through study; rather it must be accomplished by a well-organized sequence of applications to actual processes (2). Key to this success is training each team member to contribute to TQM. Commitment to total quality should emanate from the top levels of the organization. It should be communicated clearly and consistently and be reflected in all aspects of the organization's functions and systems, during recruitment, remuneration, recognition, promotion, and training. It involves the challenge of developing

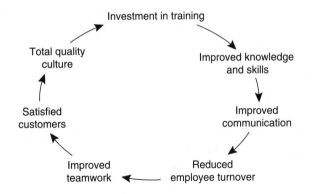

Figure 2 Training and quality interaction.

appropriate attitudes and values within the kitchen team and throughout the entire foodservice organization. Once adopted, total quality is a long-term proposition, not a "quick fix." The different systems employed will not succeed unless they are fundamentally rooted in a long-term strategy of continuous development and training of people within the kitchen. Management and the chef supervisor must recognize that total quality can be achieved only through teamwork, shared goals, and organizational vision. Applying the principles of TQM to the analysis and design of training is straightforward. The real challenge is in making it all happen. The aim of adopting a quality approach to training is to provide a service that meets and hopefully exceeds customer needs every time and to deliver what was promised. We therefore need to be aware of what is acceptable and what is not from the customer's point of view. Figure 2 demonstrates the advantages of investment in training.

A SYSTEMS APPROACH TO TRAINING

Training is a learning process that involves the acquisition of skills, concepts, rules, and attitudes so as to increase the performance of each team member. Training is not education. Training is the process of integrating personal and organizational goals. Training is used to close the gap between current and desired performance of individual kitchen team members. It is also about helping people learn and develop.

Training can be treated as a total systems approach, as a cycle with interrelated elements. These elements closely parallel the steps a person uses in solving a problem. Five steps are generally considered to be part of this closed-loop continuous process:

1. Analyze and determine training needs.
2. Develop training objectives.

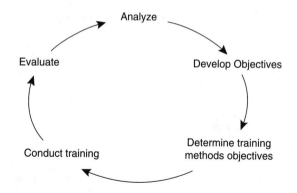

Figure 3   The training process.

3. Determine the appropriate training methods and materials.
4. Conduct the training.
5. Evaluate the training.

Figure 3 outlines the training process.

1. *Analysis of training needs*
    This step is sometimes referred to as needs analysis and has two main purposes: to determine what is needed in the first place and to ensure that the training that does occur is based on sound requirements (3). Therefore, the needs analysis process is the most important step in the development of a training program because all other activities involved in the design, delivery, and evaluation stem from this process. A needs analysis typically contains the following steps:

- Identification of the performance problems within the kitchen
- Identification of the knowledge, skills, and attitudes necessary for each team member to perform the job
- Assessment of each team member's knowledge, skills, and attitudes
- Designing the needs analysis and its specific training methodology
- Determining methods of gathering data on needs analysis
- Analyzing needs analysis data findings
- Preparing training plans based on the needs analysis

    The term *needs analysis* is best described as the difference between present performance and desired performance, that is, the gap between what is and what ought to be. "Performance problems might be reflected in high employee turnover, a decline in productivity, grievances, poor teamwork, and/or customer complaints. If this is the case, the following questions should arise as part of the needs analysis." (4):

- What are the specific problems?
- What exactly is the desired outcome of training?
- What would the effect of *no* training be?
- Is training the best method of resolving the problems?

Once the problem or problems have been identified and it has been determined that it is training related, the next step in the needs analysis process is to:

1. Identify the knowledge, skills, and attitudes essential to performing the job.
2. Assess individual team members. Analyze their strengths as well as their weaknesses. These strengths and weaknesses are measured against the specific job requirements identified in the needs analysis step.
3. Design an instrument or methods of gathering information. The basic rule of thumb in a systematic approach is to collect only that information that is necessary to design the training program.

Principal methods of data collection in the kitchen are:

- *Observations:* The process of observation involves observing team members—their work routines and behaviors and how each person interacts within the team.
- *Interviews:* The face-to-face interview is also a useful method of gathering information on training gaps. The interview technique, like the observation process, can take the form of informal interviews to discuss problems or issues related to training.
- *Work samples:* Samples of work produced by the team member can be evaluated by having the individual prepare and cook a dish from the menu.

Once the data have been collected, it is necessary to analyze the information so that specific training plans and strategies may be formulated.

The training plan should be prioritized on the basis of the needs analysis. In the needs analysis segment of a systematic approach to training the basic purpose is to uncover the quality gaps—what it is that prevents the total quality dining experience. It is also about utilizing scarce resources of time, money, and people so as to maximize the training effort in a planned, systematic, and sequential way.

2. Training objectives

Systematic and sequential planning of the training program is critical to its success. The development of precise and measurable training objectives is crucial in instructional delivery (5). Good objectives ensure that learners are aware of what will occur during training. Objectives will also provide learners with information on what they will be able to do upon completion of the training session. In addition, objectives often serve as the basis for program and trainer evaluation.

3. *Determine training materials*

The challenge here is to take the training plan outline that resulted from the first two phases and convert it into a complete set of materials that when implemented will result in the attainment of the desired learning outcomes. This is where most of the time devoted to training (apart from conducting the actual training) is traditionally spent. Depending upon the circumstances, a wide variety of materials may be utilized. *Job talks, demonstration,* and *role plays* are some of the most widely used instructional techniques appropriate to training chef team members.

4. *Conduct the training*

This is where all the preparation pays off. The chef trainer's role here is to instruct, motivate, lead, enable, and facilitate learning. In addition to serving as a training instructor, the chef supervisor should facilitate the logistics involved in the training sessions.

The first few minutes of any training session are critical. The introduction should capture the interest of the entire kitchen team. The chef supervisor as a trainer has a considerable advantage in that he or she has an existing rapport with the group, which should therefore facilitate getting the object of the training session across smoothly. However, different topics that are important to the success of the organization should be introduced to provide variety. This will help to generate additional interest. Successfully delivering the introduction will ensure that each team member is prepared to receive instruction.

5. *Evaluate the training*

Instruction is designed to bring about the learning of several kinds of skills. The outcomes of this planned training are learner performances that show that various types of additional knowledge, skills, and attitudes have been acquired. The chef trainer needs a system to determine how successful the training has been. There is a need to assess learner performance and to check learning to determine whether the designed instruction has met the training objectives. Evaluation is an essential component of training. It is often neglected because the chef trainer is not sufficiently adept at measuring learner performance. Materials that are used continuously need to be assessed so that improvements may be made. In simple terms, did the planned changes occur? Without evaluation it's impossible to quantify the results of the training plan.

Methods of evaluation include:

- Instructor evaluation of the training outcome when each segment is completed
- Learner evaluation of the course (What skills do I possess now that I did not have prior to training?)

Chef Talk: Training: "What's in It For You?"

In rough economic times, nothing comes under fire more than a training budget. It's an easy budgetary target. The alternative is just not to do any training.

Training is extremely important for the success of any foodservice operation. Without it the leader cannot motivate other members of the kitchen to achieve high-quality standards and cooking skills. Training is about setting quality objectives and then showing people how to perform these tasks to the required standard. More and more foodservice organizations are focusing on training the kitchen team.

Is it easy? No! There is often strong resistance from management because of a fear of giving up power and control. Where enlightened organizations have invested in training, their kitchen employees' success has followed. Training, in my view, is not only the path to success for the company but also sends a message to the individual being trained. Very often employees in training programs will remark, "If this company is investing in me, then they must value me as an employee." This sense of belonging engendered through training encourages greater effort by the individual.

There are all sorts of "buzz words" associated with training: empowerment, participative management, self-directed work teams, and others. What it all means is respecting the abilities of the individual kitchen employee and giving them the tools to do the job. Involve the employees in deciding what training is necessary. Ask for their input and then proceed slowly. It's really a win-win formula for success. You end up with a more productive team involved and participating in the successful accomplishment of the foodservice organization goals.

Reimund Pitz, CEC, CCE, AAC, Executive Chef, MGM Studios, Walt Disney World, Lake Buena Vista, FL

- Third-party evaluation by guests or other work centers
- Field evaluation to determine if the learners are performing well in the roles for which the training was to have prepared them (Can they perform the skills at the level desired?)

Field evaluation is the most suitable method to determine training effectiveness in the kitchen. Learners may be assessed on the job by the chef supervisor. Coaching on the job is also facilitated through this method of evaluation. Evaluation is part of the continuous loop that feeds back into the cycle (6).

TYPES OF TRAINING

There are many types of training. Each has its own relative strengths and weaknesses. The following training methods are considered appropriate to total quality enhancement training in a culinary environment. They are listed so that each may be evaluated relative to the appropriateness of the training mission.

1. *Job talk*
A speech by the chef supervisor with limited opportunities for open discussion.

Strengths

- Clear and direct method of presentation.
- Good for large groups.
- Materials can be provided to each member in advance to help with preparation.
- The chef supervisor has control over time.
- Inexpensive training method.
- Little or no equipment is necessary.

Weaknesses

- Information not easily assimilated.
- Appeals to one sense only (hearing); therefore, overloading may occur.
- Group can become easily bored.
- It is difficult to assess if your "message" has been understood and accepted by the team.
- It is difficult to pace to the learning rate of each team member.

2. *Team meetings* (group discussions)
A speech by the chef supervisor with a lot of participation and interaction with the team. Always requires leadership. Particularly useful for teams with mixed experience levels.

Strengths

- Good for a small number of people.
- All team members have the opportunity to present their ideas.
- More ideas can be generated.
- Good for total quality principles.
- Quality gaps can be identified.
- Effective for continuous improvements within the foodservice organization.

Weaknesses

- Sometimes the team may get away from the subject matter.
- The chef supervisor may be inexperienced at guiding or leading the discussions.
- Possibility of one strong individual dominating the meeting.

3. *Role Playing*

Creating a realistic situation and having team members assume parts of specific personalities in the situation. Their actions are based on the roles assigned to them. Emphasis is not on problem solving. A role play draws upon the participants' experiences and knowledge and forces them to apply theory to practice (7). Useful for attitude awareness training.

Strengths

- Good if the situation is similar to the actual work situation.
- Team members receive feedback that gives them confidence.
- Good for interpersonal skills.
- Teaches team members how to act in real situations.
- Can be used to highlight sensitive topics such as personal hygiene and/or poor interpersonal habits.

Weaknesses

- Team members are not actors.
- Sometimes role playing is not taken seriously.
- Some situations cannot be implemented in role playing.
- Uncontrolled role plays may not lead to any results.
- It requires that incorrect and correct methods being role played both be described.

4. *Demonstrations*

Actual equipment is used to demonstrate the action. The most effective method for instructing culinary manipulative skills. Makes use of the learner's visual sense.

Strengths

- Has great visual impact.
- Instruction can be built step by step.
- Demonstration ensures that instruction is given in sequence.
- Difficult tasks may be shown in easy stages.

- Makes use of the natural inclination to imitate.
- Best if preceded by study assignment.

Weaknesses

- Suitable for relatively small groups.
- A lot of preparation required.
- Pace is often too fast.
- Learners often watch the demonstrator rather than the demonstration.
- Should be avoided unless adequate time has been allowed for preparation and practice beforehand.

5. *Case study*

This is a written narrative description of a real situation faced by chefs. Team members are required to propose one or more suitable solutions and/or make appropriate decisions.

Strengths

- Individual cases can be very interesting.
- Involves the team members in a lot of discussions and interactions since there is no absolute solution.
- Develops kitchen team members' ability to communicate and encourages active participation.
- Develops the ability to analyze factors that influence decision making.

Weaknesses

- A slow method of training.
- Often difficult to select appropriate case studies for specific training problems.
- Requires a high level of skill by both chef supervisor and team members.
- Can sometimes be boring for some team participants.

6. *Apprenticeship training*

Trainee chefs work under the guidance of skilled chefs. They rotate through all kitchen departments in a planned sequential way. According to the American Culinary Federation, "the apprentice [chef] completes 6,000 hours of on-the-job training as well as the related theory courses, usually over a three year period" (8).

Strengths

- Develops culinary skills while working.
- Promotes understanding of the actual work skills required.
- Can involve extensive training over a period of years.

Weaknesses

- Takes a long time.
- Chef mentor changes may adversely impact continuity of learning, along with quality/quantity of skill development.

7. On-the-job training (OJT)

Strengths

- Can be individualized to suit the learning pace of the individual.
- Conducted on the job using actual work situations with which the kitchen team member is involved. Provides immediate job application for the new team member.
- Integrates the new individual into the team.

Weaknesses

- Requires a good deal of preparation and application by the chef supervisor.
- Sequencing of on-the-job training must be planned and then recorded.
- Not all skills are addressed within one establishment.

HOW PEOPLE LEARN

No two people learn at the same rate. Some team members will pick up new skills very quickly, while others will require repeated instruction and supervised practice. There are several ways to classify types of learning, but all basically fall into what are called "domains." These domains fall into the following four categories: cognitive, psychomotor, affective, and interpersonal skills (9).

> *Cognitive*: This means knowledge learning and includes the mental skills of classifying, identifying, detecting, and making decisions. This type of learning is experienced through self-paced individual interactive programs. The cognitive domain includes learner-controlled instruction, which is sometimes called self-instruction.
>
> *Psychomotor*: These are the manipulative, or physical, skills that require the learner to *do* something. Within the kitchen, psychomotor skills are found everywhere. Culinary art requires a great deal of manipulative skill from knife skills to whipping, chopping, or shredding.
>
> *Affective*: These skills reflect attitudes, values, and interests of the kitchen team. Personal leadership, such as the chef supervisor as coach of the kitchen team, is one way to facilitate attitudinal learning. Attitudes can be learned. The importance of good attitudes in the foodservice industry

Chef Talk: "My Way or the Highway"

To train, to form by instruction, discipline, or drill. In the kitchen, chefs are involved primarily in training two types of culinarians: the apprentice chef (who is inexperienced in the area of culinary art) and the cook (who may have had many years of experience with other establishments). From personal experience each culinarian should be handled differently when it comes to training.

In comparing the apprentice chef and the cook from a training standpoint, I feel most chefs would prefer to train apprentice chefs. The rationale is that the apprentice is new, has no preset ideas or bad habits, and is usually eager to learn. It doesn't take much for the chef to convince the apprentice of how things should be done. Let's face it, all of us chefs have different ideas on how things should be done. So with an apprentice it basically boils down to what we as chefs are willing to commit to this person, which should be everything we know about cooking and how to run a kitchen.

The experienced cook may have served an apprenticeship with another chef or be a graduate of a culinary school or of the "School of Hard Knocks." Either way they are most assuredly going to do things differently from you. How do we train such a cook? When I first became a supervisory chef, I thought it would be simple. My technique, in all honesty, was "my way or the highway." As I gained experience, I learned how to work with and train these individuals. In fact, sometimes I ended up as the trainee. Training becomes a watching process. I would watch new cooks in action, observing their skill levels, techniques, work methods, and the final product. When they prepared something that was different from our standards, I would compare both methods and discuss which method was better. If theirs made sense, we would change to that method and vice-versa. If the end result was the same, and there was no difference in the cost or time factor, then both methods could be used.

It is difficult to train persons if they are uncomfortable with the training method. I discovered that by utilizing an open training style and involving the cooks, they become more open to my suggestions because they realize their input is valued.

Aidan P. Murphy, CWC, Executive Chef, Old Warson Country Club, St. Louis, MO is vital. However, affective or attitudinal training is more difficult to do than any other method of training, because it is so difficult to measure.

Interpersonal Skills: Learning involves interaction among people. These types of skills are crucial to supporting total quality in the foodservice industry. These are people-centered skills that involve the ability to relate effectively with others. Examples include teamwork, counseling techniques, administrative skills, salesmanship, discussion activities, and customer relations (10).

Most learned capabilities actually contain elements of all domains. They entail voluntary display (affective) of some observable action (motor skill) that indicates possession of some mental skill (cognitive) and working with other people and through people so as to meet customer needs (interpersonal).

We learn through our senses: seeing, hearing, touching, smelling, and tasting. The most important training sense is seeing. When giving instruction, as many of the five senses as possible should be used to get the message across. Show things as often as possible. For example, if demonstrating sauce preparation, the method is explained (learning), skills are demonstrated (seeing), what the texture should be is determined (touching), and finally the sauce is sampled (tasting).

A major advantage in culinary skills instruction is that it has the ability to make use of the learner's five senses.

Instructional techniques may be divided into two areas: passive and active techniques. Passive techniques require little or no activity from the learner. It is therefore difficult to assess what learning has taken place. Passive instructional techniques involve:

- Telling: The use of words to explain subject matter.
- Showing: Trainers perform the activity.
- Illustrating: Use of visual materials.

Active techniques require the learner to participate by saying or doing something:

- Question and answer, checking if information is understood
- Participation and involvement by learner
- Discussion, learners involved
- Practical exercises, learners practice

The best training techniques for culinary instruction are obviously "active." They allow the chef supervisor to check if learning has taken place.

Training experts generally agree that we retain:

20 percent of what we hear,
50 percent of what we hear and see,

70 percent of what we hear, see, and say, and

90 percent of what we hear, see, say, and do.

Most of the training in the kitchen involves the hearing, seeing, saying, and doing, which indicates that this is the desired training method for all skills instruction. These methods involve breaking down training into steps that are paced to the learner's ability so that he or she may be able to assimilate this new information. Using this method, difficult tasks can be shown in easy stages. The unknown becomes known. Training is about helping people learn and develop. It should be centered on the team member, and there are no reasons why it should not be enjoyable: "Individuals learn best when they choose what to learn—that is, when they learn things that interest them, which they find personally satisfying, and when the learning environment is in harmony with their own particular learning preference or style" (11).

ADULT LEARNING

Androgogy is the concept of adult education. At the heart of this concept is the assumption that adults *want* to learn. Adults prefer training sessions that will assist them in the successful completion of their daily work tasks. Therefore, instruction should be designed relative to the needs of each participant (12). If the need or relevance of the training topic is not evident to adult team members from the start, they may soon become disenchanted with the training process. To meet this adult need, the objectives of the training session should be stated and linked to job performance in the introduction stage of the training program or module. For the most part adults enter training with a high degree of interest and motivation. Motivation can be improved and channeled by the chef supervisor who can provide clear instructional goals. Adults learn by doing. They want to get involved. Adults relate their learning to what they already know. This presents a challenge for the chef supervisor to incorporate participative activities into training such as hands-on work, discussions, or projects. Variety of training topics and methods tends to stimulate and open all five of the team members' senses.

The need for positive feedback is characteristic of all learners. Adults, especially, prefer to know how their efforts measure up when compared with the objective of the training program. Additionally, adult learners may have certain reservations when it comes to training; among these are doubts about their ability to learn and a fear of failure.

Each training session should be opened with a good introductory activity that will put everyone at ease. Adults prefer to be treated as individuals who have unique and particular talents, and they prefer an informal environment.

Learning flourishes in a nonintimidating win-win setting without grades. Facilitators of the adult learning process can be described as change agents. The role of the chef supervisor as a change agent is to present information or

Chef Talk: "Teaching Old Dogs New Tricks"

A lesson I learned many years ago about improving the standard of cooking and food presentation involved a major personal commitment and investment in training my kitchen brigade.

The Shelbourne Hotel is a first-class hotel located on Dublin's famous St. Stephen's Green. It is one of the oldest, most celebrated hotels in Ireland. When I came to it as only its fourth executive chef in 100 years, I found a traditional kitchen designed on the old labor-intensive "partie system." Its cooking philosophy was deeply embedded in the traditions of classical cuisine. My arrival there coincided with the advent of the cuisine nouvelle period of the early 1980s.

One of the major goals set for me by management was to introduce a new style of cooking in line with the modern approach and style of cuisine that reflected the needs of the discerning, health conscious customer of the 1980s. As a young enthusiastic chef, this was a challenge I was happy to accept. The a la carte menu that was in place when I arrived had not changed in many years. The repertoire of dishes included on this menu was rather limited, and my attempts to introduce new dishes and simpler methods of preparation and presentation were resisted by the older, more conservative chefs. Change was therefore necessary to bring the cuisine up to date.

Before any new dish was introduced, I had to develop an overall training plan for the traditional brigade, one that would meet with each person's schedule. Great consideration was given to the training methods to be used. The method I felt best suited my training goals was the demonstration training technique.

The problem I faced was how to convince the kitchen staff to attend my training sessions voluntarily. No budget was available to facilitate the training on company time. Because of trade union rules, I could not compel any of the chefs to attend these sessions. However, I decided to go full speed ahead with my plans. I selected Saturday mornings as the most appropriate training time and informed the kitchen brigade of my planned training sessions. For the first session, three apprentice chefs showed up, which, needless to say, was disappointing. Despite this initial disappointment, I continued with the training sessions each Saturday morning.

Key to my training philosophy and plan was my approach. I would demonstrate the preparation, cooking, and presentation of new dishes to be featured on our new menu along with explaining the relevant techniques of preparation. I did the work, and then with careful coaching and correcting on the job, the session participants grew in confidence and developed professionally. Demonstrating these new techniques showed the participants the benefits of the training sessions. Training made their jobs easier and provided them with additional culinary skills.

I believe a positive training atmosphere was set, one that was anxiety free, entertaining, and educational. What started out with three apprentices eventually grew to full participation by the kitchen brigade. When the older chefs learned of the training style adopted, they began to attend. They felt comfortable and unthreatened.

My training sessions did not happen accidentally. They were planned step by step. Careful planning made the training sessions work. The most worthwhile measurements of investing in culinary training are the increased skills and improved attitudes of those receiving the training, and that impacts on customer satisfaction. I am happy to say this happened at the Shelbourne. Within six months we had higher standards of professional practice from all our chefs, including the "old dogs." Training works, and the greatest compliment I received as a chef trainer was when the older chefs "bought into" my culinary philosophy and thanked me for sharing with them new skills that gave them a renewed pride in the culinary profession.

Noel C. Cullen, Ed.D., CMC, AAC, Boston University, Boston MA

skills in an environment that is conducive to learning, and the learner's role is to take that information (or skills) and apply it in the best way.

The establishment of a positive training environment hinges on understanding the characteristics of adult learners. The dynamics of the training process are dependent upon the instructor having a clear understanding of these characteristics. For adults, training should be a highly motivating experience, after which they should be inspired and committed to trying out new ideas and approaches. Effective adult training should be relevant, practical, inspirational, dynamic, informative, and solution centered.

BARRIERS TO LEARNING

Fatigue is a condition that prevents learning. It reduces physical and mental ability to accept and assimilate new information. It is therefore essential that training be planned and implemented at appropriate times. It should not be conducted at the end of work shifts. Monotony is also a problem. If the chef supervisor finds the training boring, it is highly probable that the team members will also find it boring. It is important for the chef supervisor to keep the sessions lively and interesting. While the information for the chef supervisor is routine, it may not be so for the team member.

Distractions inhibit training. Plan time for training so as to avoid work-related distractions. People are usually tense when confronted with the unknown. It is up to the chef supervisor to create a positive training environment that is also the motivational and quality setting environment.

Before the actual training begins, in addition to physical considerations of how, when, and where the training will take place, the team members must be analyzed to determine the following:

- What are their prior culinary work experiences, knowledge, and skills?
- What types of job duties must they perform?

A careful match must be made between what tasks each team member currently performs and what the training is preparing them for.

Before commencing the training session review the training objectives. This review will serve to focus the chef instructor on the intended purposes of the training program and what the desired outcomes are. The development of the presentation step is next. This includes the session topics and highlighting the learning activities designed to reinforce the learning. It is important at this stage to realize that excellent training session design does not guarantee excellent outcomes in terms of training.

Questions to consider with regard to creating the training environment include restating the organization's vision and outlining the goals of TQM. The next item to consider is the smooth transition from a work-driven atmosphere in the kitchen to a training one. Training sessions need not take up large chunks of the work day. They can range from 30-minute to 2-hour sessions but must be on an on-going basis. What is vital is that the training period be totally uninterrupted by the requirements of work.

Plans should include arrangements for meals or coffee breaks during the session periods. When time allocation is made part of the training plan, it must be strictly adhered to. Where will the training take place? Even the most dynamic chef trainer can fail in poorly prepared facilities. Whether training is to be conducted on site or off site, the facilities should be satisfactory:

- If the room to be used is too warm or too small, a poor instructional climate will result.
- Is lighting adequate? Can the room be darkened to show visuals, yet still allow participants to take notes?
- Is the required audio/video and demonstration equipment in working order?
- Is there a writing board or flip chart available with marking pens or chalk?

Starting Right

Training sessions that begin correctly, in a positive environment, generally have a better chance of finishing well than those that start badly. If the first training session begins properly, the chef trainer will feel good about the session. Much more learning will probably take place. First impressions can be long-lasting ones, and the first training session sets the tone for the rest of the training program.

Preparation

There are several reasons why preparation is necessary:

1. It ensures that no essential detail is omitted.
2. Instruction can be arranged systematically.
3. Topics can be assessed to determine their relevance to overall objectives and organizational vision.
4. The chef supervisor's thinking can be directed to match the training needs of individual team members, and individual needs can be addressed to allow for different competency levels.
5. Unnecessary overlapping and repetition of topics can be avoided.
6. The amount and type of learner involvement is decided beforehand.
7. It ensures that maximum benefit is derived from the time allocated for instruction.
8. Most importantly, it helps to strengthen the chef supervisor's confidence in himself or herself as a trainer.

Adequate preparation often serves as a refresher and helps chef supervisors to do their job more effectively.

On-the-Job Training

The unpredictable nature of the foodservice industry often makes it difficult to plan for training. In addition to the structured training sessions, every possible advantage should be taken for total quality training. The following are some guidelines for fitting training into the day-to-day routine:

1. Take advantage of downtime to give short pieces of training instruction or review previous training topics. If downtime can be predicted, plan to use it for training.
2. If possible, schedule team members with similar training needs to be in the kitchen at the same time so that these needs can be addressed more effectively.
3. Chef supervisors should use their own work as quality standard setting demonstrations. Have team members watch while explaining critical elements during the demonstration.
4. Take advantage of crises and problems to give on-the-spot correction and explanation of the correct way to perform tasks.

5. Assign work that will allow each team member to practice new skills as soon as possible after instruction.

6. Fit training in whenever possible. If only 5 or 10 minutes is available, cover a portion of the task.

7. Keep simple records to track the training you have given, to whom, and whether or not the training was successful.

8. In addition, other experienced team members may be used as cotrainers. However, the chef supervisor is ultimately responsible for the culinary training.

By integrating training on the job, the chef supervisor is watching for gaps between the required quality and the way that each team member is performing, while giving praise and encouragement to the team.

CONCLUSIONS

Total quality management as a philosophy depends on continuous improvement at all levels of the culinary operation. For TQM to work, investment in those providing the foodservice must be made through continuous training. Therefore, the modern chef supervisor, in addition to the other necessary skills of supervision, must be a first-class trainer.

Training is a process, and it has various forms. It is the systematic application of:

- Analyzing training needs
- Developing training objectives
- Determining appropriate training methods
- Conducting and evaluating training

There are many types of training. Those training methods that have proved most suitable for culinary training in a TQM environment are job talks, demonstration, role play, case study, apprenticeship training, and on-the-job training. Each has strengths and weaknesses. Experienced chef supervisors can assess the training needs and determine the most appropriate training methods. The secret is to develop skill in using a variety of these training tools. The most critical roles of the chef supervisor as trainer are counseling team members through the learning process and being a subject matter expert, teacher, and motivator of all team members as they rotate through the training process.

Understanding how people learn is key to effective training. No two people learn at the same rate or in the same way. There will be peaks and valleys in individual team members' progress.

Training sessions should be stimulating and inspiring and be separate from the usual work schedule. The environment in which the training session is to be conducted should be one that is conducive to learning. The duration and timing of training are important. Training must be planned in a sequen-

Chef Talk: "Rethinking Your Most Valuable Asset"

Today the hospitality industry is as dynamic as ever, full of rapid changes and opportunities to use newly learned skills. Therefore, productive training is more critical than ever.

While the concept of training is straightforward and quite basic, the true challenge is applying it to the ever-changing issues that arise on a daily or weekly basis. Well-trained kitchen team members are crucial to the culinary operation. Part of this is understanding how team members relate to the product or services you provide and realizing that their values are not necessarily the same as yours. Remember, important elements that you may consider motivating factors could be regarded as simple satisfiers in a team member's eyes.

As an exercise, view your operation from an employee's perspective. Remember you have the ability to control how your culinary operation is interpreted by your employees. If their definition of what your business is all about does not concur with yours, you are likely to be vulnerable, because they are the main link with how your customer perceives your business. Chef leaders who are involved with their employees on a daily basis encourage spontaneous communication that creates an atmosphere that can increase their ability to think and respond to the needs of your customer.

Victor Gielisse, CMC, Culinary Fast Trac & Associates, Dallas, TX

tial and logical way and should not last too long. Dynamic presentations will always ward off monotony and fatigue.

SUMMARY

- Total quality management depends greatly on training. For TQM to be effective in the foodservice organization, the chef supervisor must understand that TQM is a long-term proposition rooted in continuous improvements through training, teamwork, organizational vision, and shared goals within the kitchen.
- Training should be viewed as a total systems approach; the steps are (1) determining training needs, (2) developing training objectives, (3) determining appropriate methods, (4) conducting the training, and (5) evaluating the training.

- Types of training used for foodservice training include job talks, team meetings, role playing, demonstrations, case studies, apprenticeship training, and on-the-job training.
- People learn at different rates and in different ways. Essentially, learning falls into the categories of cognitive, psychomotor, affective, and interpersonal; these are referred to as domains. Additionally, training is conducted through either active or passive training techniques.
- Androgogy is the concept of adult education. Adults learn by doing. They want to learn, are motivated, and relate training to what they already know. Positive feedback is a characteristic of adult learning. Learning for adults flourishes in a nonthreatening environment where grading is absent.
- Training must be presented in an environment conducive to learning and at a time when the kitchen team member is ready to receive it.
- The modern chef supervisor must constantly invest in training the team for TQM to succeed.

DISCUSSION QUESTIONS

1. What is the difference between training and education?
2. What are the steps involved in a systems approach to training?
3. Before training can commence a needs analysis is conducted. What is the purpose of this step?
4. What are the strengths and weaknesses of "job talk" as a training method? When should it be used?
5. Why is demonstration as a training technique appropriate for skills training in the kitchen?
6. What are the learning domains of cognitive and psychomotor? How may they be applied to training in the kitchen?
7. What are the advantages and disadvantages of passive and active training techniques?
8. Adults learn by doing. What training challenges does this present to the chef supervisor?
9. What are the important factors the chef supervisor should ensure in order to remove training barriers?
10. In planning training sessions, what physical factors should be considered?

NOTES

1. Philip B. Crosby, *Quality is Free, The Art of Making Quality Certain*, Wiley, New York, 1989.
2. Shoji Shiba, Alan Graham, and David Walden. *A New American TQM, Four Practical Revolutions in Management*, Productivity Press, Portland, OR, 1993, p. 353.
3. Richard L. Sullivan, Jerry R. Wircenski, Susan S. Arnold, and Michelle D. Sarkeess, *Practical Manual For The Design, Delivery, and Evaluation of Training*, Aspen, Rockville, MD, 1990, p. CD 1.

4. Ibid., p. CD 2.
5. Ibid., p. CD 37.
6. Tom W. Goad, *Delivering Effective Training*, Pfeiffer & Co., San Diego, 1982, p. 169.
7. Lois B. Hart, *Training Methods That Work*, Crisp, London, 1991, p. 65.
8. American Culinary Federation (ACF), *Apprenticeship Operations Manual*, ACF, St. Augustine FL, 1985, p. 21.
9. Robert Heinich, Michael Molenda, and James D. Russell, *Instructional Media and the New Technologies of Instruction*, Macmillan, New York, 1989, p. 41.
10. Ibid., p. 42.
11. Brian Thomas, *Total Quality Training: The Quality Culture and Quality Trainer*, McGraw-Hill, Berkshire, England, 1992, p. 73.
12. Dugan Laird, *Approaches to Training and Development*, Addison-Welesey, Reading, MA, 1985, p. 125.

10

Preparing Training Objectives

Outline

- Introduction
- Definitions
- Hierarchy of objectives
- Training lesson plans
- Characteristics of a training session
- Steps in planning training sessions
- Summary
- Discussion questions

Objectives

When you complete this chapter, you should be able to:

1. Describe the components of good objectives and write a performance objective that contains each of these components.

2. Identify the hierarchical elements that reflect how team members learn and the associated behaviors.
3. List the rationale for preparing performance objectives.
4. Identify and outline steps in preparing training plans and sessions.
5. State the purpose and application of a lesson plan.

INTRODUCTION

Learning often results in an activity that can be observed, measured, and recorded, a behavior modified by past and present experience. It is gaining knowledge, experience, and understanding (1). Objectives in any of the learning domains discussed in the previous chapter may be adapted to the abilities of the individual learner. Objectives are intended not to limit what a team member learns, but to provide a minimum level of expected achievement.

Learning objectives are also called performance objectives or behavioral objectives. Whatever terminology is used, it is the concept that counts. The concept is that stating objectives for whatever type of training is undertaken in the kitchen will ensure that all efforts are directed to achieving only the desired results, and it will tell the chef supervisor whether or not the training objectives have been achieved. Knowing the objectives will force the creation of a training environment, in which the objectives can be reached. Without explicit objectives the kitchen team will not know what is expected of them. If objectives are clearly and specifically stated, learning and instructing become objectives.

A statement of objectives may be viewed as an agreement between the kitchen team and the chef supervisor, whose responsibility as an instructor is to provide training and coaching in a positive environment; as the learner, the team member's responsibility is to participate conscientiously in the training sessions.

Objectives are the instructional solutions to link what is and what is not desired through training. Problems of quality in the kitchen can be redefined as objectives that can be used to develop plans for training. Critical to all objective preparation is the statement of what the team member *will be able to do* after completion of a training session. Objectives should build the training needs of each team member in a logical and systematic way (2).

DEFINITIONS

Three basic components make up performance objectives:

1. The performance of the task
2. The conditions under which the task is to be performed and
3. The criteria or standards to which performance of the task will be compared

Expressed another way, objectives are an unambiguous statement of what the learner will be able to do as a result of some training. These can also be referred to as "enabling" objectives, which state what the team member is going to learn that will enable him or her to perform a task.

Within the stated objectives, what facilities, tools, equipment, and constraints under which the objective is performed should be included. The level of performance in terms of time, accuracy, and completeness of the tasks is also described. The statement of objectives must also have measurable attributes that should be observable in the team member upon completion of training. Otherwise it is impossible to determine whether or not the training program is meeting the stated objectives.

The essence of a good objective is the description of a measurable performance. According to Robert Mager, author of *Preparing Instructional Objectives*, a complete objective will have three parts (3):

1. The *observable performance* portion of the objective begins with an action verb and is followed by the object of that action, that is, a task the team member must accomplish, such as "identify," "describe," or "use."
2. The *conditions* portion of the objective specifies what the team member will be given in order to complete the task and will reflect the conditions under which the task is performed on the job.
3. The *standards* or *criteria* portion of the objective will indicate the level of acceptable performance of the task and reflect standards for performing the task on the job.

Examples of a training objective for the kitchen team might be:

- *Example 1*: Upon completion of the training session on sauce making the kitchen team member will be able to correctly prepare within 10 minutes 2 quarts of Hollandaise sauce from the recipe provided using the kitchen blender following all safety/sanitation procedures indicated within the lesson.
- *Example 2*: After completion of the training session on quick breads the kitchen team member will be able to properly prepare and bake five specified quick breads from the assigned list using the dough mixer and baking oven while observing correct timing and temperature.

These are precise statements. They make a futuristic promise to the team member indicating what they will be able to do when they complete a training session.

Tasks consist of a single action verb and an object. The verb may represent the cognitive, affective, psychomotor, or interpersonal domain. A task should have a definite beginning point and should be independent of other tasks. For example, the task "understand sauce making" is meaningless. What does *understand* mean? Where does it start? Similarly, the chef supervisor would have a difficult time observing the task "appreciate" in the importance of good sauce making.

Goals are statements of intent in the learning process. Goals are overall statements or general aims for a training program. They provide the chef supervisor with a general idea of what a given training session should achieve. Goals and objectives differ as follows:

1. Goals may be written to help select the area of knowledge and skills and may contain *unmeasurable* verbs.
2. Goals written as "knowing or understanding" do not provide specific actions team members should perform to show that learning has occurred. This makes evaluation of the results of training difficult.

Since attitudes are difficult to measure, we write attitude "goals." Barbee and Bott state: "Training in the hospitality industry involves more than just the technical skills common in other industries. Interpersonal skills are as important, if not more so" (4). At times with attitude goals it is difficult to find precise words for the objective.

However, objectives should always communicate the same intent to all people. One way of testing whether a written objective clearly defines a desired outcome is to answer the following two questions:

1. How exactly do you intend the training to change the learner?
2. How exactly will you know if the change has occurred?

A final criterion for a set of training objectives is to ask yourself if you would be fully satisfied if the team members achieved only the stated performance objectives and nothing else.

Objectives must be examined as a complete set of topics, levels, and skills of the overall training plan. Some of the more subtle quality objectives concerning attitudes or even the more complex kind of understanding may be missing. Whenever possible these subtle objectives should be included.

Objectives must be attainable. While this may seem an obvious point, the objectives must be assessed carefully in relation to the knowledge, background, and expectations of the team along with the resources available and the duration of the training session.

Performance objectives should fall into the category of learning the team member "needs to know" rather than what may be "nice to know." In searching for the neatness of fit between the culinary quality training plan and the team member's needs, performance objectives must contain the essentials that the person needs to know first and those that are desirable second.

HIERARCHY OF OBJECTIVES

Objectives should be prepared in a hierarchy that reflects how a person learns and associates behavior within each level of learning:

1. *Knowledge*: This refers to remembering previously learned materials.
2. *Comprehension*: This is defined as the ability to grasp the meaning of the materials.
3. *Application*: This refers to the ability to use learned material in new and concrete situations.
4. *Synthesis*: This is separating ideas into component parts and examining relationships.
5. *Evaluation*: Involves judging by using self-produced criteria or established standards (5).

The following is a list of action verbs used in preparing performance objectives. The areas that most kitchen training objectives fall under are the first three: knowledge, comprehension, and application.

Action verbs

1. *Knowledge*: define, state, list, name, write, recall, recognize, label, underline, reflect, measure, reproduce.
2. *Comprehension*: identify, justify, select, indicate, illustrate, represent, name, formulate, explain, judge, contrast, classify.
3. *Application*: predict, select, assess, explain, choose, find, show, demonstrate, construct, compute, use, perform.
4. *Synthesis*: combine, restate, summarize, argue, discuss, organize, derive, select, relate, generalize, conclude.
5. *Evaluation*: judge, evaluate, determine, recognize, support, defend, attack, criticize, identify, avoid, select, choose.

Objectives can be best described as:

- A statement of intent about what the team members will be able to do when they have successfully completed a learning experience.
- An intent communicated by describing a proposed change in a team member.
- Precise statements of desired learning outcomes.
- Worthwhile, nontrivial learning activity unambiguously stated that is necessary to both the team member and the culinary operation and is perceived as a benefit for the team member to progress in his or her job.

Performance objectives are written in the compilation of training plans because they:

- Limit the scope of training tasks
- Remove ambiguities and difficulties of interpretation
- Ensure that measurement is possible
- Define the desired level of attainment and depth of treatment of each topic area
- Provide a basis for the selection of appropriate materials, content, and training methods
- Ensure no essential details are left out
- Organize training instruction systematically
- Avoid unnecessary overlapping and repetition of training information
- Ensure maximum benefit from the often limited training time available in the kitchen
- Strengthen the chef supervisor's confidence in the instructional role

Complete objectives also state *standards* of performance and the conditions under which performance is to be evaluated.

TRAINING LESSON PLANS

Just as training objectives serve as a road map and a check to see if training is accomplished, the training lesson plan guides the chef supervisor through the process of instruction that causes training to occur. A lesson plan may be thought of as a combination of speaker's notes, recipes, and scripts. It is an outline of everything that is to happen during the training event.

In the case of individual team member instruction, the lesson plan serves as the lesson specification from which text is derived. One of the requirements for being prepared is to have a lesson plan. Even if the training is a short 30-minute presentation, a plan is essential. Learning is stimulated and aided when the chef supervisor can present a coherent and sequential series of training sessions, each of which has a clear-cut training objective.

The four-step training method has been widely utilized in training in the kitchen. These four steps have been tried and found to be a successful pattern around which every training session can be planned and instructed. These four steps are:

1. Preparation
2. Presentation
3. Application
4. Evaluation

CHARACTERISTICS OF A TRAINING SESSION

1. The training session must be a complete unit of learning. What is to be learned should be made apparent to the team members in the title of the session.

2. Each training session should contain new material exclusive of review or some other training topic, previously instructed material for reinforcement, and new material for progression. Sullivan states: "Our primary duty is to teach our staff something new every day. Training is a philosophy not a department" (6).

3. Each training session should be adapted to the needs of the team member. The material should be within the capabilities of the team member and it should be consistent with the needs of the team in keeping with the purpose of the training and according to the progress of the entire kitchen operation.

4. The session should be reasonable in scope. It should be balanced, interesting, and neither too simple nor too complex.

5. It should have a clear-cut beginning, a presentation, and an end. The language of the chef instructor should enable the team member to follow, comprehend the presentation, and finally absorb the material with a feeling of understanding and accomplishment.

6. The session should require a measurable standard of achievement in terms of TQM. Each session should contain a TQM element. High-quality standards of performance should start at the beginning and continue throughout each training session.

Types of Training Lessons

The type of training session presented will depend on the type of lesson:

1. The manual skills lesson
2. The informational lesson

It is from these materials that the chef supervisor will develop training topics:

1. The skill lesson is a type of instruction in which the chef supervisor instructs team members in using physical skills in performing the manual phases of a culinary skill. The skill lesson is generally taught by demonstration. To further simplify and clarify the intent of any skill lesson, the question should be asked: "Am I going to teach the team member how to do something?" If the answer is yes, then the lesson will be a skill lesson.

2. The informational lesson is a type of instruction in which the team member is instructed in the theory and basic fundamentals of the area being taught. The area covered by a "theory" lesson appears to be broader than

that covered by the skill lesson because so many subtopics can be included. This type of lesson is also referred to as "job talks."

STEPS IN PLANNING TRAINING SESSIONS

Careful and thorough preparation is essential to successful instruction. The effectiveness of the other stages of instruction will depend upon how well the chef has selected training tasks and adapted this training material to the special needs, abilities, and interests of the kitchen team, arranged for equipment and materials needed, planned for activities, and anticipated problems peculiar to TQM. Many chef supervisors often feel there is never enough time for adequate planning. One solution to this problem is to use a systematic procedure in the preparation of training sessions. The following is a simple, yet effective procedure.

Step 1: The objectives   This is the starting point for all planning of training activities. The chef instructor must realize from the start just what can be accomplished and the limits of time. (The objective when well developed and written will serve also as a tool to evaluate the training.)

Step 2: Analysis of the training topic   This involves determining the specific objectives, skills, knowledge, or techniques the team member must learn for successful performance of the task. For example, the objective of a training session may be using the meat thermometer. An analysis of this subject, or breaking it down into instructional steps, would result in these teaching points: Describe a meat thermometer, show and explain the thermometer, demonstrate how to read the thermometer, and have team members measure internal temperature with the thermometer and sanitize after use. Each step would have subpoints in the presentation, but in the analysis only the major instructional steps required to accomplish the training are considered.

Step 3: Equipment, facilities, and training aids   Requirements for and availability of training aids, equipment, training areas, and facilities need to be considered. Advance notice may be required to obtain training films, videos, or other media. Frequently chef supervisors must improvise, and this often takes time. Last minute arrangements for training aids or equipment usually result in slipshod instruction. The ingredients used for demonstrations must be selected and checked well in advance for quality and portion size.

Step 4: Time available   If time is short, the training subject matter should be limited to the items essential for accomplishment of the training objectives. If time is available, more team participation can be used and more supporting material can be included.

Step 5: Training condition   Instruction must be flexible enough to remain effective even when obstacles to training arise. The basis of such flexibility is careful planning.

Step 6: Select and organize material   Identify essential manipulative skills and related knowledge. Then organize the materials for demonstration. Examples and stories can be used to make the lesson presentation or skill demonstration more interesting and meaningful. They should be related to the overall quality objectives of the foodservice organization and should be used whenever possible.

The lesson plan ensures that the training session will be complete. It shows what material is to be instructed and in what order and what procedures and training methods will be used.

Each training lesson plan is an outline for one segment of the training plan.

Purpose of the lesson plan

- Ensures a wiser selection of material and a more complete coverage of the topic and assists the chef supervisor in focusing on training objectives
- Assists in the presentation of training material in the proper sequence for effective learning
- Ensures that proper consideration is given to each part of the plan, that essential points are included, and that irrelevant material is omitted
- Provides time control
- Provides an outline of the training methods and procedures to be used in the instruction
- Assists in the proper use of presentation media technology
- Serves as a record of training provided to each team member
- Refreshes the chef supervisor's memory and keeps topics current

The lesson plan should be reviewed each time it is used. Few chef supervisors are gifted with such phenomenal memories that is it not necessary to refresh themselves on what is to be taught and how the training is to be conducted. This review will help to keep the training progression smooth and effective.

Requirements of a good training lesson plan

- Must focus on one main thing to be learned
- Must contain something new
- Must not present too much material at one time
- Must be suited to teams members and their past experiences

- Team members must derive satisfaction
- Achievement should be measurable

Once a lesson plan has been completed, it should be thought of as a dynamic entity. Each time it is used, apply the tenets of TQM to it, that is, continuous improvement. Make notes each time the training lesson plan is used. It is a tool to help prepare for effective training.

SUMMARY

Training objectives are the starting point in an overall plan for continuous improvements in the kitchen:

- Learning objectives are also known as performance objectives.
- They facilitate objective instruction and define the task performance.
- They are an unambiguous statement of what the team member will be able to do as a result of training.
- They provide criteria, standards, and conditions under which different tasks are to be accomplished.
- They allow for measurement of the training.
- They provide the basis for determining the *essential* and *desirable* training objectives.
- They separate tasks between knowing and doing.
- They provide time control, organize training systematically, and avoid unnecessary overlapping.
- Training plans are a road map to guide the chef supervisor through the process of training.
- Training plans require four steps: preparation, presentation, application, and evaluation.
- Each training session must be a complete unit of learning and should contain some old material for connection along with some new material.
- Training plans are classified as (1) manual skills and (2) the informational areas of the training topic.
- The needs and capabilities of the kitchen team should be an important consideration of the training plan.
- Equipment and material needs for the training session must be planned for and secured prior to the commencement of the training session.
- Training lesson outlines are prepared so as to ensure complete treatment of the training objectives.

DISCUSSION QUESTIONS

1. Why is it necessary to prepare explicit objectives?
2. What are the three basic components that make up a performance objective?
3. Why is the essence of a good objective the description of a measurable performance?
4. What are the primary differences between goals and objectives as they relate to training?
5. Why are action verbs used in the preparation of performance objectives?
6. What are the four essential characteristics of a well-planned training session?
7. What method of instruction is generally considered appropriate for culinary skills?
8. What is the purpose of lesson plans as they pertain to training?
9. What are the requirements of well-developed training lesson plans?

NOTES

1. Lois B. Hart, *Training Methods That Work*, Crisp, London, 1991, p. 15.
2. Robert F. Mager, *Preparing Instructional Objectives*, 2nd ed., Fearon, Belmont, CA, 1971.
3. Ibid.
4. Cliff Barbee and Valerie Bott, "Customer Treatment as a Mirror of Employee Treatment," *Advanced Management Journal*, Spring 1991, p. 31.
5. Benjamin S. Bloom, *Taxonomy of Educational Objectives: Book 1*, Longman, New York, 1977.
6. Jim Sullivan, "Making It Stick: How To Eliminate Teflon Training," *Nation's Restaurant News*, April 1993, p. 22.

11

Understanding Instructional Delivery

Outline

- Introduction
- Getting started
- Dealing with nervousness
- Effective interpersonal communication
- Training and diversity
- Trainer styles and attributes
- Getting the team involved
- Understanding group behaviors
- Summary
- Discussion questions

Objectives

When you complete this chapter, you should be able to:

1. Describe the factors that contribute to an effective training presentation.
2. Identify elements conducive to creating a professional training atmosphere.

3. Describe methods used to deal with nervousness.

4. Understand the appropriate communication style used for effective training.

5. Describe the steps appropriate to training a diverse kitchen team.

6. Define training styles, trainer attributes, approaches, and attitudes toward training.

7. Recognize the differences between open and closed questioning techniques.

8. Define the dynamics of group behaviors and the activities associated with kitchen team training.

INTRODUCTION

Every time a chef supervisor enters the training room, what follows should be a dynamic and effective training session. An effective presentation can be the most exciting and rewarding aspect of the chef supervisor's job. The time invested in determining the needs analysis and preparing training objectives pays off as the chef supervisor becomes an instructor and learns to interact, discuss, question, and work with the kitchen team to reach the training objectives. Chef supervisors who are able to maintain team member interest with a dynamic delivery using a variety of instructional techniques are more likely to be successful in helping the kitchen team succeed.

The purpose of instruction is to communicate knowledge and skills from the chef supervisor to the team member. It is only successful when at the end of the training the individual team member can safely perform skilled activity to the required standard. Therefore, it is essential that the chef supervisor choose the instructional method most suited to the training topic and the needs of the team member. Do the following before proceeding with training:

- Specify to the team what needs to be learned.
- Decide on training priorities.
- Decide appropriate techniques of training.
- Specify when and how often training can take place.
- Decide on how much instruction can be given at one time.
- Decide over what period of time training will take place.

Every presentation should begin with an interesting introduction to capture the kitchen team's interest and to prepare them for learning. Good introductions will prepare the team members, boost their confidence, and also set the stage for a positive learning environment. Dugan Laird states: "In professional instruction, learning processes are not blurred by an instructor's awkwardness or amateurism. Professionalism is often based on the mastery of a few teaching techniques" (1).

The training session introduction may be used to review the objectives, restate the culinary mission, and describe the activities of total quality that will be occurring during the training session. During the introduction step it is necessary to ensure that all of the team members participating in the training session are aware of what you are trying to achieve by the training and what is expected of them as a result of the training. The first 5 minutes of the training session can be the most important. Start off the session with an icebreaker, the purpose of which is to relax everybody.

GETTING STARTED

Appearance is very important. Choose your attire carefully. The best attire for the chef is, of course, a clean, crisp, smart chef coat. This helps the chef to bond with the kitchen team members. Overdressing can cause alienation from the group: "Be respectful. Right or wrong, some listeners will make judgements about your message based on their interpretation of the respect you are showing by your choice of dress" (2). The training environment is the same as the normal working environment of the kitchen team. A general rule to follow is, the more formal the training session, the more formal the attire.

Be conscious of body language. Good posture is important. Use body language that expresses confidence and that enhances the training presentation. Maintaining eye contact is essential. Put enthusiasm in your voice, speak clearly, and don't start with an apology for being there. Create a comfortable atmosphere. There is no reason why a warm, friendly atmosphere cannot be created and maintained throughout the training session. Try to establish this at the beginning. Other helpful suggestions are:

- Use effective facial expressions.
- Use and maintain eye contact.
- Move around the room and gesture.
- Use gestures that are not distracting.
- Communicate with the team members in the training session on a personal level.
- Vary tone and pitch of voice.
- Emphasize key points and use relevant examples.
- Be certain to talk to, not at, the kitchen team.
- Select and use appropriate media technology.
- Plan to make logical, smooth transitions between topics.
- Give clear directions for all subsequent activities.
- Greet all team members as they arrive for the training session.
- Be available during breaks to visit with each member to answer individual questions.

- Be available after the training session to answer any additional questions or to discuss concerns.
- Provide clear oral and written instructions for all assignments and activities.
- Maintain alertness.

DEALING WITH NERVOUSNESS

Relax, do not get a death grip on the podium. You are literally "on stage," but as long as you maintain control, success can be expected. The best defense against nervousness is to be fully prepared for the training session. The following are some suggestions for dealing with nervousness:

- Don't fight it.
- Don't call attention to your nervousness.
- Breathe deeply.
- Turn your thoughts inward, focusing on your inner self.
- Practice giving your presentation in front of a mirror.
- Talk to yourself before talking to them.
- Pretend you are wearing an overcoat and "feel" it resting on your shoulders.
- Picture the group eating spaghetti.

Slow down. Be more deliberate. This is a good way to avoid becoming tongue-tied: "Don't worry about it, this may actually be the best advice. Worry is like a rocking chair. It gives you something to do but it doesn't get you anywhere. Don't worry—do something about your fears" (3). Observe other, more experienced trainers. Rehearsing until you are confident that you are ready will help enormously, mentally walking through the training session from beginning to end, picturing in your mind everything that you expect to happen.

EFFECTIVE INTERPERSONAL COMMUNICATION

Simplicity is the key to effective communication in the training setting. Simple clear language usually is all that is required. Use of terminology and jargon causes problems. Use culinary terms with which the team members are familiar. This can build rapport within the group but must be handled carefully. The intention is to communicate, not to intimidate or impress. Therefore, the team will not be insulted if simple language is used. The following are suggestions to improve verbal training skills.

- Eliminate "er," "ah," "ok," and "you know what I mean," and similar nervous expressions from your vocabulary.
- Communicate on a personal level with each team member by pronouncing and spelling new terms or culinary terms that are used in the kitchen.
- Deliver important concepts and points slowly and cover less important material at a faster pace.
- Avoid long monologues. Make your presentation as natural as possible. Break up your speaking with other activities. Ask questions.
- Facilitate open communication by inviting the team to participate in identifying training that will provide continuous improvements in training plans.
- Do not appear to be reading aloud. An outline is better than a complete script.
- Avoid all "isms" (ageism, sexism, racism).
- Use appropriate gestures and visual aids to illustrate what you are saying.
- Avoid using slang.
- Use correct grammar and avoid "talking down" to the team.
- Demonstrate respect, awareness, and kindness.
- Give a little of yourself to the session. Empathize with the individual team members.
- Watch for loss of attention. Change direction or involve the team quickly in order to get back on track.
- Avoid undesirable habits, such as fumbling with your hair, picking at your face, or cleaning your nails.

Imagery is an important part of the communication process. When speech is used to create a picture or scene, that image helps facilitate learning. Perception also plays an important part in interpersonal communication. It can either help or destroy the most sincere effort to communicate. People often only hear what they want to hear. Problems in perception can be caused by team members with dissimilar attitudes, different cultural or educational backgrounds, and difficulty with the language used.

The cultural background of kitchen team members has a strong influence on their receptiveness to new information. This includes verbal and nonverbal communication. A big consideration in nonverbal communication is distance (4). The distance that people maintain when communicating has been determined as follows:

Intimate distance

- Close phase: close physical contact
- Far phase: 6 to 18 inches; not considered proper in public by Euro-Americans

Personal distance

- Close phase: 1½ to 2½ feet; comfortable if the people know one another
- Far phase: 2½ to 4 feet; arm's length.

Social distance

- Close phase: 4 to 7 feet; impersonal business
- Far phase: 7 to 12 feet; more formal communication.

Public distance

- Close phase: 12 to 25 feet; can get away
- Far phase: 25 feet or more; set around important public figures

The distance that is accepted is based on the relationship between people involved and the circumstances. Depending on the physical nature of the training environment and the type of training to be given, the chef supervisor and the kitchen team's personalities can be categorized within the personal and social distance scales.

TRAINING AND DIVERSITY

According to the U.S. Bureau of Labor Statistics, by the year 2000, women and minorities will make up the largest percentage growth in the work force. The number of white males will drop to 39.4 percent, down from 48.9 percent in 1976 (5).

American culture is becoming increasingly diverse. It is no longer a melting pot where new ethnic groups attempt to leave their original cultures behind them: "A more accurate image is a tossed salad, where various ingredients remain distinct even as they are mixed together" (6). Embracing cultural diversity in the kitchen requires the chef supervisor to adopt training skills and styles that are sensitive to valuing the differences within the kitchen team.

Diversity includes everyone. It is not something that is defined by race or gender. It extends to age, education, lifestyle, sexual preference, geographic origin, exempt and nonexempt status, physical abilities, religion, and where a person lives. There are also subcultures within any one of these categories. In practice, however, the word *diversity* has become synonymous with "people" who are other than white men (7).

When viewed from a TQM standpoint, cultural diversity in the foodservice industry is an advantage. Diverse points of view can breathe life into a culinary operation. Better customer service can be offered by a diverse kitchen team who can reflect the differing needs and preferences of those who make up the foodservice establishment customers. Key to developing this talent pool is training. What is required, according to R. Roosevelt Thomas, Jr. is "a new way of thinking about diversity, not as an us/them kind of problem to be solved but as a resource to be managed" (8).

The foundation for training and teamwork in a culturally diverse kitchen is valuing and appreciating *all* the differences within the team. This can be achieved by:

- Fostering awareness and acceptance of individual differences
- Helping team members understand their own feelings and attitudes about people who are different
- Exploring how differences might be tapped as assets in the kitchen
- Enhancing relations between people who are different
- Finding or inventing ways for each team member to collaborate

Thomas also stated: "You can manage diversity without valuing differences, but you can't manage diversity without understanding differences"(9). Tapping the team's full potential is about *empowerment*, and success depends on the ability to empower the entire work force. However, acceptance, tolerance, and understanding are not by themselves enough to create an empowered team. To empower a diverse kitchen team to reach their full potential, training is needed. It is therefore important to understand the cultural values, attitudes, and beliefs of the team and the uniqueness this brings to the kitchen.

TRAINER STYLES AND ATTRIBUTES

Leadership is an important element of successful training. (See Chapter 8, The Chef as Leader.) There are many styles that chef supervisors can adopt, ranging from extensive use of media technology to informational sheets to using humor. A chef supervisor's training style will almost always be a reflection of his or her personality. The purpose of any training is to facilitate learning, and it will require the chef supervisor to switch training styles in any given situation. As such a repertoire of diverse styles is required. In addition to various styles, chef supervisors are called upon to play different roles. Among these roles are:

- Subject matter expert, counselor
- Leader, motivator, psychologist
- Role model, communicator, performer
- Manager, listener, learner
- Diplomat, friend, evaluator

All of these training roles are obviously those that make up the profile of a successful chef supervisor. The point is that there is an appropriate time and place for each of these roles to be applied. Recognizing when to apply each role is important, as is the ability to blend them effectively. This can be one of the most important achievements of the chef supervisor in the training role.

Apart from the roles the chef supervisor has to play during the training process, he or she must have and be aware of certain other requirements:

Qualities required by chef supervisor

- A good attitude toward TQM and the job
- Technical skill
- Openness to learn more and to new ideas
- Belief in the potential of each team member
- Good relations with the kitchen team and others
- Dedication to the goals of continuous improvement by investing time and effort in training
- An understanding that total quality is a never-ending quest
- Active listening for feedback

Attitude to instruction

- Interested in all aspects of training
- Understands methods and techniques of instruction
- Knows subject matter and be enthusiastic
- Able to choose techniques appropriate for individual team members
- Willing to allow sufficient time for planning and preparing training sessions

Relationship with kitchen team during training

- Maintain positive discipline
- Be sympathetic and approachable
- Understand the learning difficulties of all team members
- Use persuasion whenever possible
- Demonstrate interest in imparting knowledge
- Allow for divergent views
- Do not criticize destructively

As in situational leadership, different approaches to training are used. The particular approach used depends on the combination of the performance tasks, the team members, and the chef supervisor's experience. No one single approach is the best. However, some or all of the following approaches may be used to create a positive training environment that enhances the training process. Brian Thomas, in his book, *Total Quality Training* (10), observed the following approaches:

The controlling approach

Positive effects: Learners know where they are in terms of discipline, standards, and expectations.

Negative effects: Some learners may feel dominated, powerless, and over-controlled and may rebel or leave. Learners are unlikely to approach the trainer for help with personal problems.

The supporting approach

Positive effects: Learners receive high levels of personal support from their trainer. There is generally a caring, friendly atmosphere.

Negative effects: There may be an overemphasis on personal problems, with a negative effect on the training.

The informing approach

Positive effects: The trainer is highly knowledgeable about the subject matter. Training materials are meticulously prepared and there are lots of explanatory materials. The trainer is not easily distracted from the subject.

Negative effects: There is very little person-to-person contact between trainer and learners. There is little if any humor. Learners are unlikely to approach the trainer for help with personal problems.

The enthusing approach

Positive effects: There are high levels of commitment and personal enthusiasm from the trainer. There are good interpersonal skills. It is a creative training style. A wide variety of training methods are used.

Negative effects: Such trainers are often poor at administration. They may have unrealistic expectations of learners and the pace may be too fast.

The adapting approach

Positive effects: High levels of negotiation are included in the training program. The trainer is prepared to expend a great deal of effort to identify and meet learner's needs.

Negative effects: The trainer may become dominated by the learners, being excessively anxious to please. The trainer may resist any leadership role.

The chef supervisor as a trainer is a person of many roles, has strong attitudes, and uses different approaches to achieving successful training, the most important being that of facilitator of the learning process. This is the function of doing everything possible to cause learning to take place. The skill is to develop a sense of understanding in using a wide variety of training tools, approaches, and styles at the right time and with the appropriate team members.

GETTING THE TEAM INVOLVED

Vital to the efforts of all quality improvement training sessions is getting each kitchen team member involved. The quality and the quantity of learning and continuous improvement are directly proportional to the degree of involvement by the kitchen team. Most people learn by doing. Key to the success of this method is to shift responsibility for learning to the team member. This technique is sometimes referred to as learner controlled or self-paced instruction. Interacting with the team in this way requires the skills of a group facilitator. Team activities such as discussion, role plays, or case studies provide an opportunity for team members to explore topics, interact with each other, and share information by expressing their views and responding to each other's ideas and opinions. While these group activities may be perceived by the team as informal, as an instruction method they need to be carefully planned. The role of a "group facilitator" consists of managing group discussions and group processes so that individuals learn and group members feel that the experience is positive.

Typical activities for a facilitator are group activities in which quality improvements are assessed. In group discussions whereby all team members feel committed to the quality improvement actions there exists an enhanced awareness of team efforts. Participation by all team members is facilitated. They are invited to present their viewpoints, levels of knowledge, and attitudes regarding various topics of culinary quality. Group activities stimulate thinking, create enthusiasm, and assist in analyzing different approaches to food preparation. The environment and characteristics of good team involvement are:

- An informal relaxed atmosphere
- Understanding of the TQM philosophy
- Willingness to act as a group, communicate, and listen to each other
- Willingness to share new ideas
- Willingness to focus on differences about concepts, not about team members
- A readiness for action once a course of action has been arrived at through consensus.

Questioning is a tried and true method for getting each team member involved.

Questions arouse interest in the team member. They stimulate thinking, keep the team member on track, solicit information, and get individual team members involved. Questions can be classified in at least two ways. It is necessary to understand both types in order to become successful using the technique. These are categorized as open/closed, and direct/indirect questions. Other descriptions of these question types are overhead, direct, relay, and return (11). Open questions are the most suited to group discussions. They arouse interest, stimulate creative thinking, keep the chef supervisor and team on track, and provoke feedback. However, questioning, if overused, may send a message that the chef supervisor lacks confidence. Overuse of questioning can suggest to the team that constant reassurance is needed on topic matters being discussed. Open questions are questions asked of the entire training group. After each answer the question is repeated to generate more answers. These types of questions are typically used to open discussions, introduce new topics, and give each team member a chance to comment.

Examples of open questions

- What do you ask for in quality food presentation?
- How would you explain why this is so?
- Can anyone suggest a better method?
- What do you think would happen if?

Open questions are recommended, as they arouse interest and encourage the team member to think creatively.

Examples of closed questions

- Can anyone tell me who has ultimate responsibility in the kitchen?
- What are the ingredients for this recipe?
- How many methods of cooking fish are there?
- What is the order of preparation of this dish?

Closed questions, no matter how carefully they are asked, require only one answer. They don't contribute to advancing discussion or encourage the development of new ideas or concepts.

Examples of direct questions

- Jennifer, now that we have discussed our new menu composition, what other items should we include?
- Frank, how do you feel about the total quality program within the kitchen?
- Scott, tell me how you would prepare chili?
- Jude, what would you do to improve foodservice quality?

Direct questions are used to call on individuals for specific information and may be used to involve a team member who has not participated in the discussion. Directing questions to specific team members also helps to even out the distribution.

Examples of indirect questions

- The question that calls for an opinion—what are the team's views?
- How does the team view the new menu?

- Can anyone suggest new ways?
- What other methods might we try?

Indirect or rhetorical questions can be used to avoid giving an opinion on a topic but encourage team member's opinions. Indirect questions are aimed at the entire team and can be useful for brainstorming.

Effective questioning means knowing how to seek information and stimulate insights. A question is defined as an inquiry designed to test, stimulate thought, or clarify. Questions can serve as an on-going assessment of the learning taking place. Use as often as possible questions that allow the learner to respond (12). When team members respond correctly, the chef supervisor can feel confident that the information or topic matter has been received. Questioning also provides the opportunity for dealing with any concerns individual members have before proceeding with training.

The primary purpose of questioning is to encourage team members to think about the training session topic. Involving the team through questioning helps to maintain interest and attention. The following are suggestions that can help to ensure success:

- Ask open-ended questions, the how, when, where, and what; they inspire thinking.
- Using questions during the topic introduction helps to establish what level of knowledge of the training session topic the team has.
- Using questions during the session allows the chef supervisor to check learning.
- Using questions at the end of the session helps to summarize and reinforce the training content.
- Variety in questioning keeps things more interesting.
- Avoid continuously calling on certain individuals even if they appear to be motivated.
- Keep things simple; keep questions confined to one main thought.
- Maintain eye contact; it enables the chef supervisor to gauge reactions.
- Use the right tone of voice and the right body language.
- Respond to the emotions of the team. Start with the easy questions and proceed to the more difficult (13).
- Play one response off against another: "Are there any other views?"

Brainstorming

While brainstorming is a means of generating new ideas, it can only be made to work effectively within a formal structure in which every participating kitchen team member must know and understand:

1. A brainstorming session should be limited to a defined place and time. It is useful to precede it with a 10-minute warm-up session on a totally un-

related and even trivial subject. Plan 30 minutes on the real session objective. It should stop on time even if it is in full flight.

2. The session should be held in a relaxed atmosphere. The team must be encouraged and motivated to generate *their* ideas; evaluation of the ideas generated is strictly avoided during the sessions.

3. The procedure requires each team member to come forth with new ideas no matter how extreme they seem. They should not switch off to other people's ideas and wait for a chance to have theirs included, but rather should develop the other members' ideas.

The functionaries during these sessions are the chairperson (who need not be the chef supervisor) and the note taker. The chairperson's functions are:

- Defining the objective or problem at the outset
- Being independent of the issues that arise and resisting interference or domination
- Directing the discussion and keeping it on track
- Acting to control input from everyone at once, facilitating the less vociferous to be heard
- Contributing to idea generation
- Stopping any form of evaluation during the session
- Involving each team member and providing positive feedback to encourage more team member input

The note taker's functions are:

- To write down ideas as they are generated
- To review written suggestions and stimulate additional ideas

Using brainstorming in a structured way is an excellent method of resolving problems within the kitchen. It is also an excellent way of identifying training gaps.

Getting the people involved is one of the best methods to facilitate training. It is the single most positive contributor to successful training.

UNDERSTANDING GROUP BEHAVIORS

Within groups people often act out roles that are closely related to their individual personalities. Each person plays out a particular role or assumes a certain mental posture during training. Chef supervisors should be aware of these various roles. These roles can be divided into building and supportive roles, self-centered roles, and task roles. Team members within each category may be subdivided as follows:

Building and supportive role

- Supporter: praises, agrees, goes along with the team
- Harmonizer: mediates differences between team members
- Tension reliever: jokes or brings out humor
- Facilitator: opens channels for communication

Self-centered role

- Blocker: constantly raises objections, revisits topics when others have moved on
- Aggressor: expresses ill will and makes sarcastic remarks
- Recognition seeker: calls attention to themselves during the training session
- Dominator: tries to run the session by giving orders, interrupting, and attempting to get their own way
- Apathetic member: nonparticipant in team activities

Task role

- Problem solving and task performance

Within groups many other roles are played out, including:

- Initiator: proposes new ideas, goals, and procedures
- Information seeker: seeks facts and additional information before making decisions
- Information giver: offers facts and information
- Opinion seeker: seeks clarification of the values involved
- Opinion giver: states own opinions
- Clarifier: elaborates on ideas offered by other team members
- Coordinator: brings together ideas offered by the team
- Energizer: prods the team to a greater level of activity (14)

By carefully listening and watching the various verbal and nonverbal clues, each of the described roles may be observed. Recognizing these behaviors is the first step in developing a method of coping with them. Each team training session will take on a culture and personality of its own. The most serious lapse is when a chef supervisor appears to be taking over. This alienates the other team members, who may consequently lose sight of the objective of the training session. An inexperienced chef supervisor new to the training role often defers to a dominant type, which also has the effect of alienating the group, causing them to lose confidence in the chef supervisor. Another signal to watch for is the question that does not relate to the topic under discussion. This may be an indication of boredom or a team member who is having difficulty.

The TQM process relies greatly on team/group activities such as meetings, discussions, and training. Understanding the dynamics of the group enables the chef supervisor to recognize and deal with them. Each team training session will almost certainly have a selection of these various personality types. Expect to have them, but learn to cope with them. Continuous improvements within the kitchen cannot be made by one person. It takes the entire kitchen team. This is where the chef supervisor demonstrates leadership skills by overcoming these personality obstacles.

SUMMARY

Vital to effective training is the understanding of all the elements that can lead to its success. Good introductions by the chef supervisor facilitate the training process. The first 5 minutes of the training session sets the scene for the training that will follow. Attention to detail ensures success with training. Among the important elements of this process are:

- Explaining the objectives of the training sessions
- Capturing the kitchen team's interest and preparing them for training
- Being cognizant of the message being sent through appearance and individual demeanor
- Creating a warm, friendly atmosphere, which facilitates training
- Being able to deal with nervousness and adapting presentations to cope with it
- Using effective, clear interpersonal communication skills, avoiding the use of jargon
- Recognizing the nonverbal and distance aspects of communication
- Understanding the advantages of a diverse team in the kitchen and actively fostering training toward empowerment
- Understanding the training attitudes toward TQM, the job, instruction, and relationships within the kitchen team during training
- Recognizing the dynamics of group behavior and the role of the chef supervisor as team facilitator
- Using correct and appropriate questioning techniques
- Facilitating and planning the kitchen team's brainstorming sessions
- Understanding the dynamics of group behaviors, arranging meetings to elicit feedback, and identifying training gaps

DISCUSSION QUESTIONS

1. Why is it important to outline to all team members what is expected of them as a result of training?

2. What are the methods that can be employed to deal with nervousness?
3. What are the four levels of distance that team members often maintain when communicating?
4. What are the significant elements to be considered for training a diverse kitchen team?
5. What are the qualities, attitudes, and styles used by chef supervisors in their training roles?
6. What are the key points that contribute to getting team involvement in training?
7. What are the closed, open, and directed questioning techniques?
8. What are the primary uses and benefits of brainstorming as a training technique?
9. Within groups each member plays out a certain role. What are the three categories into which these roles fall?

NOTES

1. Dugan Laird, *Approaches to Training and Development*, Addison-Wesley, Reading, MA, 1985, p. 76.
2. Dennis Becker and Paula Borkum Becker, *Powerful Presentation Skills*, Mirror Press, Boston, MA, 1994, p. 65.
3. Ibid., p. 33.
4. Edward T. Hall, *The Hidden Dimension*, Doubleday, New York, 1966.
5. U.S. Department of Labor Bureau of Statistics, Washington, DC, 1991.
6. Sally J. Walton, *Cultural Diversity in the Workplace*, Irwin, New York, 1994, p. v.
7. Julia Christensen, "The Diversity Dynamic: Implications for Organizations in 2005," *Hospitality Research Journal*, Vol. 17, No. 1, 1993, p. 70.
8. R. Roosevelt Thomas, *Beyond Race and Gender*, AMACON, New York, 1991, p. 10.
9. Ibid., p. 169.
10. Brian Thomas, *Total Quality Training: The Quality Culture and Quality Trainer*, McGraw-Hill, Berkshire, England, 1992, p. 144.
11. David Wheelhouse, *Managing Human Resources in the Hospitality Industry*, Educational Institute of the American Hotel and Motel Association, East Lansing, MI, 1989, p. 170.
12. Bruce B. Tepper, *The New Supervisor Skills For Success*, Mirror Press, Boston, MA, 1994, p. 85.
13. David Wheelhouse, *Managing Human Resources in the Hospitality Industry*, Educational Institute of the American Hotel and Motel Association, East Lansing, MI, 1989, p. 171.
14. Richard L. Sullivan, Jerry R. Wircenski, Susan S. Arnold, and Michelle D. Sarkeess, *Practical Manual for the Design, Delivery, and Evaluation of Training*, Aspen, Rockville, MD, 1990, p. 37.

12

Training Methods

Objectives

When you complete this chapter, you should be able to:

1. List the major techniques of training used for instructing within the kitchen.
2. Explain which training techniques can be used to achieve specific learning objectives.
3. Understand and describe the elements of training reinforcement.
4. Identify negative training methods and state their effect.

5. Identify characteristics of those team members with potential for development.

6. Specify designs for evaluating training.

INTRODUCTION

All modern learning theories stress involvement by the learner. Learners should have a degree of ownership of the learning process. Training is therefore a learning process that involves the acquisition of skills, concepts, rules, or attitudes that serve to increase the performance of the kitchen team. These acquisitions are best gained through methods that actively involve the learner. Training and *retraining* can be accomplished by using individualized or group training techniques. This chapter will explore the instructional techniques and methods that best serve members of the kitchen team.

People grow to a point where they are ready for new responsibilities beyond their initial assignments. When this happens, the foodservice organization can help them to develop and assimilate new roles and understanding of all the elements necessary to continuously improve themselves and the organization. Training is the critical factor. Training all employees, with special attention to hourly employees, will enable the kitchen to recruit and retain workers and keep a well-run foodservice establishment afloat and realizing its potential even in hard times (1). To become customer focused and for the establishment to succeed, new team members must master the skills, concepts, attitudes, rules, and philosophies of TQM.

SPECIFIC TRAINING METHODS

Job talks are a method of instruction whereby the chef supervisor provides verbal information about a particular job. These are typically used in the kitchen when the chef supervisor is presenting information concepts and theories that are found in the cognitive learning domain. They are delivered by way of an illustrated lecture and may be supplemented with a variety of instructional materials such as slides, transparencies, projected computer displays, flip charts, instruction sheets, and/or video tapes. Job talks are, by definition, words spoken by the chef supervisor. It is thus a verbal medium, offering a passive, unstimulating experience for the kitchen team member, unless the chef supervisor has unusual vocal talent. Interesting examples as well as colorful and persuasive language are needed to illustrate the job talk (2). Job talks offer many advantages to the chef supervisor. They can be an effective method of reaching mixed groups of learners. Job talks can ensure that a large amount of information is delivered in a relatively short period of time.

Strengths of the job talk lecture are:

- Job talks get the message across to a large group.
- The chef supervisor can communicate enthusiasm for the subject matter.
- Job talks can cover material not otherwise available.
- Chef supervisors can serve as effective role models for the kitchen team.
- Job talks are nonthreatening to the individual team member.
- The chef supervisor controls the material and time involved in the job talk.
- It is not necessary to plan group involvement.

Some weaknesses of the job talk as an instructional technique include the following:

- Job talks often do not allow for feedback from the team.
- They are passive methods of training.
- It can be difficult to maintain listeners' interest.
- They appeal to one sense only—hearing (unless illustrated).
- Overloading may occur.
- It is difficult to assess if the "message" has been understood.
- Successful job talks are totally dependent upon the public speaking abilities of the chef supervisor.
- Job talks are unsuitable for certain higher forms of learning such as analysis and evaluation.

Maximum value from job talks can be gained if the chef supervisor observes the following:

- Makes the subject matter interesting
- Makes the job talk relevant to the needs of the kitchen team
- Presents job talks in an interesting and varied way
- Supplements and supports the "talk" with instructional media
- Communicates the job talk on a personal level
- Avoids repeating certain words, phrases, or gestures
- Projects voice
- Demonstrates enthusiasm during the job talk
- Moves throughout the training area and maintains contact with each individual person
- Checks for understanding by asking questions
- Provides positive feedback
- Uses team members' names as often as possible
- Displays a sense of humor

- Becomes a role model in terms of dress, appearance, support for the quality objectives, and enthusiasm for the training program and by facilitating each team member to grow and succeed

There are three parts to the structure of a job talk:

1. *Introduction*: State what you are going to talk about and why. Start positively; go over previous information pertaining to the job talk.
2. *Presentation*: Avoid reading word for word; use key words to revolve around. Develop the talk from the known to the unknown, from the simple to the more difficult. Build information in a logical way. Try to develop a picture in the team member's mind. Media technology may be used to emphasize and support the job talk. Vary tone of voice, observe each person, and don't fix your gaze on a "challenging" individual. Avoid rushing the job talk and attempt to pace it to the learning rate of the group. Do not allow too many long pauses.
3. *Summary*: Restate the key points of the job talk. Allow time for team members to ask questions. Use questions to determine what learning has taken place. Praise the team for their interest and link forward to the next job talk or training session.

Schedule job talks close to the time the knowledge and skills will be used by each team member. Break the job talk down into fairly simple steps, then progress through each step until the entire job is learned. This provides an opportunity for the team member to experience success along the way, to remain interested, and to be motivated to learn the job. Team members can be overwhelmed if too much information is presented all at once. This causes frustration.

When a highly experienced person attempts to instruct the details of a job, significant points may be omitted, assumptions may be made that "everyone knows that," or some detail is so routine that it is overlooked. Do not assume anything. Concentration on the key points should help simplify the job talk. If the job talk preparation process is complete, then repetition and emphasizing of key points becomes easy to do. The tried and true method of preparing job talks may be summarized as:

Tell them what you're going to tell them
Then
Tell them
Then
Tell them what you told them.

Put another way, let the kitchen team know what the training objectives are.

Role plays   In role plays, team members simulate or act out a real or hypothetical situation in order to acquire the skills needed to manage the interpersonal dynamics of that situation. This training method can be used to build skill and confidence. It is usually followed by discussion and analysis among the kitchen team participants. Team members are asked to act out certain roles (such as a dissatisfied customer) in order for others to be able to practice how to handle such problems. The idea is for the team members to learn from playing out the assigned roles. In this way team members can be exposed to both sides of an issue. Role plays are one of the training methods that offers participants the opportunity to be actively involved in the learning process. Videotaping role plays allows for review and evaluation to improve their effectiveness.

Advantages of using role plays as a training method are:

- Team members are directly involved in the training.
- The role play highlights key attitudinal issues.
- The role play develops awareness of other people's feelings.
- Similarity between role play and work situations becomes clear to team members.
- Team members receive instant feedback that gives them confidence.
- The role play is good for interpersonal skills.
- The role play allows team members to "see" problem areas as they exist.

The main disadvantages of role plays are:

- They require a lot of preparation.
- They are suitable only for small groups.
- Sometimes role plays are not taken seriously by team members.
- They require close monitoring and control by the chef supervisor.

The following are recommended guidelines for using role plays:

- Allow plenty of time for each role play.
- Introduce role plays when team member's knowledge of the subject will assure success.
- Fully explain the purpose of the role play (outline training objective) as well as the expected results.
- Always demonstrate role plays before team members try them.
- Keep the tone of the training session "serious."
- Invite the team member to choose a particular role; seek attitude changes during the role play.
- Coach and correct team member during and following enactment of the role play.
- Give positive reinforcement and praise and link forward to further training.

Total immersion in the learning process can be achieved by using a role play. It is particularly useful for awareness training with regard to customer satisfaction and may also be used to demonstrate correct and appropriate interpersonal transactions. If done with enthusiasm by the chef supervisor, it can become a very effective method of training.

Role plays may be highly structured, with the roles well defined, or they may allow the team members who are playing the roles a great deal of flexibility in acting them out (3). Role plays cast participants into real-life situations. Real-life situations within the kitchen take on special meaning when dealing with personal sanitation, grooming, and hygiene. Sensitive topics such as these are ideal subject matter for role plays. Crucial to the success of these sessions are prior explanation of the training objective and follow-up discussions on the role play content. In this way sensitive topics can be treated as part of a group role play with critical sensitive elements being highlighted. Remember, role plays only work if the participants are able to let go of their inhibitions, feel empathy for the role they are asked to play, and really get into the situation. The chef supervisor's ability to understand team members' attitudes toward role play training, hopefully, will enable him or her to improve personal awareness of individual shortcomings.

Training in the foodservice industry involves more than just technical skills. Interpersonal skills are as important, if not more so. Chef supervisors must not assume that team members know how to treat customers or other members in the foodservice organization in a polite and friendly manner. Instructing interpersonal skills by using role plays is an efficient training method that results in increased motivation. Role plays do not, however, guarantee that the desired behavior will be used on the job, but they do provide examples of expected behavior. This method of training should be used with care and is most appropriate when the social competence of the team member is low.

Demonstrations   Demonstration as a training method is very effective in skills training. By showing team members how to perform a task while explaining the procedure, the chef supervisor enables the kitchen team members to use more than one sense and one learning mode at the same time. They can listen to the chef supervisor while observing the proper performance steps of the task or skill being demonstrated. Follow-up activity on the job then allows the team member to practice while being coached and corrected by the chef supervisor.

In a demonstration actual kitchen equipment is used to demonstrate the steps involved in the task. Demonstration alone makes use primarily of the team member's visual sense. He or she may hear and/or smell, which reinforces learning.

The advantages of using demonstration as a training method are:

• Demonstration has great visual impact.
• Instruction can be built step by step and can be given in sequence.

- Difficult steps or tasks can be shown in easy stages.
- It makes use of our natural inclination to imitate.
- It is the most effective method of instructing a skill.
- Emphasis on safety/sanitation practices can be included.
- Food product quality and specifications can be observed.
- Required job skills or tasks may be repeated.

Disadvantages of demonstrations as a training method are:

- They are only suitable for relatively small groups.
- A great deal of preparation is required.
- Pace of demonstration is often too fast.
- Team members may watch *you* rather than *what* you are doing.

Suggestions for effective demonstration include the following:

- Ensure that your actions can be seen easily.
- Arrange all food ingredients, equipment, and tools needed for the demonstration in advance.
- Introduce the demonstration by reviewing previously instructed information and/or skills that are relevant to the demonstration.
- Introduce any technical/culinary terms that are relevant to the demonstration.
- Demonstrate the manipulative skill or task in a way that closely resembles the actual kitchen environment.
- Prepare a "procedure sheet" for team members' reference.
- Use supporting materials (or preferably the "real thing") to reinforce the performance steps being demonstrated.
- Stop and explain new terms.
- Explain the underlying rationale for each skill.
- Stress safe food handling.
- Check learning during the demonstration; be sure each step is understood.
- Ask questions and provide positive feedback.
- Repeat demonstration if necessary for team members who did not fully grasp all the steps.
- Keep it short (15 to 30 minute cycles). Assign a related activity following the demonstration.
- Supervise the activity or practice session.

Demonstration as a training method should be avoided by the chef supervisor unless practiced beforehand and adequate time for preparation and checking of equipment and food materials has been allowed. The demonstration can be reinforced with an effective review and summary (4).

A common mistake made is to complete a demonstration and ask whether each team member feels he or she can perform the steps or understand the basic skills involved. The usual response in this situation is silence or affirmative nods. An excellent summary technique is to ask the team member to repeat the demonstration while the chef supervisor or another team member reads each of the steps. Following the second demonstration the individual is ready to practice the steps.

Demonstrations are especially suitable for skills training (psychomotor objectives) but can also be used as modeling to illustrate interpersonal, interviewing, or communication skills. Within the kitchen, demonstration is by far the single most effective method for instructing culinary art: the preparation, cooking, and presentation of menu items. As a method, it has the benefit of utilizing all five senses of the team member, and no other training method affords this total sensual integration.

Effective questioning and reinforcement techniques are employed during and following the demonstration to encourage team members to think about the training topic. In addition, questioning helps to maintain the individual's interest. It provides the chef supervisor with feedback regarding team members' understanding of the topic and allows for feedback to strengthen the training climate in the kitchen.

Case study   This method of training presents to the kitchen team real or hypothetical situations for them to analyze. Ideally, the case study should force the team member to think through problems, propose solutions, choose among them, and analyze the consequences of the decision. Case studies are a popular way to get involvement by the team so that discussion and resolutions of problems may be brought down to the level of concreteness.

In traditional case studies, team members receive a printed description of a problem situation. The description contains sufficient details so that the individual can make recommendations for appropriate corrective actions.

Some of the major advantages of case study as a training method are:

- Cases emphasize the analysis of a situation typical of a training need.
- The case method may improve the team members' communication skills.
- Cases expose team members to true-to-life problems in the kitchen.
- Cases may inspire interest in otherwise theoretical and abstract training materials.

Disadvantages of case study as a training method are:

- Cases focus on past and static considerations.
- Case analysis often lacks emotional involvement on the part of the team member and therefore can become unrealistic in terms of what the team member would actually do in the situation.
- There are time limits on analysis and discussion.

Areas in which the use of case studies as a training method are particularly appropriate in the kitchen are:

- Safety
- Analysis of sanitation procedures
- Food-borne illnesses and contamination
- Teamwork, work flow, and work organization
- Customer relations
- Analysis of quality in the foodservice organization

While many cases exist under these headings, it is possible for resourceful chef supervisors to create their own. Additionally, team members can be encouraged to write their own case studies from past real-life situations, and these may then be shared with the rest of the kitchen team. To increase total participation, team members may be split into small "buzz groups." When there are fewer people in each group, individuals are more inclined to participate at higher levels than if only one large discussion group was going on.

Case studies are particularly relevant to the entire issue of TQM (5). By focusing on past case studies of foodservice operations that failed and by placing high importance on customer satisfaction, quality or operational gaps can be identified. Discussions, comparisons, and observations on shortcomings can be noted. To achieve total quality, each team member can draw comparisons between what was in a case study and what should be. People can relate to problems associated with quality issues when they are presented in a carefully prepared case.

To facilitate and enable success with case study training methods, the technique of structured discussions is used. Structured discussions are conversations between team members aimed at specific learning objectives. These objectives distinguish them from more social conversation. The learning objective for the case study analysis should be announced in advance. Structure in the ensuing discussions can be facilitated by the use of an agenda with time controls. Agendas and timetables developed by the team afford ownership of the session to the kitchen team.

Attempting to conduct a structured discussion when team members have had a limited exposure to the case study topic often will result in little or no interaction and an ineffective discussion.

Suggestions to enable a purposeful structured discussion include the following:

- Create a forum where each team member can interact and learn from each other.
- Establish the purpose of the session and what the desired outcomes are.
- Consider the nature of the session topic.
- Arrange seating so that each team member can hear and see each other.

- Give the team guidelines.
- Moderate the session.
- Provide feedback.
- Identify issues for consideration.
- Ensure that the case under study is real to the team.
- Stimulate discussion and debate.
- Encourage all team members to be involved.
- Ensure that no one team member dominates the discussions.
- Use the contributions of each team member and provide positive rein-
  forcement. Conclude the discussion with a summary of the main ideas.

Structured discussions are appropriate for use with case studies. They
should have predetermined objectives. The chef supervisor must ensure that
team members do not bring a negative viewpoint to these objectives. When
used with case study analysis, structured discussions can be a motivating and
useful training method in the kitchen.

On-the-job training   This is the most commonly used method to train
kitchen team members. It is not necessarily the best training method for culinary standards of quality. It is usually conducted by the chef supervisor, and it
has the advantage of providing "hands-on" experience under normal conditions. Although on-the-job training (OJT) is commonly used in the kitchen, it
also is one of the most poorly implemented methods of training.
Common drawbacks of OJT are:

- Lack of a well-structured training environment
- Poor chef supervisor training skills and the omission of a well-defined
  high-quality job performance criterion

On-the-job training can be successful when the chef supervisor as trainer
has an objective, a plan, and the knowledge that quality and continuous improvements can only be implemented on the job.
One benefit of OJT training is that it provides immediate application and
satisfaction for the new team member who may often be anxious and fearful.
The chef supervisor can determine which training method is most suitable for
instructing different job duties. Additionally, for retraining or cross-training,
different methods and techniques and/or combinations of these methods may
be appropriate.
The following are the steps and structure of an OJT training session:

1. *Introduction*
- Introduce what the team member *will be able to do* at the end of the ses-
  sion.
- Indicate why you want the team member to learn.

- Discuss how this training relates to what the team member already knows.
- Demonstrate equipment to be used during the training session.
- Explain the steps involved in the task and the overall purpose.

2. *Presentation*

- Highlight key points.
- Demonstrate the procedure in sequential order.
- Explain the what, why, who, when, how, and where.
- Use training aids where appropriate.
- Instruct at a pace that allows the team member to understand the task.

3. *Summary*

- Demonstrate the task a second time, if necessary; repeat the key points and steps.
- Encourage questions on points of clarification.
- Give specific feedback.
- Give praise when due.
- When satisfied that learning has occurred, move to next step.

4. *Practice*

- Team members practice under supervision.
- Ask questions to assess team members' understanding.
- Coach and correct team members.
- Praise when correct quality standards have been achieved.

5. *Follow-up*

- The team member puts into practice what has been instructed under supervision.
- Encourage further questions from the team member.
- Decide on follow-up talk.
- Show how every job relates to the importance of every other job and that failure of one affects the value of all of the others.

6. *Coaching*

- Allow all team members to become involved with the procedures they will use.
- Conduct correction interviews in private.
- Permit team members to evaluate their own performance.
- Allow ample time for skill development.
- Use open questions to establish work problems.
- Provide positive reinforcement.

The first step of coaching is to observe team members doing their job. If they are doing the job well, don't hesitate to tell them. Everyone likes to be praised; try to catch team members doing good things.

Training is progressive. It must be continuous. Repetition is the key to learning. Therefore it is important that the chef supervisor demonstrate a good deal of patience. If there appears to be a problem with some aspect of the team members' performance, check the following:

- Are they fully aware of what is supposed to be done?
- Do they have adequate equipment and materials to perform the task?
- Did they receive adequate feedback during the practice stage?

The next step is to confront, not criticize, the team member's poor performance. Confronting is a positive process used to correct job performance problems. Chef supervisors who confront are more interested in helping team members feel confident about improving future performance, rather than making them feel inadequate and guilty about past performance. Praise in public, correct in private. Training means directing the growth of an individual. In the total quality kitchen environment, cross-training is becoming more important. Cross-training prepares individual team members to fill in as needed on jobs. This is also an excellent method of eliminating job monotony and fatigue. Another advantage of cross-training is that is makes flexibility possible; for example, when one team member is absent, another can perform that job.

Apprenticeship training   This is designed to provide young chefs entering the culinary profession with a comprehensive training in the practical and theoretical aspects of work required in a highly skilled profession. Apprenticeship programs combine OJT and classroom training with a skilled and experienced chef conducting the OJT training during the apprenticeship period. The purpose of this training is to learn practical culinary skills on the job. Apprentices learn the theoretical side of the culinary profession in classes they attend outside the job. Subjects covered in classroom training are safety, sanitation, communication skills, mathematics, supervisory management, law, food cost control procedures, purchasing, and nutrition.

The culinary apprenticeship program in the United States is sponsored by the American Culinary Federation's Educational Institute in cooperation with local chapters of that organization. It is the only national apprenticeship training program for chefs and operates in cooperation with the U.S. Department of Labor, Bureau of Apprenticeship and Training (BAT). The apprenticeship program also operates in conjunction with local post-secondary schools and colleges providing culinary theory courses (6).

The culinary apprentice completes 6000 hours of OJT training as well as theory-related courses, usually over a three-year period. Wages paid to apprentices usually begin at half those paid to fully trained chefs. However,

Chef Talk: "Do Not Assume"

I remember the incident that made me realize the need to rethink my methods of training. This incident might be funny and I guess in retrospect it was, but it could have spelled big trouble. I was the executive chef at a hotel in Germany with an extensive banquet business. It was one of those extremely busy days, with many banquets and functions. All day I had given out work orders to the crew. One apprentice was charged with arranging an ice cream coupe. In my usual stern manner, I informed him that he was to produce 250 of these coupes and he was to use three different ice creams and a garnish; and he was to do it quickly.

I didn't give him any details, never checked his background and experience level, and never gave a demo of how to prepare this dish. So off he went to the production kitchen. After a while, he came back and reported that the dessert was finished and in the freezer. I immediately assigned him to another task. I never checked his work. As the time of ser-vice approached, I instructed him to bring out the dessert to be served. As the cart rolled to the service line, I almost had a heart attack. There were 250 desserts all right, and they each had three scoops of ice cream, vanilla, chocolate, and strawberry, and a garnish of whipped cream, *cucumber slices, tomato wedges, and a sprig of parsley.* I thought my head would explode. I started to scream at the top of my lungs, then I stopped, and walked out of the kitchen after telling my sous chef to do the best he could. I sat down in my office and asked myself over and over why this had happened. It was just like a big awakening inside. I realized that I had never asked the person how long he had worked in the kitchen. As a matter of fact, he had started only two days before. I had never instructed him or given all the information he needed to know to do a proper job. So, in other words, besides the commonsense aspect, I was mostly to blame for this mistake. I came to realize more and more the importance of training.

Carl J. Guggenmos, CEC, CCE, Director of Education, Johnson & Wales University, Charleston, SC

---

wages are generally advanced rapidly at six-month intervals. The BAT has established the following minimum standards for apprenticeship programs:

1. Nondiscrimination in all phases of apprenticeship employment and training
2. Organized instruction designed to provide the apprentice with a knowledge in technical subjects related to the trade or skill

Chef Talk: "Apprenticeship"

Although my earliest memories of cooking are as a young child helping my mother in our family restaurant, I began my formal culinary apprenticeship in 1949 at age 13 in the kitchens of the distinguished Grand Hotel de l'Europe, in my hometown of Bourg-en-Bresse, near Lyon.

As was traditional in France at the time, my apprenticeship lasted three years, the first of which I was not even allowed to approach the stove. My earliest duties included cleaning the floors, the walls, the refrigerator, and the stove. After I'd been there a while, I was assigned innumerable small chores, among them chopping parsley, cutting up vegetables, trimming meat, plucking and eviscerating poultry, and gutting and scaling fish. Going to the stove, finally, was such a big deal that it was almost like a graduation. We worked seven days a week, with a few days off at the end of each month, and received no pay.

Soon after completing my apprenticeship, I went to Paris and continued my training under Executive Chef Lucien Diat at the world-renowned Plaza Athenée. At that time, there were 48 professional chefs among the hotel's 130-member kitchen brigade. The world of the chef was structured and disciplined then, with recipes seldom deviating from the classic origins. Improvisation and personal interpretation were not permitted.

Basically, apprentices back then had to steal the craft. Chefs did not explain anything to us; we watched and we imitated. We didn't question the chef's orders, but did what we were told.

This old visual and osmotic system of training had its merits, however. As apprentices, we repeated and repeated procedures until our hands could accomplish them without our even thinking about what we were doing. This taught us discipline and a great appreciation for fundamental skills. I don't think you can be a good chef until you are a good craftsperson, and, in my opinion, it takes at least 10 years to learn the craft. Not until the basics are understood and mastered can a chef begin to create dishes and develop a personal culinary philosophy.

Nouvelle cuisine opened the floodgates of culinary creativity, which resulted in more opportunities for apprentice chefs. Now they can participate in the cooking process early on, and their opinions are appreciated. They should remember, however, the importance of mastering techniques and continuing to learn in this profession.

Jacques Pépin, master chef, author, and host of PBS's "Today's Gourmet"

3. A schedule of work processes in which an apprentice is to receive training and experience on the job
4. A progressively increasing schedule of wages
5. Proper supervision of OJT training with adequate facilities to train apprentices
6. Periodic evaluation of the apprentice's progress both on the job performance and related instruction
7. Recognition for successful completion

Upon graduation the apprentice receives a Department of Labor certificate and/or a certificate of the American Culinary Federation and is admitted as a member of that organization.

TRAINING REINFORCEMENT

People strive to achieve objectives they have set for themselves. The most frequently identified objectives of kitchen team members are job security, rewarding work, recognition, status, responsibility, and achievement. If training assists team members in achieving these objectives, then the learning process is greatly facilitated. When training provides greater opportunities for job advancement, team members will be highly motivated because they can see that greater rewards and job security will likely result. Knowledge of results (feedback) influences the training/learning process. Keeping team members informed of their progress as measured against a quality improvement standard helps in setting goals for what remains to be learned. The on-going process of analyzing progress and setting new objectives greatly enhances learning.

Reinforcement theory states that behavior appearing to lead to a positive consequence tends to be repeated, while behavior appearing to lead to a negative consequence tends not to be repeated. A positive consequence is rewarded (7). Praise and recognition are two of the most important rewards used in training. Each segment of training should be sequentially organized so that the individual can see, not only its purpose, but also how it fits into the overall quality training program.

Perfect practice makes perfect, and bad practice will not make perfect. This is applicable to training in the kitchen. Repeating a job task several times develops facility in performing it. Practice and repetition almost always lead to effective training.

NEGATIVE TRAINING METHODS

It is impossible to effect standards of quality food production if chef supervisors do not actively engage in training their team. Yet it is not uncommon to observe poor or no training in some kitchens. Many chef supervisors assume that experience in a previous job takes the place of training. They assume that new team members know how to do the job to the quality standards that they have set. There is also a misguided assumption that once a team member is hired, he or she will learn the job from other team members. Known as the "buddy system," this is rooted in the mistaken belief that other team members can train the new team member, often while still doing their job. Probably the most common negative training method is the one that allows the person leaving the job to train the person who will take over the job. Other negative training methods are:

Spectator method   The new team member does not have the right to do anything and can only watch others. This is boring for the individual, produces nothing, and simply prolongs the training period.

Unskilled labor method   The team member can perform only trivial jobs, for example, cleaning up or getting coffee. Nothing is learned and the team member feels useless and is not stimulated for the job.

Do-it-yourself method   New team members are left on their own to "sink or swim." This method can be successful with individuals who catch on quickly and who like to show off what they are capable of. The down side to this method is the risk that a new team member will develop bad habits, and this can harm team spirit. Later, these team members are usually unwilling to pass on to others what they know.

DEVELOPING THE TEAM MEMBER WITH POTENTIAL

Training deals with the immediate concerns of the kitchen team; development deals with recognizing team members who posses obvious talent for leadership roles. Developing individual team members into capable chef supervisors of the future is the answer to continuous improvements necessary to provide better quality food and service to customers. The team member with potential for growth needs nurturing and encouragement.

Human resources development is generally a combination of OJT training and educational opportunities that will help a team member develop into a more productive and responsible member of the foodservice organization. Although there are no foolproof methods of determining who has the greatest potential for development, there are some observable characteristics that help identify potential leaders:

- Are able to cope with problems and seek help when it is needed
- Are able to act without supervisory direction
- Are open-minded, calm, and tolerant

- Accept responsibility for their actions and don't try to blame others
- Maintain a level disposition
- Display high energy levels

There are two important steps in developing a team member:

1. A series of jobs through which a team member can be promoted
2. Opportunities to receive training beyond each job for each team member who shows potential for leadership

Each job can be an opportunity for the team member to prepare for something better. Internal job mobility means that team members have a chance to grow and the foodservice organization has a reliable source of labor without the high cost of turnover and of training someone new.

TRAINING EVALUATION

Evaluation is necessary to determine whether training in the kitchen has had an impact on improving team members' knowledge, skills and attitudes, and job performance related to total quality. Evaluation of training is part of the cycle of the training process. Without it, the chef supervisor is unable to determine if he or she has been simply "spinning wheels."

Evaluating is the final step before reviewing and renewing training objectives and before starting the process again. Training is a very dynamic process. Its elements cannot be left for long without the possibility of their becoming stagnant, outdated, or inaccurate, even harmful to the total quality efforts of the organization. Additionally, team members do not always learn precisely what the training was intended to teach them. Evaluating the impact of training on kitchen team job performance revolves around certain basic questions:

- Did training make a difference?
- Is the team member able to perform the skills presented during the training session?
- How has training affected team attitudes?
- Were interpersonal skills improved?
- Were the resulting changes in team members worth the investment in training?
- Did team members provide suggestions for improving the training sessions?
- Did training correct identified problems?
- Were deficiencies related to method of training, content, format, and delivery identified?
- What recommendations are there for improvement?

If most of the feedback is positive, it can be assumed that the training was effective. If specific concerns were expressed, the data must then be compared to other methods of evaluation.

The kitchen team members who received training are the most obvious source of data regarding the impact of training. Through the evaluation process, team members are asked to express their opinions and make observations about the effectiveness of the training. In addition to asking them to respond to specific questions related to tasks addressed within the training program, a number of general questions can be built into a survey instrument that will provide valuable information. Typically, participants are asked to complete a questionnaire with regard to the training they received. These questionnaires may be quite elaborate or simple. The following simple example details elementary questions to be asked:

- Are job elements different than those taught during training?
- Was the benefit from training worth the effort spent?
- Were the course objectives explained clearly?
- Did the instructor demonstrate technical knowledge?
- Were the training topics sequenced logically?
- Were all your questions and concerns regarding training answered?
- Were facilities adequate and suitable for training?

This type of training participant evaluation is not too tedious to complete and is easy to follow. This "form type" of evaluation should be used at the end of the training session or segment of a teaching program. It is important that they not be overused. Evaluation tests can be administered at any appropriate time or when they will help. The reasons for testing are essentially the same as the reasons for asking questions.

When training is effective, team members completing a training program are able to perform the skills or apply the knowledge necessary to correct quality or implement correct standards. Evaluation also monitors the team members' performance OJT as well as the entire training process. Continuous monitoring and feedback ensure that the training process is successful and that the chef supervisor is able to fulfill the roles and responsibilities required in the design, delivery, and evaluation of training.

SUMMARY

Attaining maximum involvement of the kitchen team member in the training process is one of the greatest objectives of the chef supervisor. People learn best by doing.

Specific training methods suitable for the implementation of training in a culinary environment include the following:

- Job talks, which by definition are a one-way process by the chef supervisor, can be boring, and can be unproductive unless considerably enhanced and supported by stimulating visuals, good preparation, and interesting delivery.

- Role play participants are asked to act out certain roles in order for other learners to be able to practice how to handle such problems. In this way, participants can be exposed to both sides of the role play issue. It offers full participation in the training process by the kitchen team member.

- Demonstration is a widely used training method in the kitchen. It offers the chef supervisor a method to carefully and slowly instruct skills. Team members can then practice under supervision while the chef supervisor coaches and corrects.

- Case study team members develop solutions and approaches to situations that are presented by means of written cases. Proposed and actual solutions and their results are discussed.

- On-the-job training is the most widely used method following demonstration. This is a combination of all methods of training and retraining. In this method the team member is placed into the real work situation and trained to do the different parts of the job by an experienced team member or the chef supervisor. It includes the following steps: introduction, presentation, summary, practice, follow-up, and coaching.

- Apprenticeship training in the kitchen is organized according to guidelines and structures set forth by the American Culinary Federation Educational Institute and the U.S. Department of Labor. Apprenticeship offers the foodservice establishment a long-term training program that can provide a long-term commitment from those in the program.

- Reinforcement training theory is based on studies that show that behavior that leads to a positive consequence tends to be repeated, while behavior that leads to a negative consequence tends not to be repeated. Praise and recognition are two of the most positive elements of reinforcement training.

- Negative training methods involve skills that the chef supervisor assumes team members either bring to the job or learn from others on the job. The results of negative training are that team members learn bad habits and are unaware of objectives or the quality vision of the kitchen team.

- Developing the team member with potential is necessary to identify future leaders. Characteristics of these potential leaders manifest themselves in high energy levels. These people are problem solvers. Promotions and further training opportunities are ways to develop these potential leaders.

- Evaluation of training is necessary to determine the success of the planned training. Evaluation is the final step in the training process. It provides the basis for a review of the objectives and applied methods.

DISCUSSION QUESTIONS

1. What are the merits of using case study as a specific training technique in the kitchen?

2. What are the main disadvantages to apprenticeship training?

3. Why is on-the-job training sometimes considered to be one of the most poorly implemented training techniques in the kitchen?

4. In your opinion, what training technique(s) are most suited to implementing total quality management?

5. Describe reinforcement theory. How can reinforcement facilitate quality improvements?

6. What are negative training methods? What is their impact on new team members?

7. What team member characteristics demonstrate potential for further development?

8. Why is evaluation of training programs necessary?

9. What are the links between training objectives and training evaluation?

NOTES

1. Francine A. Herman and Martha E. Miller, "Training for Hospitality," *Training & Development*, Sept. 1991.

2. Robert B. Maddux, *Team Building: An Exercise in Leadership*, Crisp, Los Altos, CA, 1992, p. 33.

3. Lois B. Hart, *Training Methods That Work*, Crisp, London, England, 1991, p. 70.

4. Herman Zaccarelli, *Training Managers to Train*, Crisp, Los Altos, CA, 1988, p. 48.

5. John Bank, *The Essence of Total Quality Management*, Prentice-Hall, New York, 1992.

6. American Culinary Federation, *Apprenticeship Operations Manual*, St Augustine, FL, 1985.

7. B. F. Skinner, *About Behaviorism*, Alfred Knopf, New York, 1974.

13

Induction and Orientation Training

Outline

- Introduction
- Induction training
- Orientation training
- Duration of orientation training
- Communicating induction and orientation training
- Topics for kitchen training
- Follow-up and evaluation
- Summary
- Discussion questions

Objectives

When you complete this chapter, you should be able to:

1. Differentiate between induction and orientation training programs.
2. Identify the elements and essential information that form part of induction and orientation training.

3. Describe methods of communicating induction and orientation programs and outline how they can benefit the foodservice organization and new team member.

4. Describe topics for inclusion in kitchen orientation training programs.

5. Explain the value of follow-up and evaluation of induction and orientation training.

INTRODUCTION

A new team member's first impressions about his or her job can make all the difference. The foundation for attitudes that may stay in place as long as that team member remains in the foodservice organization is established during orientation and induction. Orientation and induction training describe the types of training given to a new kitchen team member. They provide information about the total quality culture, mission, philosophy, job, and working conditions and cover the main activities and duties in which the new team member will be involved. They state the area of training in which the new team member will be instructed and the quality levels of performance expected. They also provide a systematic plan to accomplish these goals. By providing an orientation program, you communicate to new employees what is expected of them and how their job fits into the overall operation. It also helps employees fit into their jobs faster, be more productive and satisfied, and realize you care. Also, remember that how employees treat customers is often a reflection of how they are treated by management (1).

INDUCTION TRAINING

Induction implies the absorbing of a new team member into the culture of the foodservice organization. It is separated deliberately from orientation as a training method. It is different from orientation insofar as it is not process oriented. Typically, induction will cover issues such as customer focus, philosophy, total quality management, team focus, mission statement, corporate culture, commitment to goals, concepts of empowerment, and individual attitudes toward these goals. Induction does not need to cover specific job details, since its purpose is to evoke feelings and generate commitment. The chef supervisor conducting the induction should sell the organization's philosophy along with security, caring, and peace of mind by talking in general terms about benefits, recognition programs, and salary policies. New team members want to be part of a successful organization. Induction is introduced on the first day the team member begins the new job.

While written policies concerning these issues are contained in an orientation kit, most induction training is conducted by the team. It is not just a series of slogans but a calculated rationale that is lived by each member of the team daily. Induction training is shared rather than lectured. When an employee leaves an organization, needless staffing expenses are incurred and service to customers is likely to decline. Potentially good employees may be "turned off" through improper orientation and poor training (2).

When tactfully and correctly implemented, induction will result in a committed team member armed with the expectations of the mission of the organization.

ORIENTATION TRAINING

This is the umbrella under which induction is carried out. However, orientation is more of a systematic method to acquaint the new team member with all aspects of the new job. Orientation can be defined as a two-way informational and introductory session conducted by the employer to educate and excite all participants (3). Its purpose is to make the new team member an effective contributor to the kitchen team in the shortest time available.

New team members receive orientation from their fellow team members and from the organization. The orientation received from fellow team members is usually unplanned and unofficial, and it often provides the new team member with misleading and inaccurate information. This is one of the reasons why the official orientation provided by the foodservice organization is so important. An effective orientation program has an immediate and lasting impact on the new team member and can make the difference between a new team member's success or failure. Studies have identified a strong correlation between customer satisfaction and the employee's view of service quality. When employees view an organization's human resources policies favorably, customers tend to view the quality of service they receive favorably (4).

The highest proportion of employee turnover occurs within the first 30 days. This is due largely to poor or nonexistent orientation training. A planned approach to orientation will ensure that:

- All new team members will receive information to allow them to fit into the kitchen team as quickly as possible.
- The new team member is working productively from the first day.
- The new team member is assigned duties and is informed of the quality standards required.
- The new team member will be more inclined to have a sense of belonging and will consequently be motivated.
- The new team member will be more inclined to be confident and loyal.
- The scene is set for further training.
- Job expectations are fulfilled.

It is ultimately the responsibility of the chef supervisor to carry out induction and orientation training. Each new team member brings to the work-

Chef Talk: "My First Day"

It will remain with me forever, my first day in the kitchen. As an innocent young apprentice chef filled with expectations of my future in the culinary profession, armed with my new chef uniforms and my meager set of chef's knives, I began my "orientation" to the chef's profession, which I still love to this day. However, my first day on the job as an apprentice chef in Jury's Hotel in Dublin, Ireland, was anything but a pleasant experience. Induction and orientation training sessions were unheard of back then. In fact, the only information I was provided with was a duty roster in which I was listed as the "new body." Nobody had bothered to even find out what my name was. The roster as I remember was an 11-day cycle spread over 2 weeks. It was broken down into 7 late days, 6 early days, with every second Sunday off and a day off each week. Late days began at 9 a.m., off at 3 p.m., return at 6 p.m., until 10.30 p.m. Early days were 9 a.m. to 6 p.m.

On my first day I reported to the "back office" for a time card. I was directed to the male changing room. After considerable effort I eventually found this room. When I got there, there was no available locker to store my street clothes after I had changed into my chef uniform. I reported to the head chef and introduced myself to him. He barely acknowledged my presence, and with a grunt waved me toward the sous chef, who assigned me to the garde manger department. The chef garde manger's method of induction and orientation was to give nicknames and engage constantly in ridicule. At the end of my first period that day I returned to the locker room to discover that my street clothes had disappeared. I had to cycle home that afternoon in my chef uniform. My parents were furious. They wanted me to remain at home and to consider some other profession. In any event I did go back to the hotel that evening. Orientation was by the sink-or-swim method by the other chef apprentices. This was probably the worst type of orientation anyone could receive. As a result of that first day I formed attitudes about the organization that took many years to undo. If I had been inducted and orientated in a planned and sequential way, I know I would have been a much more productive worker. I have often wondered since then how many potential "escoffiers" were turned off simply because of poor initial orientation or no orientation training at all.

Noel C. Cullen, Ed.D., CMC, AAC Boston University, Boston, MA place his or her own set of values. The new employee's values and attitudes may be quite different from those of the supervisor and other employees. The background of the new employee will have some effect on the way this person relates to the supervisor and to the new job (5). In view of this, orientation training should be prepared with the same attention to detail as any other training program. It can be one of the best and most complete training investments made by the foodservice organization.

The first three days for the new team member at work is a critical time and will have a definite effect on his or her future performance. The first day is an opportunity to set a positive tone and thereby avoid problems that might occur later (6).

The topics presented in the training plan should be based on the needs of the organization and the new team member. Generally, the foodservice organization is concerned with meeting the needs of its customers, making a profit, satisfying team member needs, and being socially responsible. New team members, on the other hand, are generally more interested in pay, benefits, and specific terms and conditions of employment. A good balance between the foodservice organization and the new team member needs is essential if the orientation program is to be successful.

Arrangements should be made to tour the foodservice facilities. In addition, comprehensive orientation kits should be prepared for all new team members. Contained in this kit are:

- Map of the foodservice organization's facilities
- Organizational chart
- Organization's policies and procedures handbook, which typically features information and guidance on the following topics:
  - Sanitation procedures
  - Safety procedures
  - Uniforms, dress code
  - Personal appearance and grooming
  - Union policies (if applicable)
  - Payroll procedures
  - Vacation policy
  - What public holidays are allowed
  - Group health insurance
  - Meals and break policies
  - Pension/savings plan
  - Attendance, hours of work
  - Incentive programs
  - Performance evaluations
  - Emergency procedures
  - Promotion policy

- Harassment policy
- Employee assistance programs
- Days off for religious observations
- Security department's authority
- Disciplinary rules and actions
- Key telephone numbers
- Training programs

The chef supervisor might want to conclude the explanation of the orientation handbook policies and procedures by reviewing the most important points. Additionally, the forms that the new team member will need to complete should be highlighted within the orientation. *Reassure new employees. Let them know you are confident they can do the job and that they will get all the support they need from the team.*

Many foodservice organizations require team members to complete a questionnaire on the policy notebook. The questionnaire is not graded, but it is checked. Others require passing a test on safety and sanitation, emergencies, hazardous materials handling, and harassment policies. This shows whether there are areas of the notebook that are unclear and need further explanation. The policy notebook will contain policies on topics such as vacations, holidays, sick leave, absenteeism, tardiness, health examinations, accidents, safety, parking regulations, disciplinary actions, grievance procedures, health and group insurance, and other policies and benefits.

DURATION OF ORIENTATION TRAINING

It is impossible for a new team member to absorb in one long session all of the information in the foodservice organization's orientation program. Brief sessions should be used. These may last up to two hours, spread over several days. This increases the likelihood that the new team member will understand and retain the information presented. Frequently when new team members arrive in the kitchen they are handed a departmental procedures handbook and are told to read the material and to ask any questions they may have. Task and station orientation should be well planned and conducted by the chef supervisor using appropriate menu and recipe guidance.

It is important to introduce the new team member to the other kitchen team members on the first day. During these introductions each team member's function and position within the team should be indicated and an explanation of how each one fits into the department should be given. Ensure employees are told about company goals and visions and their role in the dream (7).

As with any training, 'ime is involved: the new team member's and the chef supervisor's. However, induction and orientation training are truly a quality investment of time, one that can contribute to effective integration of the new team member and set the foundation for a long association with the organization.

COMMUNICATING INDUCTION
AND ORIENTATION TRAINING

If the chef supervisor does not communicate and deliver the induction/orientation program, other team members will. This may not be the type of orientation you wish the new person to receive. Unplanned orientation can be harmful. Existing team members can paint an unfavorable and untrue picture of the kitchen operation. Most people will have a tendency to relate and listen to those they feel are their peers, rather than the supervisor. Therefore, it is very important that the first impressions of the organization be created by the chef supervisor and that they be in the framework of real work situations.

New team members come with a certain amount of anxiety. They will have feelings of insecurity regarding confidence in their abilities to do the job and fit into the team. The type of positive work environment the chef supervisor creates can reduce these anxieties and facilitate a feeling of worth and belonging in new team members. It is much better to invest in training at this stage because they will become productive in a shorter period of time.

In communication, an open style should be adopted. Speak to the team member in a bilateral way, as if to say "we picked each other." Speak clearly and directly as one human being to another. Provide any background information he or she will need. Explain any technical terms and avoid using kitchen jargon. Too much information at one time is as bad as too little; break it into parts. Without making it obvious, repeat anything that is important for the team member to remember. Use open questions as much as possible. Listening to the new member during the orientation is important, not just because of what you might find out, but because it means a lot to the new team member. The intention is to communicate, not to intimidate, during this phase. Avoid "talking down" from a position of power. Show respect for the individual. A little awareness and genuine kindness go a long way. Develop an orientation program that not only goes over the rules but also stresses a "spirit of hospitality" (8).

Perception plays an important role in communication during an orientation or induction session. It can help immensely and it can also devastate the most sincere effort to communicate effectively. The fact is that people often only hear what they want to hear. Knowing this, the chef supervisor should keep trying until the correct feedback is received. The negative aspect of this is that it can cause the new team member to become defensive, which will hinder the communication process. Problems in perception are often caused by differences in ethnic or cultural backgrounds, different educational levels, and difficulties with the particular language used. The cultural background of people has a strong influence on the communication process, which includes non-

Chef Talk: "Induction by Fire"

Being a country boy with little exposure to the European culinary scene, I was a prime candidate for induction ceremonies that I later found out took place in almost every kitchen. The first night on the hot line, while setting up garnishes for the self-professed "king of the broiler," I ran out of oval platters, which were the only appropriate frame for the masterpieces coming hot and sizzling from the "master."

After being duly reprimanded for allowing the platters to run out, I was told to hastily retrieve platters from the dish room. Upon entering the dish room, I discovered there were no oval platters. With the screams of the broiler chef getting louder, I ran back to inform him of the situation. He glared at me and told me to go to the storeroom and get

a "plate stretcher." Not thinking, I ran to the storeroom. I was directed to a cabinet, opened it, and rifled through not even knowing what I was looking for. Suddenly it dawned on me. Plate stretcher! I turned and walked out of the storeroom to the laughs and howls of those who witnessed what I had just done. From that moment on I was adopted into the kitchen brigade and no longer felt an outsider. Rightly or wrongly this method of passing through the gate to the inner circle of acceptance still goes on today. In the pressured, highly technical world of culinary art, humor and acceptance go hand in hand. It is a necessity to laugh together, to perform together, to depend on each other. That's a team. And it's always apparent (from the food served) if there is a team in the kitchen.

Keith Keogh, CEC, AAC, Executive Chef, Research and Development, Walt Disney World, Lake Buena Vista, FL

verbal and verbal communication. Investing time so as to start the new team member on the correct path will make things easier for the chef supervisor. Induction and orientation training assist in developing the quality management philosophy in the new person.

TOPICS FOR KITCHEN ORIENTATION

1. Kitchen department functions
Goals, objectives, and standards
Organization and team structure
Operational activities: hours of operation, range of menus

Working relationships between "front of the house" and "back of the house"

Relationship of jobs and functions in the kitchen

2. Duties and responsibilities of kitchen team member

Detailed explanation of total quality as a business philosophy

Discussion of common foodservice problems and how to avoid and overcome them

Quality performance standards and the basis of performance evaluation

Number of daily work hours and reporting times

Overtime requirements and needs

Extra duty assignments, i.e., covering for other employees

Dress codes, uniforms, who furnishes them

Professional conduct policy

Use and maintenance of kitchen equipment

Food controls and requisitioning

3. Pay and benefits

Review the pay and benefits the new team member will receive, where, and when.

Explain amount of sick time, holiday time, personal time, and vacation time allowed.

4. Rules and procedures

Handling emergencies

Safety, sanitation: codes, practices, and inspection

Reporting accidents

Assignment of lockers, changing room areas

Security, theft, and costs

Time clock and time sheets

Breaks and dining arrangements

Communication and reporting channels

Unions (if applicable)

Recognition program

Promotions and transfers

Disciplinary procedures

Termination

Rules on telephone use

Procedure for requesting time off

Smoking policy

Calling in if unable to come to work

Approved entrances and exits
Time scheduling
Use of kitchen side towels
Use of cleaning materials

5. *Tour of kitchen and related areas*
Rest rooms and showers
Fire alarms and fire extinguishers
Store rooms, recycling areas, dish rooms
First-aid kit
Employee cafeteria
Pantry, restaurants, banqueting
Reach-ins, walk-ins, and freezers
Dry goods stores
Introduction to entire kitchen team
Automobile parking

FOLLOW-UP AND EVALUATION

Formal and systematic evaluation of the induction and orientation training program is essential. New team members should receive a set of contingency plans and contacts in the event they need further clarification or assistance to ensure their careful induction and orientation into the foodservice organization. The chef supervisor should regularly check on how well the team members are doing and answer any questions that may have arisen after their initial induction and orientation. A formal scheduled follow-up should take place within one month after the team members become part of the kitchen team. The actual induction and orientation training plan should be reviewed at least once a year. The purpose of this evaluation is to determine if the plan is meeting the foodservice organization and new team members' needs and to ascertain ways of improving the current program.

Feedback from new team members is one method of evaluating the induction and orientation program. This can be achieved by asking new team members to complete unsigned questionnaires or through in-depth interviews. Feedback of this type enables the chef supervisor and the foodservice organization to adapt and modify the program. Induction and orientation training programs for new team members take priority in development and implementation; once completed, work on other training aspects can begin. The first day on the job is an opportunity for the chef supervisor and the foodservice organization to set a positive tone and thereby avoid problems that might occur later. The way a new kitchen team member is treated during the induction and orientation period conveys an impression of you as the chef supervisor and the organization as having a well-planned, well-executed induction and orientation program.

SUMMARY

Induction and orientation training programs are vital to assimilating new team members into the foodservice organization's philosophy. They also provide for clear understanding of what team members' jobs are and the level and standards of quality performance expected.

- Induction is different from orientation in that it covers issues of corporate culture, philosophy, mission, total quality, customer focus, concepts of individual empowerment, and expected team member attitudes. Induction training is eventually conducted by the entire team.
- Orientation training is the umbrella under which induction takes place. The purpose of the orientation training plan is to systematically and sequentially orient the new team member to the job, the kitchen, and the other team members so as to enable him or her to effectively contribute to the organization in the shortest possible time. The first 30 days of the new team member's tenure in the job are vital. It is during this period that most employee turnover occurs, due largely to poor orientation training.
- Orientation training should include an information kit that enables the new team member to fit smoothly into the foodservice organization. It is the chef supervisor's duty to ensure that the new member is armed with the necessary information to understand rules and procedures.
- Induction and orientation training should take place over a period of time in a planned way, rather than as one long session. Formal and systematic follow-up should be planned.
- If the chef supervisor does not conduct the induction and orientation of the new team member, others will. Unplanned induction and orientation usually result in a negative view of the new job, the organization, and the chef supervisor by the new person.
- The communication style of the chef supervisor during induction and orientation should be open and concentrate on removing anxiety and building feelings of security in the new team member.
- Topics for the induction/orientation training sessions should include the kitchen department functions, team members' duties and responsibilities, pay and benefits, rules and procedures of the organization, and a tour of the entire organization.
- Formal evaluation of the induction and orientation training program should take place annually to ensure it meets with the needs and requirements of the organization and its future employees.

• A systematic follow-up to the initial induction and orientation should take place within at least one month to check on new team members' comfort with their new position.

DISCUSSION QUESTIONS

1. What are the major difference between induction and orientation?
2. Why conduct induction training programs?
3. Why does the highest proportion of team member turnover in the kitchen occur within the first 30 days?
4. What 10 critical items should form part of an orientation packet for new kitchen team members?
5. What are the advantages of receiving feedback on induction and orientation training programs?
6. What are the effects of unplanned induction and orientation with regard to new kitchen team members?
7. How long after the initial induction and orientation should systematic follow-up take place?

NOTES

1. Karen Eich Drummond, *The Restaurant Training Program*, John Wiley, New York, 1992, p. 1.
2. Herman Zaccarelli, *Training Managers to Train*, Crisp Publications, Los Altos, CA, 1988, p. 56.
3. Vincent H. Eade, *Human Resources Management in the Hospitality Industry*, Garsuch Sciarisbrick, Scottsdale, AZ, 1993, p. 173.
4. Cliff Barbee and Valerie Bott, "Customer Treatment as a Mirror of Employee Treatment," *Advanced Management Journal*, Spring 1991, p. 31.
5. Anna Katherine Jernigan, *The Effective Food Service Supervisor*, Aspen Publications, Rockville, MD, 1989.
6. Marion E. Haynes, *Stepping up to Supervisor*, Crisp Publications, Los Altos, CA, 1990, p. 76.
7. Jeff Weinstein, "Personnel Success," *Restaurants & Institutions*, Dec. 1992, p. 113.
8. John J. Hogan, "Turnover and What To Do About It," *Cornell HRA Quarterly*, Feb. 1992, p. 41.

14

Training Media and Technology

Outline

- Introduction
- Overhead projection
- Video tape and film
- Slide presentations
- Interactive computer training
- Multimedia technology
- Job aids
- Summary
- Discussion questions

Objectives

When you complete this chapter, you should be able to:

1. Describe major elements of media technology used to support the training efforts of the chef supervisor.

2. Outline applications of different media formats.

3. Understand the prior preparation required to use media technology effectively.

4. Define job aids and state the elements of good design for job aids.

INTRODUCTION

Instructional training media and technology provide powerful tools for making the training process highly effective. The two most important aspects of using instructional training media are knowing when it is appropriate to use during the training process and selecting the appropriate media. Instructional training media technology refers to those items that help the chef supervisor train and the kitchen team member learn.

Instructional media and technology have developed and expanded beyond the traditional scope of what were known as "audiovisual aids." Today, technology provides the training process with many media formats that enhance the chef supervisor's ability to effectively train. Among the most popular options available are:

- The overhead projector
- Video tape and/or film
- Slide presentations
- Interactive computer training
- Multimedia technology

Additional training aids include the chalkboard, flip-charts, and wall-charts. We learn more through our sense of sight than from any of the other senses. The best visual aid therefore is the real thing—the kitchen, its equipment, and food. Visual aids and technology are used when the real thing is not available or it costs too much or when giving job talks or providing background information such as costing, portion control, menu terms, and customer service focus. Use of media technology will stimulate interest and provide variety to your training session (1).

Instructional training media comprise a vast subject area. As in other brands of technology today, many people have become experts in small, narrowly defined segments of media, such as video or computer-assisted instruction. Progression from still visuals to the more complicated combinations of media increases costs. The main considerations in choosing and using media technology are its ease of preparation and use, its flexibility, its impact, and the relative costs associated with purchase or preparation. For each training topic the media technology that best supports the main idea of the training session should be selected.

Instructional media are tools. They can simplify instruction and help to achieve desired training results. They should be used to complement the chef supervisor's training skills, not replace them. The rules associated with media technology are:

1. They should be simple and uncluttered so that all kitchen team members can relate to them.
2. They should be planned and selected well in advance and be relevant and related to the training topic under instruction and associated with the training objective.
3. They should be used to reinforce and supplement the speech message, not as an end in themselves (too much media use during the training session is as bad as too little).
4. They should be clear, concise, and able to get the message across succinctly, particularly visual aids. They should not contain too much information and should contain material that is better illustrated visually rather than verbally.
5. They should be current.

OVERHEAD PROJECTION

Because of its many virtues, the overhead projector is the preferred piece of media technology of many trainers. This is because of its simplicity and ease of operation in normally lighted rooms. This allows the trainer to face the group, maintain eye contact, and observe the reactions of the group. This permits the trainer to adjust the training presentation if required. No special skills are required to operate the projector. Transparencies can be readily "home made." Materials for transparency production are inexpensive and simple to use.

Suggestions for using the overhead projector

- Ensure the projector is in working order before starting the presentation.
- Make sure each team member can see the screen clearly.
- Arrange transparencies in the correct order before the presentation.
- Use the on/off switch to control attention and place each transparency on the glass plate before switching the projector on.
- Turn off the projector if your discussion does not refer to a transparency.
- Always turn to face the group.
- Use the "revelation technique" by placing a sheet of paper under the transparency and revealing information one line at a time to control pace and attention.
- Do not block the view of the group by obstructing the projection.
- Practice using the projector and sequencing the transparencies.

Creating transparencies

- Keep them simple, no more than six words per line and six or fewer lines for each transparency.
- Select only key words and phrases that assist the team to remember each point. Don't put too much information on a transparency.
- Ensure each letter is readable from at least 10 feet away; use graphics or charts as appropriate.
- Check each transparency to ensure a united, informative, simple message.
- Do not copy prepared typewritten text onto acetate as overheads.
- Mount all transparencies in frames; use the frames to make prepared notes.
- Words alone seldom cover the entire message; consider the visual image.
- Use color functionally; we do not live in a black and white world, and color can add realism and evoke moods.

Overhead transparencies can be made with the use of hand-drawn colored letters and traced images using permanent felt-tipped markers. Additionally, modern computer software packages are readily available to produce overhead transparencies. These computer packages can also be projected onto a large screen with the aid of an LCD (liquid crystal display) unit positioned on the stage of an overhead projector, or by using a computer to TV monitor adaptor.

VIDEO TAPE AND FILM

Video tapes and films have particular advantages within the training arena. These two visual aids help stimulate interest on many topics. They can help motivate kitchen team members to try new behavior patterns. The content of videos and films can provide illustrations and models for the ideas and skills being presented.

Critical to the success of using video and film for training sessions is the preparation of the group prior to showing the film or video. This involves setting the scene by introducing the training context of the video or film and outlining the relevant learning objectives. Appropriate questions should be developed for evaluation and follow-up at the conclusion of the training session. There are many reasons why video and film are used in training; among these are:

- Orientation for new team members
- Training in job-related skills
- Development of interpersonal skills

- Introduction of new menu items
- Role plays
- Customer focus training

Before using video or film, some important steps must be considered:

- Check that the video tape or film is the correct size for the available equipment.
- Preview and identify the important points you want the group to get from viewing the video or film.
- Check that for groups of 25 or more, there is more than one TV monitor.
- Introduce the video or film; tell the group what they will see and why.
- Inform the group that there will be discussion after the presentation.
- Cue video or film to the beginning.
- Whenever possible, use a remote control.
- Monitor the training group's reaction to the video/film.
- At the end of the presentation, have the group discuss their reactions.
- Summarize the key points you wish the group to retain.
- When using film ensure that the screen is well positioned so that all training session participants can view the film comfortably. The size of the screen is determined by the 2×6 rule: The width should be half the distance from the first row of seats to the screen, and the height should be one-sixth of the distance from the last row of seats to the screen.

Part of the preparation for any training activity must be a thorough orientation to any equipment to be used. Chef supervisors, in their training role, must know how the equipment works and ensure that back-up equipment is available. Nothing is more awkward than when a VCR or a film projector does not work. This undermines the effectiveness of the training session. Finally, always practice before each presentation.

SLIDE PRESENTATIONS

Slide projectors are widely used as training visuals. A wide variety of "off-the-shelf" programs are readily available in many areas of kitchen training, including safety and sanitation procedures and processes. The use of color and photographs along with graphics is possible with these relatively easy-to-operate devices. Programs can be upgraded with little difficulty with sound (music and narration) played simultaneously. The same rules that apply to overhead transparencies equally apply to slides. However, slides are somewhat more expensive to produce. Slide presentations can be effectively generated using computer software packages. One drawback with using slide presentations is the requirement for a darkened room.

The assembly of slide programs is facilitated by today's automatic projectors, which advance sets of slides in sequence. Most automatic slide projectors also offer the convenience of remote control advancing of slides, allowing the chef supervisor to remain at the front of the room or off to the side while advancing the slides with a push button unit connected by wire to the projector. Wireless remote control is also available. A variety of slide projectors exist. The differences in most slide projectors generally refer to the receptacles that hold the slides. Slide projectors can be simple or they can include such capabilities as multiple projectors and fade-in, fade-out, and dissolve units. The use of these devices requires greater skill, preparation, and investment on the part of the chef supervisor. The most frequently used slides are the 2 × 2-inch 35-millimeter format (2).

There are eight possible ways a slide can be placed in a projector tray; seven of them are wrong. The following steps will assist in utilizing the slide projector more effectively:

- Number all slides in the order of presentation.
- Take each slide and hold it the way it is supposed to be seen on the screen, that is, right side up with the lettering running from left to right. Then place a spot on the bottom left-hand corner. This is known as the "thumb spot method" because the slide is turned upside down in the projector tray, with the thumb covering the "spot" as it is placed in the tray.
- Turn on the lamp, project a slide, and adjust the elevation of the front of the projector to center the light on the screen.
- Focus the image by adjusting the lens.
- Use a remote control advance device. This will allow you to stand at the side of the room and allow eye contact with the team.
- Employ visual variety. Mix the types of slides. Use word slides to break up the presentation.
- Limit discussion to each slide being presented.
- Begin and end with a "black" slide. A white flash on the screen at the beginning and end of a presentation is irritating to the eye.
- At the end of each presentation, turn off the lamp; allow the fan to run until the bulb is cool. Remove the electrical cord from the socket and fold it into place under the projector.
- Rotate the carousel to a position where it can be removed. Press the button down and lift off the carousel. Return the elevation knob to its storage place.

INTERACTIVE COMPUTER TRAINING

Undoubtedly the most exciting area of training media technology development has been the computer. Without a computer many training delivery systems would not be possible (3). With its virtually instantaneous response to trainee input and its extensive capacity to store and manipulate information, the computer can serve foodservice training enormously. As a training device it can include complete systems with which trainees interact.

Computer-based interactive training refers to a system that requires decisions and input from trainees. As technology expands and advances, more use of this training medium will be made in kitchens. Computers simplify the chef supervisor's job with regard to cost control procedures, pricing, nutritional analysis, product price variation, and inventory controls. Additionally, menu and recipe ingredients and numbers can be manipulated. Many prepared software programs are available for use in training in the kitchen.

Perhaps the greatest potential for using the computer as a training device lies in the application of *virtual reality*. It has been said that virtual reality's capabilities will revolutionize training. In its fullest realization virtual reality is "being there" with all the senses intact and enhanced, navigating through an artificial three-dimensional environment (4).

Advantages of this training format are that chef trainees can prepare, cook, and present dishes utilizing all essential culinary skills without the need to use high-cost food ingredients each time. Other possibilities of virtual reality as a training medium in the kitchen are:

- New team members could learn about the job by using computer simulations.
- Role plays could be developed to assess potential team members' hospitality attitudes.
- Menu items could be manipulated with regard to presentation.
- Touch screen responses from trainees can provide interaction on information presented.

One of the major advantages of interactive training is its requirement for trainee responses. Learners can respond by typing on a keyboard, touching the computer monitor screen, or manipulating objects connected to the system. By requiring frequent responses, interactive computer training captures a trainee's attention and holds that interest.

MULTIMEDIA TECHNOLOGY

Multimedia refers to the ability to use a computer to combine multiple media, text, graphics, sound, still images, and video in one single presentation. The key component is the computer because it enables interaction with these materials. Multimedia, in and of itself, is not instructional; it is simply a technology (5). Only when multimedia is applied to training objectives does it become a powerful training resource. Multimedia can make training materials more engaging through the provision of high-quality images and sound that engage multiple senses in the trainee. Additionally, multimedia can offer to the chef supervisor the ability to provide team members with a far greater degree of personal control over the training materials they are studying than is possible with more static training media. For example, team members can advance through a multimedia presentation at their own speed, reviewing where necessary and following up on topics of interest. Multimedia technology can allow the chef supervisor to tailor materials to the individual team member and to allow them to interact with these materials.

Computer-based multimedia sources include CD-ROM drives (compact disc read-only memory), VCRs (video cassette recorders), camcorders, broadcast TV, and videodisc players.

Learning happens via interaction. Multimedia technologies are not and never will be complete trainers. Learning will always require the input of the instructor (6).

JOB AIDS

The job aid is anything that will help the trainee to do the job when the chef supervisor is not present. Job aids include display boards with photographs of completed menu items and other items that assist memory. Additionally, reading materials can enhance learning as long as they are relevant and their purpose is clearly understood. The positive impact of job aids is increased when visual and reading materials are relevant to the team member's job situation and are used in conjunction with other training methods. Examples of job aids are:

- Books
- Pamphlets
- Checklists
- Wall charts
- Diagrams

A good job aid should:

- Be relevant
- Be simple
- Be well laid out
- Make an impact

Situations where a job aid might prove useful are:

- Where 100% observance of standard practice is required
- Where frequent changes occur that do not affect basic skills

- Where key procedural areas exist
- Where knowledge is infrequently desired but must be recalled accurately
- Where large "chunks" of memory are involved
- Where off-the-job training is brief and infrequent

Job aids can also shorten training time by helping the team member do the job and learn or acquire skills at the same time. They can supplement, but never replace, practical skills training. Reading materials alone may have little impact unless they are somehow tied to other follow-up activities.

SUMMARY

In general, instructional training media technology is used to support the speech element of instruction. Its main purpose is to increase understanding, *not* as a replacement for the training skills of the chef supervisor. It is possible to reduce a complex subject to simple understanding with the addition of media technology. The chief principles to observe in using media technology are knowing when to use it during the training process and selecting the appropriate technology. Too much media technology is as bad as none at all.

In using media technology, be sure the group can see the visuals you are presenting:

- They should be as clear, concise, and current as possible and be able to get the message across quickly and succinctly.
- They should not contain too much information and it should be material that is better illustrated rather than verbally described.
- Use color wherever possible in designing visuals.
- Design of projected visuals should be such that they draw the viewer's eye to the essential message.
- Projected visuals require special consideration. Check all equipment before training begins; ensure that the sound is loud enough. Match the correct format to film and video tape. Check the room lighting and locate the light switches.
- Do not use sophisticated computer media technology unless you are familiar with the software and the methods of integrating it into the training process. Finally, media technology is used to reinforce and supplement the training, not as an end in itself. Plan and develop the most attractive aid possible.

DISCUSSION QUESTIONS

1. What are the most popular media options used by the chef supervisor to support training?
2. What are the general rules associated with the use of media technology?
3. What are the advantages of using an overhead projector?
4. What are the conventions associated with creating transparencies?
5. What is critical to the success of using video and film for training?
6. What are the training topic areas where film or video presentations are particularly useful?
7. What advantage does the use of an overhead projector have over a slide projector relative to room lighting?
8. What are some of the potential training applications of interactive computer technology?
9. Why can multimedia offer a greater degree of control over the learning process?
10. When is it appropriate to use job aids?

NOTES

1. Robert Heinich, Michael Molenda, and James D. Russell, *Instructional Media and the New Technologies of Instruction*, Macmillan, New York, 1989, p. 7.
2. Ibid., p. 142.
3. B. Farnsworth and A. Shaw,"The Academy of Multimedia: A Quest for New Destinations," *T.H.E. Journal*, Feb. 1993.
4. "How Real Is Virtual Reality?" *New Media*, Jan. 1993.
5. Diane M. Gayescki, "De-mystifying Multi Media," *IABC Communications World*, April 1993.
6. Margaret Newman Wilson, "Multi Media: The Revolution Has Begun," *IABC Communications World*, Nov. 1993.

15

Training and Transactional Analysis

Outline

- Introduction
- Identifying ego states
- Crossed transactions
- Psychological games
- Summary
- Discussion questions

Objectives

When you complete this chapter, you should be able to:

1. Understand the elements of transactional analysis and its benefits to the training process.
2. State the physical and verbal aspects of the parent, adult, and child ego states.
3. Indicate differences between crossed and uncrossed transactions.

4. Recognize the benefits of using ego states to stimulate discussion relative to training sessions.

5. Identify psychological games that are often used by team members to mask hidden agendas.

INTRODUCTION

Transactional analysis is a wide-ranging set of theories and techniques that can be used by individuals and groups to enable them to grow and develop to their full potential. The framework of transactional analysis is based on the theory of personality and communication founded by Eric Berne, a Canadian psychotherapist who wrote the founding work of transactional analysis, *Games People Play*, in 1964 (1). It captured the interest of millions worldwide and has been reprinted many times. The book was well written, easy to understand, and made use of ordinary language. Many people felt the theories detailed in the book made sense of their experiences; helped them to understand their feelings, thoughts, and actions; and offered them alternative behaviors to cope with the difficulties encountered in personal and working life (2).

Essentially, transactional analysis is a tool that can help to improve interpersonal relations. It is a method of analysis by which one person can determine the basis from which another individual is communicating or interacting. Once this is established, it is then possible to decide how best to respond. It is a tool that can be used easily in the kitchen and in everyday work situations as well as during the training setting. As a trainer, anything the chef supervisor can do that helps to better understand where each individual team member is "coming from" and what their true feelings and dispositions are will contribute to successful training and supervision.

If an individual's behavior is observed over a period of time, it becomes clear that individual disposition changes. These changes manifest themselves in modes of speech, body language, interest, and attitudes. They do not remain constant; they fluctuate over time. According to transactional theory, there are three aspects or roles within each of us, the ego states of *parent, adult,* and *child*. These different ego states determine the way in which we communicate.

Berne based his theory on three obvious assertions:

1. Everyone has had parents (or substitute parents or caregivers) and everyone will have internalized consciously or unconsciously some of the views of these parents or parent figures.

2. Everyone is capable of behaving in a rational way, which means that each of us is capable of behaving according to the realities of the situation rather than reacting irrationally or purely in terms of emotions or prior conditioning.

3. Everyone sometimes reacts to situations the way they reacted to similar situations in the past.

IDENTIFYING EGO STATES

The following guide provides the basis for some of the verbal and physical aspects of the parent, adult, and child ego states:

Parent

Physical: Severe or stern expression, folded arms, furrowed brow, pointing finger, the "horrified" look, eyes to heaven; aggressive tone of voice, talking down to others; gestures of concern and helpfulness, patronizing others

Verbal: "Never, do, don't, ought, should, must, if I were you, the best thing for you to do . . . , don't worry, I'll take care of it." Examples of automatic responses are "disgusting, shocking, ridiculous, not again, stupid, typical, will they ever learn, what can you expect from them." These words MAY identify the parent, but the adult can also decide on the basis of reasoning that certain things are shocking, disgusting, stupid, etc.

Adult

Physical: The adult face is open and expressive. It shows interest and listening when appropriate. Active listening is one of the recognizable behaviors of the adult.

Verbal: The adult vocabulary includes such words as "what, where, why, when, who, how." Other words are "how much? comparative, true, false, I think, in my opinion, probably, possibly, likely, apparently, it seems," showing reflection and evaluation.

Adult-to-adult interaction provides the basis for both groups to be productively engaged in training, planning, decision making, and organizing. Crossed transactions between unparallel ego states will usually be counterproductive. Therefore, recognition of the ego state will direct the course of the interaction and determine its possible outcome.

Child

Physical: Teasing, carefree excitement, laughter, curiosity, giggling, pouting, tears, temper tantrums, sulking, downcast eyes, anxiety.

Verbal: "I wish, I want, I don't care, big, better, best, hey that's fantastic, what am I going to do now." The tone of voice can be loud, energetic, compliant, whining, defiant, and demanding.

The three ego states are commonly represented as three circles arranged vertically:

(P) The parent ego state

(A) The adult ego state

(C) The child ego state

The arrangement of these circles will have the parent on the top, the adult in the middle, and the child at the bottom. This does not imply a hierarchy exists. This is the basic structure of personality as described by Berne. It is the basis upon which the chef as supervisor or trainer can attempt to determine what ego state each kitchen team member is transacting in.

In most cases the adult creates the most positive basis for communication by treating the receiver on an adult or an equal basis. However, the parent and child ego states also have their use, the child for humor and the parent for directive behavior.

The following examples of how transactional analysis (the ego states) is related to the chef supervisor's role as a trainer demonstrate situations in which these ego states might be encountered in the kitchen:

Parent ego state: "You have to learn this technique."

Adult ego state: "You have been able to master all the other techniques up to now. I'm certain that with some coaching you will master this one too."

Child ego state: "I'll never be able to do this"

In some cases it appears as though some team members are programmed to communicate in certain ways. Many times this is true. If chefs adopt the parent ego state, they will automatically respond just as their parents did. The adult mode is somewhat more difficult to achieve and maintain. The three ego states identified by Berne—parent, adult, and child—can be further divided into different styles. Subdivisions of the parent ego state are *controlling parent, nurturing parent, natural child,* and *adapted child.* These different ego states are also sometimes referred to as the "tape recorder in your head." People function from the point of view of these remembered ego states.

Generally, parent and child are replays from our past; for example, in the parent ego state, attitudes, values, thoughts, and behaviors are copied from our parents, mainly during the first eight years of our lives. Similarly, Berne's theory states that the child ego states are replays of thoughts and feelings from our childhood. The adult ego state includes the ability to deal with situations in the "here and now" and involves being objective, logical, and rational.

The adult ego state is associated with the skills of problem solving and decision making: "Employing the concept of ego states gives us a method for checking our behavior and consciously selecting the most appropriate option for our current objective" (3).

The key contributing qualities of each ego state are:

Natural	Child: Friendliness, creativity
Adapted	Child: politeness, courtesy
Nurturing	Parent: nurturing, caring
Controlling	Parent: firmness, control
Adult:	Problem solving, identifying compromises

Problems may include:

Controlling parent	Being righteous, their way is best
Nurturing parent	Desire to take care of everyone
Adult	Clinically dismissing every idea
Natural child	Being silly, horseplay
Adapted child	Not participating, waiting to be asked

CROSSED TRANSACTIONS

Communication is a two-way process, and in this process transactional analysis is most beneficial. An example of transactional analysis might be: If a team member speaking in the adult mode is responded to as an adult, the communication is likely to be successful. If the responding team member is also speaking from the adult mode, so much the better. However, communication problems arise when one is speaking as an adult and is responded to in the child or parent mode. This is called a crossed transaction. First an example of an uncrossed (adult-to-adult) transaction:

| Chef supervisor | Tomorrow will be a busy day for the kitchen (*adult*) |
| Kitchen team member | Good, we'll be well prepared (*adult*) |

An example of a crossed transaction is:

| Chef supervisor | Tomorrow will be a busy day for the kitchen (*adult*) |
| Kitchen team member | Not again, I don't know how we are going to cope (*child to parent*) |

Uncrossed transactions occur when the ego state addressed is the ego state that responds. If, for example, the controlling parent is used to address the adapted child and the reply is from the adapted child, we have an uncrossed transaction. The rule for an uncrossed transaction is that communication can continue indefinitely. However, crossed transactions usually mean that a break in real communication will occur. This does not necessarily mean that all crossed transactions are bad and that all uncrossed transactions are good. If, for example, a team member is shouting at the chef supervisor from a controlling parent ego state about a mistake made and the responding supervisor is in an adapted child ego state, he or she may respond with an uncrossed transaction by apologizing. If the apology is ignored, it is appropriate to break the communication and for the chef supervisor to shift to adult-to-adult communication for some problem-solving discussion.

Know your ego states. Use the adult to stimulate healthy discussion on the kitchen training sessions. Use the controlling parent to tell team members what the rules are concerning the sessions. Use the nurturing parent to reassure team members regarding their ability to assimilate the training methods to be used. Use the natural child to bring fun and excitement into the training sessions. Use the adapted child to be polite and courteous to team participants. At the end of each training session review what happened. Select some areas of the training session you were unhappy with. Analyze the transactional ego state used and consider what other ego states might have worked better. Determine what the likely effects might have been, decide which offers the best ego state for future training sessions, and resolve to handle these areas more skillfully next time.

PSYCHOLOGICAL GAMES

In *Games People Play* Eric Berne outlined a series of psychological games that people engage in. These repetitive and unsatisfactory interactions usually have negative effects.

People play psychological games, often in an unaware way, and tend to choose as spouse and business associates those people who will play the role opposite to their own. This also holds true for foodservice organizations. Although there are many different games, in each one there are three basic elements:

1. A series of complementary transactions that on the surface seem plausible
2. An ulterior transaction that is the hidden agenda
3. A negative payoff that concludes the game and is the real purpose for playing

Games tend to be repetitious. People find themselves saying the same words in the same way, only the time and place may change. Perhaps the replay contributes to what is often described as "I feel as if I've done this before."

Even though some people have favorite ego states, they also have a favorite game role. Games may involve two or three of the dramatic roles of *victim, persecutor,* and *rescuer*—the manipulative roles learned in childhood. Games played from the persecutor or rescuer role serve to reinforce a negative position about others.

Games prevent honest, intimate, open relationships between the players. Yet people play them because they fill up time and provoke attention (4).

The Game of Yes, But!

The game is likely to be Yes, But if the chef supervisor in a meeting presents a problem and then shoots down all suggestions. A person who plays Yes, But does so to maintain positions such as "nobody's going to tell me what to do" or "people are stupid." In childhood they had parents who either tried to give them all the answers or didn't give any answers, so they took a stand against them.

To initiate this game, one player presents a problem in the guise of soliciting advice from one or more other players. If hooked, the other player advises, "Why don't you . . . ?" The initiator discounts all suggestions with "Yes, but . . . ," followed by *reasons* the advice won't work. Eventually the "why don't you" advice givers give up and fall silent. This is the payoff of the game to prove the position "parents can't tell me anything" or "parents are stupid."

In this game the child ego state "hooks" the nurturing parent in the other player. Although the transactions may appear to be adult to adult on the surface ("I've got a problem. Tell me the answer."), the ulterior transaction is child to parent ("I've got a problem. Just try to tell me the answer. I won't let you.").

The Game of Kick Me

In the game of Kick Me the player does something to provoke another player to put him or her down. Team member states, "I stayed out late last night and didn't prepare the mise en place for this morning." Chef supervisor responds, "Sorry about that. This is the last day I can give you extra time off." (Ulterior: Yes you are a bad boy and here is your kick.)

Though he or she may deny it, a person who is used to the game of Kick Me tends to attract others who can play the complementary hand and are willing to "kick."

The Game of Harried

Harried is a common game acted out to justify an eventual collapse or depression. Chef supervisors who play Harried say "yes" to everything, volunteer to come early and work late, take on additional assignments, and bring work home. For a period of time they are able to act like Superman, but eventually appearances begin to reflect this harried state. They are unable to finish work and their physical and mental health deteriorates. They collect and save so many feelings of depression that they finally collapse, so depressed they are unable to function. Other variations of this game are Harried Chef, Harried Manager, Harried Purveyor, Harried Waitperson, Harried Supervisor, etc.

The Game of See What You Made Me Do

This game is played in the kitchen when a team member makes a mistake while the chef supervisor is watching from behind. Rather than taking responsibility for the error, the team member turns to the supervisor and angrily says, "See what you made me do!" thus blaming someone else for the mistake. If this happens often enough, the supervisor may feel guilty and leave the team member alone. In this way the purpose of the game is fulfilled—isolation. Another See

What You Made Me Do player may be collecting feelings of purity instead of anger, "After all, it's not *my* fault. It's *your* fault I made my mistake. I'm pure."

The Game of Stupid

Stupid is a game played when a secretary "accidentally" puts a letter in a bottom drawer and then, later, when it's rediscovered, makes a fuss, complaining, "How could I have done such a stupid thing! This was that letter that you wanted in Washington, DC last month."

Other Popular Games

Themes of other games that are often easily recognized are the following:

> *I'm only trying to help you*: "My advice is so good, why do you want to think for yourself and reject my ideas when I'm only trying to help you?"
>
> *Wooden leg*: "Surely you can't expect much from me when I have such a handicap," i.e., wrong race, wrong background, etc.
>
> *See how hard I tried*: "Don't blame me if things turn out wrong. After all, see how hard I tried."
>
> *Uproar*: "I'm stronger than you are. You stupid fool; you never do anything right."
>
> *Now I've got you*: "I've caught you making a mistake and will now make you suffer."

Games may be foiled by a refusal to play the expected hand or a refusal to give a payoff. For example, refusing to give advice or suggestions to a Yes, But player usually stops the game. There are many ways to stop a game. Team members may:

- Give an unexpected response
- Stop exaggerating their own weaknesses or strengths
- Stop exaggerating the weaknesses and strengths of others
- Structure more of their time with activities, intimacy, and fun
- Stop playing the rescuer, helping those who don't need help
- Stop playing the persecutor, criticizing those who don't need it
- Stop playing the victim, acting helpless or dependent when really able to stand on their own two feet

Why do we play psychological games? One of the major problems is that most people are unaware that they are. There are, according to Julie Hay, writing in *Transactional Analysis for Trainers*, "apparent advantages that accrue from playing psychological games, we find it hard to stop the repetitive sequences, even when we become aware of them" (5). When the game preferences of different team members have been identified, it is possible to determine how these interactions impact the culture of the training session or activity in the kitchen. Having spotted a game, it is then possible for the chef supervisor to work out how to behave differently so as to avoid it in the future. Thomas Quick states: "Transactional Analysis doesn't provide a universal explanation for every aspect of human behavior, but it provides some realistic bases. In a very short time using the transactional model you could train employees, especially those who deal with the public, so as to effectively deal with the various kinds of behavior they encounter" (6).

SUMMARY

Transactional analysis is a tool that can help to improve interpersonal relations. It is a method of analysis by which one person can determine the basis from which another individual is communicating or interacting. Understanding transactional analysis contributes to successful training and supervision.

Developed by Eric Berne—who noted that if an individual's behavior is observed over a period of time, it becomes clear that that individual's disposition changes—it assumes three aspects: the ego states of parent, adult, and child, and each determines the way in which we communicate.

These different ego states may be subdivided again into the natural child, adapted child, nurturing parent, and controlling parent. Ego states are also referred to as the "tape recorder in your head." Generally, parent and child ego states are replays from our past. Each is indicative of a particular set of values, attitudes, thoughts, and behaviors from our past. The adult ego state deals with the "here and now." Knowing and understanding crossed and uncrossed transactions from different ego states facilitate successful communication, supervision, and training.

People play psychological games, often in an unconscious way. Although there are many different games, each has three basic elements:

1. A series of complementary transactions that on the surface appear plausible
2. An ulterior transaction that is the hidden agenda
3. A negative payoff that concludes the game and is the real purpose for playing

Chef supervisors can assess the climate and culture that exist in the kitchen for training by spotting the various games that team members play.

DISCUSSION QUESTIONS

1. How can transactional analysis assist the training effort?
2. What are the three ego states?

3. Why is the adult ego state conducive to learning?
4. What are the subdivisions of the parent and child ego states?
5. What are crossed transaction and uncrossed transaction?
6. Why do most psychological games have hidden agendas?
7. How can transactional analysis improve interpersonal relations within the kitchen?

NOTES

1. Eric Berne, *Games People Play*, Grove Press, Penguin, London, 1968.
2. Brian Thomas, *Total Quality Training: The Quality Culture and Quality Trainer*, McGraw-Hill, Berkshire, England, 1992, p. 122.
3. Julie Hay, *Transactional Analysis for Trainers*, McGraw-Hill, Berkshire, England, 1992, p. 83.
4. Adapted from Eric Bern, *Games People Play*, Grove Press/Penguin, London, 1968.
5. Julie Hay, *Transactional Analysis for Trainers*, McGraw-Hill, Berkshire, England, 1992, p. 136.
6. Thomas Quick, "Simple Is Hard, Complex Is Easy, Simplistic Is Impossible," *Training & Development Journal*, May 1990, p. 96.

16

Managing and Utilizing Time

Outline

- Introduction
- Time management misconceptions
- Choosing priorities
- Time leaks
- Time management skills
- Summary
- Discussion questions

Objectives

When you complete this chapter, you should be able to:

1. Identify issues associated with unproductive time use.
2. Develop a plan for effective use of time.
3. Recognize the pitfalls of procrastination.

4. List the steps that cause time leaks.

5. Distinguish between being busy and productive.

INTRODUCTION

Lack of time is perhaps the most often used excuse in kitchens for not doing certain things: "It's a great idea, but we don't have time to do that here." How often have chef supervisors been overheard to say, "If we only had more time" or "We don't have time to get too heavily involved with fancy dishes or presentations here." Therefore, often things that impact on TQM, such as quality culinary practices and motivating the kitchen team, are not done because of "lack of time." The fact is that implementing agreed-upon quality standards of cooking and presentation of menu items is not a question of time, but rather a question of poor planning, supervision, and leadership and a failure to execute good mise en place.

Timing is a fundamental element of all chef training, and it is ingrained in every aspect of cooking, preparation, and presentation of food items.

Lack of sufficient time to implement quality foodservice often results from the selection of complex recipes inappropriate for the skill level of those preparing them. Failure to use a team approach to menu development and a failure to anticipate the constraints of busy meal service periods along with the absence of training plans all contribute to a sense of lack of time. Therefore, lack of time is not the culprit of shoddy culinary practice; poor supervision, training, and management are.

Time management means organizing yourself better to get what you want from your time. Its aim is not to fill up your life with activity, but to help you identify what you want out of life and plan how to go about getting it (1).

Perhaps you have read these lines from an unknown author:

> If you had a bank that credited your account each morning with $86,400, that carried over no balance from day to day, allowed you to keep no cash in account, and every evening cancelled whatever part of the amount you failed to use during the day, just what would you do? Draw out every cent, of course!
>
> Well, you have such a bank and its name is *Time*. Every morning it credits you with 86,400 seconds. Every night it rules off as lost, whatever part of this sum you failed to invest in good purposes. It allows no overdrafts. Each day it opens a new account for you, each night it burns the record of the day. If you fail to use the day's deposits, the loss is yours. There's no going back; there's no drawing against tomorrow.
>
> You must live in the present . . . on today's deposits. Invest it so as to get from it the utmost in health, happiness, and success.

If you agree with this message, then a logical question you should ask yourself is: How am I using my time in relation to personal goals and the goals of my foodservice organization?

When work time is managed effectively by the chef supervisor, it can be prioritized so as to organize all of the elements crucial to the TQM of the kitchen operation. The fact is, most people waste time, but productive chef supervisors waste less of it. There is no secret to the principles and techniques of time management. However, they can only work if they are adhered to.

Time management on an individual level is not concerned solely with the amount of time spent on certain issues in terms of minutes, hours, days, or months. It is of course wise and prudent to track how you spend time every day. This helps to determine where you might be wasting it. The real goal is to free up time to get more done. The first step is to examine often-held assumptions about time and how these assumptions may prevent time from being used productively in the kitchen.

TIME MANAGEMENT MISCONCEPTIONS

There is never enough time to accomplish what is important in the kitchen. Wrong. There is always enough time to accomplish what is important, and what can be postponed should be. It is this decision that determines whether time is being used wisely.

Some chefs use the following as an excuse for poor time management practices: "Other people make too many demands on my time." Others do not control how you choose to spend your time, you do. If other people have that much control over your time, you are letting them intimidate you and are not behaving as a leader. Learning to say no can be one of the most effective time savers. When saying no, be courteous; give a brief explanation of why you cannot comply with a request and avoid a prolonged discussion about the reasons.

Busy schedules are used as reasons for not being able to prioritize work: "To control your time and your life, it is not only possible to prioritize, it is essential. Set priorities and stick to them" (2). Learn to delegate. This frees up time to tackle more creative projects that require attention. Other erroneous misconceptions of time management frequently cited by chef supervisors are:

- "I'm much too busy to plan any activities."
- "If only there were more hours in the day."
- "I can't devote that much time every day to one project."
- "I've so much to do I don't know where to start."
- "I prefer to do the simple tasks first and save the big ones for later in the day."

These statements usually are reasons to cover the lack of self-discipline and poor individual planning ability. Working more hours every day produces mental and physical fatigue and devours personal time. Work smarter, not longer. The busier the chef supervisor, the more important it is to take time out to plan. Planning is key to effective time management. Without a plan chef supervisors are unlikely to be in control of their workday. They will react to events as they happen rather than being the ones who set the agenda.

Procrastination is the thief of time. Sometimes procrastination kicks in as a way to avoid tasks that are unpleasant or uninteresting. Determine to deal with these areas head-on; steady progress is a great motivator. The most misleading of all assumptions about time is that "later" seldom arrives. Time cannot be lengthened or shortened, only used, and it cannot be saved and used later. You cannot choose to not use it. Either you use the moment or you lose it forever.

"Never put off until tomorrow what you can do today" (3). This familiar adage was written by the Earl of Chesterfield in 1749 and is clearly a warning against procrastination. However, just because you can do something now does not necessarily mean that you should do it now. Sometimes you need to choose priorities.

CHOOSING PRIORITIES

Obviously, all tasks and projects do not have the same importance. Chefs often feel as if they are under pressure to respond to situations or to persons exerting the greatest pressure. This causes some chefs to solve problems in the order in which they arise, do easy work first, or take care of the hard work first, on the assumption that doing so is the fastest way to get rid of it. Dealing with matters in this way should be avoided at all costs. "Lining up your ducks . . . its origins are obscure, but its meaning is transparent: if you're dealing with things in a logical, orderly sequence, you're sure to bring efficiency and results to your efforts" (4). Dealing with matters in the order they occur in the kitchen is fine in some circumstances, for example, expediting table orders. But in most other situations it is an unproductive use of time: "Important does not necessarily mean urgent, nor does urgent necessarily mean important" (5).

The simplest and most effective way to prioritize your time is to analyze how you spend your time in an average day and week. Since everyone has the same amount of time, the key question is, are you using the time effectively? Are you doing things that are unnecessary? If you are satisfied that you are doing necessary work only you can do, the next step is to set priorities: "Make a list of things to do. Compare what you want to do with what you are already doing or planning to do. The result will be a priority list that tells you what to do first, what to do next, and what to do last" (6). Keep a time log of a typical week. Disorganized priorities are common ground for procrastination. Of all TQM procedures, none is more relevant to time management than choosing to prioritize issues of quality.

TIME LEAKS

Time "leaks" are working habits and practices that eat up time unproductively. From the following list, check if these time leaks apply to you:

- Spending too much time on problems brought to you by a team member
- Oversupervising the kitchen team
- Undersupervising with consequent crises
- Scheduling less important work before more important work
- Starting a job before thinking it through
- Leaving jobs before completion
- Doing things that can be delegated to a team member
- Doing things that can be done by modern equipment
- Doing things that aren't part of your job
- Spending too much time on your previous area of interest or competence
- Doing unproductive things from sheer habit
- Keeping too many, too complicated, or overlapping records
- Pursuing projects you probably can't achieve
- Paying too much attention to low-yield projects
- Failing to anticipate crises
- Handling too wide a variety of duties
- Shrinking from unfamiliar duties
- Failing to build barriers against interruptions
- Allowing conferences and discussions to wander
- Allowing conferences and discussions to continue after their purpose is fulfilled
- Conducting unnecessary meetings, visits, and phone calls
- Chasing trivial data after the main facts are in
- Engaging in personal work or conversations before starting business work
- Socializing at great length between tasks

TIME MANAGEMENT SKILLS

You can make the most effective use of your time by planning and getting organized. The reason for managing time is to be sure that you have enough of it to meet specific goals at some point in the future. Most people are familiar with personal planners or calendars. They can provide a convenient place to keep daily lists, plus extra space to keep records and charts that are essential for planning and are simple, yet powerful time management aids. It is important to remember that calendars and personal planner diaries are only useful if you use them. Reserve blocks of time to get the job done and develop the habit of planning your time effectively:

- Make weekly and daily to-do lists in order of priority. Check off each task as it is completed. This will provide a feeling of accomplishment at the end of the day.
- Plan what you are going to do at least one day in advance. If you know what tasks await you tomorrow, organize tomorrow's to-do list today. Schedules serve as a disciplining tool. They help you do what you plan.
- Plan telephone calls in advance. By doing this, you will know what you want to cover and can reduce time spent on the phone.
- Plan meetings (one-on-one or with the entire kitchen team) in advance. If you call the meeting, take control of the agenda and stay on the subject.
- Evaluate your time management several times during the day. Take a look at how you're doing about one-third of the way through the work day and again two-thirds of the way through. Will you meet your objectives for the day? If not, what got in the way? Should it take priority over what you planned to do?
- Learn to handle common distractions. Controlling the time taken by drop-in visitors requires both courtesy and good judgment. Limit the number of people you invite to the kitchen. If you need to be with someone, go to his or her work area. It is much more difficult to get people to leave your work area than it is for you to leave theirs.
- Unsolicited business mail, often referred to as "junk mail," often arrives daily in an unending flood and makes demands on your time. Have someone sort your mail, giving guidelines on what you want to see and what should be routed to other team members.
- Communicate efficiently. Keep memos and phone conversations short. You save your time thinking, speaking, and writing and team members' time listening, reading, and understanding.
- The ability to make timely decisions is often hampered by an unwillingness to face unpleasant decisions and being overcautious.
- Complete one job at a time. Important tasks need plenty of uninterrupted time and cannot be completed between other activities. This wastes time. Each time you restart, you need to get familiar with the project again.
- Meetings should be planned with objectives in mind. Avoid unnecessary behavior; keep input relevant and factual. Some of the reasons people consider meetings time wasters include that they can take too much time to cover too little material or they don't start or finish on time.
- Learn to say no. In some cases, the demands placed on your time will exceed your ability to accommodate all of them. When you take on more than you can handle, quality begins to suffer. Saying no does not have to offend someone. When you can offer an alternative, things can be worked out to everyone's satisfaction.

Chef Talk: "Plan the Work and Work the Plan"

It has been said that time can't be managed. But what can be managed are activities and how we "spend" time! And all the experts agree. Managing our activities begins with good planning. So, by knowing what's important for us—planning our work and working our plan—we become wise chef managers.

We have to make time for getting big tasks done every day. Plan your daily workload in advance, single out relatively small tasks that must be done immediately, then tackle the large tasks to completeness. In all, planning is the power tool for achievement!

In the foodservice industry today there are greater demands and challenges than ever before. Especially as chefs we don't always believe we have enough time to meet our re-

sponsibilities to our company, our employees, and our families. That's a negative belief, not a positive belief.

My day starts with an exercise program at 6.30 a.m.! After this is completed, I am ready to face number 2 on my list of priorities, networking with my staff regarding their needs for the day. So, as each item on the list is completed, I move to the next task.

In addition, there are other ventures or affiliations that I am involved with, and thus, I need to balance my time, concentrating on accomplishing the greatest results with the least effort expended. Thus, making decisions and acting on these decisions will reflect leadership and a positive image to my staff.

Through dedication, planning, and goal-oriented thinking, I believe any chef can achieve great success in his or her future endeavors.

Bert Cutino, CEC, AAC, Co-Owner, The Sardine Factory, Monterey, CA

- Delegate tasks to other team members. To delegate (not dump) tasks is a key time management skill. Sometimes you do not have time to delegate—the unexpected happens, and you must deal with it yourself. There is only one protection here: Anticipate the unexpected before it occurs.

- Organize your work area. Do you spend valuable time looking for things? Consider how often you need each item in the kitchen. The kitchen should be organized so it is easy to complete your normal tasks.

- Avoid diversions and interruptions to the extent that you can. Some chef supervisors achieve this by scheduling an hour of quiet time during the day. During this quiet time, close your door, turn off the phone, and concentrate on whatever needs attention.

- One of the greatest time cheaters is spending too much time talking to people who won't go away. Learn to be firm; say "I don't mean to be rude, but I must get back to my work."
- Be flexible. Allow some slack time in your schedule. Emergencies occur. Projects will occasionally run over the time allocated.

Bruce Tepper states: "Being busy has nothing to do with productivity. Maximizing how [to] use your time means a great deal more. It will open either more free time, or more time for creating new ideas" (7). Get an accurate indication of how you actually use time and decide where you can make improvements. Work you don't have to do is work you don't need time to do. This does not mean shrinking your responsibilities or "passing the buck." An important part of being a good chef supervisor is knowing what tasks can be best done by you and those you can delegate to other team members. As a supervisor your job is not just to do things, it is also to organize and coordinate the kitchen team. The following are some time savers:

- Use waiting time. If you find yourself waiting for an appointment, don't think of it as a waste of time, but as a gift of time. Use it constructively: to relax, to ponder a decision, to review your daily checklist, to read a food book or foodservice industry magazine article. Always carry a pen and notebook to write down ideas.
- Combine activities. Discuss related matters over lunch.
- Have a place for everything and keep everything in its place. (mise en place). If something is worth having, it's worth knowing where it is when you want it.
- Learn to master computer programs relative to kitchen operations. Maintain all menus and recipes in computers. Learn to type. Reduce the amount of paperwork in the kitchen.
- Schedule some "togetherness time." Time management should not segregate you from the rest of the kitchen team. It should help you to reach your team-building, coaching, and TQM goals by enabling you to communicate with all team members.
- Spend your time as if you had to buy it. Before you spend an hour reading a report or going to a meeting, ask yourself, "Would I spend my own money to do this?" If you look at your time as a financial investment and monitor how you spend it, you will waste less of it.
- Maintain a regular physical exercise program. Exercising can help reduce stress. It also helps to maintain a sense of balance, discipline, order, and control in your life. You'll feel better, look better, and like yourself more. Personal time is not a luxury or something to postpone until you can fit it into your schedule. It is a requirement for maintaining a proper sense of balance and control in your life.

- Constantly ask yourself, "Is this the best use of my time right now?" Time management aims to make you more relaxed and gives you more time to relax in.

SUMMARY

Everyone can use their time better, particularly busy chef supervisors. Look at how your time is presently being used. Be sure you are doing necessary work and work that only you can do rather than busy work. Do not confuse lack of time to complete tasks with lack of self-discipline or poor supervisory skills. Maintain a balance between you controlling your time and other people controlling it. Learn to prioritize tasks and say no to demands of low priority that may overload you. Trade off low-priority commitments for high-priority ones that come up unexpectedly in the kitchen. Learn to plan time. The busier a chef supervisor is, the more important it is to take time out to plan. Planning is key to effective time management.

Time leaks are working practices that eat up time unproductively. The reason for managing time is to ensure that there is enough of it to meet specific goals at some point in the future. Develop time management skills and become disciplined in their application in terms of personal planners, diaries, and calendars. Provide time in schedules for the unexpected. You cannot anticipate everything that will happen, so leave time each day to handle crises. Consider investment time. This is the careful investment of time that not only is useful but also has the benefit of further payoff in terms of new skills. Time management is not a matter of dealing only with isolated activities. It is a process that goes on and on over a lifetime, involving thousands of activities.

DISCUSSION QUESTIONS

1. Why is effective use of time critical to the success of total quality management?
2. Why is the real goal of time management to free up time?
3. What are the elementary techniques that may be used to free up time?
4. How can the use of a time log assist the chef supervisor in prioritizing work?
5. What are time leaks?
6. How does the use of calendars or personal planners aid in time management?
7. What is the meaning of the statement "Being busy has nothing to do with productivity"?
8. What is investment time and how might it be used by chef supervisors?

NOTES

1. Barrie Hobson and Mike Scally, *Time Management: Conquering the Clock*, Pfeiffer & Co., San Diego, CA, 1993, p. 84.
2. Thomas J. Quick, "The Art of Time Management," *Training*, Jan. 1989, p. 60.

3. Robert Hochheiser, *Time Management*, Barron's, New York, 1992.

4. Marc Mancini, *Time Management*, Irwin Inc., New York, 1994, p. 73.

5. Alfred W. Travers, *Supervision Techniques and New Dimensions*, Regents/Prentice-Hall, Englewood Cliffs, NJ, 1993, p. 111.

6. Robert Hochheiser, *Time Management*, Irwin Inc., New York, 1992, p. 15.

7. Bruce B. Tepper, *The New Supervisor Skills for Success*, Irwin Inc., New York, 1994, p. 43.

17

Recruiting and Selecting Kitchen Team Members

Outline

Objectives

When you complete this chapter, you should be able to:

1. Identify the use of job descriptions.
2. Define various recruitment techniques employed to attract a pool of qualified job candidates.

3. Describe the legal issues associated with recruitment and selection of job applicants.

4. Understand the steps in the screening of potential new team members.

5. Describe different types of interviews used to screen applicants.

6. List the steps to be considered when interviewing potential team members.

7. State appropriate and inappropriate questioning techniques.

8. Understand elements associated with the hiring decision-making process.

INTRODUCTION

Finding and hiring the best people for the kitchen team is an important element of the chef supervisor's job. All recruitment and hiring decisions should be consistent with the vision and TQM philosophy of the foodservice organization. Good chef supervisors recognize that the main contributor to the success of an organization is the quality of its team members. People do make the difference. When the right people are chosen as the kitchen team, a winning total quality culinary operation develops.

Recruiting and staffing have received great attention these days because of the many laws and procedural safeguards in place, and the chef supervisor has an important role to play in this process. The notion is that the foodservice TQM mission is better served when staff is involved. The staffing process within the kitchen is no more complicated than most other aspects of the chef supervisor's job.

Clearly, what is required is a shared responsibility in this area. All involved management and team leaders should be allowed to contribute, but the final word should be left with the chef supervisor and not management. Making the chef supervisor responsible for final selection will result in a more cohesive and productive kitchen team. After all, the chef understands best what qualities are required to make a winning kitchen team and can usually better determine who is qualified. Involving chef supervisors in the selection process will also ensure that those selected for the kitchen team will have a greater sense of commitment to the team, since it was the team leader, the chef supervisor, who hired them. Conversely, the supervisor will have a greater stake in the new team member's success.

JOB DESCRIPTIONS

Job descriptions are used to format what the essential and desirable skills of a team member should be. They are similar to a good recipe. Just as a recipe helps the chef assemble the ingredients and states the time and temperature required to complete the dish, so does the job description help in choosing the

Job description
Advertising
Recruitment
Selection
Orientation
Training
Appraisal

Figure 4   Sequence from job description to appraisal.

right person. However, to make a great dish, the chef also needs intuitive skills based on experience. A well-developed job description can also be used as a checklist for orientation, training, and performance appraisal and evaluation. (See Figure 4.)

RECRUITMENT

Recruitment involves seeking and attracting a pool of people from which qualified candidates for a kitchen team position can be chosen. The more applicants there are for a position on the team, the better chance the chef supervisor has of selecting the right person. The key to successful recruitment is to begin the process well in advance of any openings within the team.

It has often been said that a foodservice organization's reputation precedes them. Therefore, the level of perception of a quality work environment can determine the quality level of a job applicant.

There are many ways to begin searching for new team members. Recruitment can be formal or informal. It can be done internally or externally. The most reliable methods include:

- Advertising in newspapers and trade publications
- Asking friends, customers, or suppliers
- Culinary colleges, local chefs' associations, and employment agencies
- Reviewing past applicants
- Job fairs and networking with other foodservice organizations

In some areas of the United States, the public employment service is also a good source for recruitment. Private employment agencies provide another route. When using this service, the new team member in some instances pays the agency, but in most cases it is the employer who pays. Charges can range from 10 to 50 percent of the first month's or year's salary.

Networking is mostly a positive recruitment source. It can yield good results but can also cause problems. If a team member is recommended by a colleague and turns out to be unsatisfactory and must be "let go," the colleague who made the recommendation may be unhappy or angry about the outcome.

Whatever the method used, it must always be done in compliance with civil rights legislation in order to avoid discrimination.

Obviously, the best recruitment philosophy is to seek out quality people rather than accept what comes through various routes. This is the essence of recruitment. Active recruitment is the basis on which good chef supervisors acquire the best team members. They work on attracting talented chefs rather than hoping that qualified people will appear. This process of recruitment says to a potential team member "you are someone special and I want you on my team." In the world of TQM and empowered teams, recruitment is all important. It is the basis for culinary success.

Finding people who respond to your quality operational goals is critical. Without the right esprit de corps it will be almost impossible to effect quality at each step. When the best possible "neatness of fit" between people and organization occurs, you have recruited an asset to the organization, not just a "warm body."

Seeking out qualified people through recruitment helps to reduce training costs and contributes to retaining that team member for a greater length of time. One of the disadvantages of active recruitment is that other foodservice operators see this practice as "poaching," stealing another organization's employees. In the final analysis, however, it is the recruit who decides whether to take the job offer.

LEGAL IMPLICATIONS

It is important that chef supervisors and management consider the potential for discrimination in employment advertisements or notices. Title VII of the 1964 Civil Rights Act prohibits the use of phraseology that may be discriminatory. Care should be taken with regard to gender as part of the job title. The best descriptions of team openings should be gender neutral. Other potential descriptions or requirements that contravene the act are the requirement of a photograph, any reference to disability, religion, age, health, height, weight, marital status, citizenship, or ethnicity; or disbarring in some way any applicant who may be qualified. However, if there is a bona fide occupational qualification (BFOQ) related to the advertised team position, then it is reasonable to include certain elements and requirements. According to Vincent Eade, in his book *Human Resource Management in the Hospitality Industry*: "If a hotel wanted to staff its Asiatic restaurant only with Asiatics in order to create an authentic atmosphere, pre-employment inquiries aimed at determining national origin would be considered a BFOQ inquiry and not designed to discriminate" (1).

Additionally, the Equal Employment Opportunity Commission (EEOC) encourages all organizations to avoid recruiting primarily by employee referral because this practice can perpetuate the current composition of the foodservice organization. If, for example, minorities and females are not well represented at all levels, then reliance on employee referral can also be considered discriminatory.

Legislation covering equal employment opportunities sets out strict legal criteria. Its purpose is to acquaint employers with the legal framework for recruiting and selecting new team members. Numerous laws influence recruitment and selection, and most are concerned with providing equal employment opportunity for all potential team members.

Civil rights laws state that employers may not discriminate in employment on the basis of an individual's race, religion, color, sex, national origin, marital status, age, "family" relationship, mental or physical handicaps, or juvenile record that has been expunged (2). Foodservice employers may not retaliate against in any way or discharge employees who report, complain about, or oppose discriminatory practices or file or participate in the complaint process. The following list summarizes the major pieces of employment legislation.

Equal Pay Act of 1963: Prohibits sex-based discrimination in rates of pay for men and women working in the same or similar jobs.

Civil Rights Act (1964): (as amended in 1972): Prohibits discrimination based on race, sex, color, religion, or national origin. Title VII of the Civil Rights Act of 1964 applies to private sector employers with 15 or more employees.

Executive Orders 11246 (1965) and 11375 (1967): Prohibits discrimination on the basis of race, sex, color, religion, or national origin; requires affirmative action. Federal contractors and subcontractors with contracts in excess of $10,000; employers with 50 or more employees and contracts in excess of $50,000.

Age Discrimination in Employment Act (ADEA) (1967): Prohibits discrimination against individuals who are at least 40 years of age but less than 70. An amendment eliminated mandatory retirement at age 70 for employees of companies with 20 or more employees.

Pregnancy Discrimination Act (1978): This act was an amendment to Title VII of the 1964 Civil Rights Act. Its purpose is to prevent the exclusion of a pregnant woman from an employment opportunity based on pregnancy.

Immigration Reform and Control Act (1986): Prohibits the hiring of illegal aliens. The act also prohibits employers from discrimination against job applicants on the basis of their citizenship status or national origin.

Americans with Disabilities Act (ADA) (1990): Prohibits employers from discrimination in employment decisions against qualified individuals with disabilities. Employment activities covered under this law include job application procedures, hiring, firing, advancement, compensation, training, recruitment, tenure, layoffs, leaves, fringe benefits, and all other employment-related activities.

Equal Employment Opportunities Commission (EEOC): This agency was created under the Civil Rights Act of 1964 to administer Title VII of the act and to ensure equal employment opportunity. Its powers were expanded in 1979. Originally, the EEOC was responsible for investigating discrimination based on race, color, religion, sex, or national origin. Now, however, it is also responsible for investigating equal-pay violations and handicapped and age discrimination. Preemployment guidelines have been developed by the EEOC to help employers to phrase application forms and interview questions in a nondiscriminatory manner. The EEOC ensures that all applicants are afforded the same employment opportunities. Chef supervisors and managers must be aware that discrimination practices, even if they unintentionally violate individual civil rights, are against the law. Discrimination is not only unfair, it is illegal and ignorance of the law is no defense.

(See Appendix A for an extended listing of federal regulations relative to the workplace.)

SCREENING

The recruiting process yields applicants whose qualifications must be assessed against the requirements of the job and the vision of the foodservice organization. Making a selection from among potential team members from within or outside the organization to fill existing or projected job openings is a major element of TQM that has far-reaching effects. Today, greater attention is being given to the selection process than ever before. Those potential team members who are thoroughly screened against developed criteria, specifications, and a TQM culture learn their tasks readily, are productive, adapt to the team philosophy, and generally adjust to their new jobs with the minimum of difficulty. As a result, the team member, the kitchen team, the foodservice organization, and customers benefit from a careful selection process. It is in the final selection of new team members that chef supervisors play a vital role. Therefore, they should fully understand the objectives and policies relative to evaluating and selecting these new team members.

What skills are required? Are there people available with these skills or will they have to be trained? Careful screening may reduce the amount of training needed. Screening should produce a slate of potential team members who are best able to meet the job requirements and fit the rate of pay available. Screening and selection in some instances may also be impacted by union contracts.

In matching people and kitchen team positions, research has demonstrated that complete, clear, and unambiguous job criteria and specifications reduce the influence of ethnic and gender stereotypes and help the chef supervisor differentiate between qualified and unqualified potential team members.

Most organizations require application forms to be completed because they can provide a fairly quick and systematic means of obtaining a variety of information about the potential team member. As with interviews, the EEOC and the courts have found that many questions asked on application forms disproportionately reject females and minorities and often are not job related. To keep in line with this legal requirement, application forms should be developed with great care and revised as necessary.

The information on the application form is generally used as a basis for further exploration of the applicant's background. It should be designed to provide as much information as possible that is predictive of job success. Even though potential team members come armed with elaborate and impressively designed resumes, it is still important that application forms are completed early in the application process.

Essentially, an applicant's resume will tell us what *they* want us to know, not necessarily what we need to know. Some applicants engage the services of so-called employment consultants to assist them in designing attractive and elaborate resumes that enlarge their abilities. These resumes are often works of literary art and are simply examples of the writing skills of the proposer. One technique used to check the needed skills of these people is to ask them to transcribe specific resume material onto an application form. The applicant can then be asked to sign a statement that the information contained in the application form is correct and that he or she accepts the employer's right to terminate employment if any of the information is subsequently found to be false.

Studies have shown that a high proportion of people lie on some aspect of their resumes. Therefore, background investigations are necessary. Inadequate reference checking can be a major cause of high employee turnover. If sources in addition to former employers are used, it is possible to obtain valuable information about the applicant's character and habits. Other points to remember are that the information should be job related and that written documentation exists outlining that the employment decision was based upon relevant information (3). It is generally advisable to ask the applicant to fill out forms permitting information to be solicited from reference sources. Even then, many organizations are reluctant to put in writing an evaluation of former employees. One reason for this trend is that several firms have been sued by former employees who discovered that they had been given poor recommendations. Individuals have a legal right to examine letters of reference about themselves (unless they have waived the right to do so or were protected by the Privacy Act of 1974 or by state laws).

INTERVIEWING

The most crucial step in selecting potential team members is the face-to-face interview. An interview is a conversation or verbal interaction between two people (in this case the chef supervisor and the applicant) to evaluate compatibility for a particular reason. It is a process for choosing the applicant who is most suited for the team position to be filled. The interview has three main purposes:

1. To validate previously submitted information
2. To discover those skills and attitudes necessary to achieve "neatness of fit" within the kitchen team
3. To predict the successful integration of the applicant into the foodservice organization's environment.

When we meet somebody for the first time we react to them in some way. Sometimes we go further and make some definite judgments about them based only on the first impression we take. If we do this, we will usually tend, often without realizing it, to listen to them selectively and observe them selectively. In other words we will see and hear only those things that confirm our first impression and will filter out anything that contradicts it.

Research indicates that our first impressions are based to a large extent on nonverbal cues: 55 percent on what we see, 9 percent on what is said, and 36 percent on how it is said. Nonverbal cues are based almost entirely on our reliving old memories. They are therefore based, not on the person in front of us now, but on others in the past.

There is no best way to interview. Interviews can be structured or unstructured or conducted in groups. These three interview types are the most commonly used method of interviewing in the foodservice industry.

Structured interviews: These consist of a series of carefully designed and structured questions that are asked by the interviewer of each job applicant. This type of interview is based on a clear set of job specifications. Through this type of interview, the interviewer maintains control of the interview by systematically asking prepared questions. An advantage of using a structured interview is that it provides the same criteria for all interviews.

Unstructured interviews: As the name implies, this requires very little preparation on the part of the interviewer. These type of interviews are conducted without a predetermined checklist of questions. Open-ended questions are used. This type of interview may pose problems of subjectivity and bias on the part of the interviewer. However, unstructured interviews can provide a more relaxed atmosphere for interviewees.

Group interviews: These are interviews in which several applicants are questioned together in a group discussion. They typically involve a structured and unstructured question format.

Other types of interviews are:

- Board interviews
- Stress interviews
- Counseling interviews
- Evaluation or job appraisal interviews
- Exit interviews

Chef Talk: "Team Players"

One of my most difficult tasks as an executive chef is hiring the right players for my kitchen team. Because we have a strong team philosophy at our hotel, we go to great lengths to get the best possible people. I therefore look for individuals who can fit our high standards.

Among the qualities I consider important in a potential new kitchen employee are of course experience and how employment candidates present themselves for interview, but more importantly, I look for that special "hospitality attitude." For me that's a critical quality. People who possess hospitality attitudes are usually those who will also make good team players. These attitudes are not hard to tease out. I simply ask who the most important person is in the hotel. When the answer indicates that it is the guest, chances are they understand the concept of hospitality.

Previous work experience in similar establishments is not the only deciding factor in the hiring process. If the person's disposition is positive, then that can be a good basis to invest in developing and training that person.

Key to putting a great team together is "keeping them together." Therefore, investing in the existing team ensures that there is as little turnover as possible.

We employ a variety of screening processes before we to get to the interview stage. Even then not everyone that comes for interview will be determined to be suitable. For the interview I involve my existing team members. I seek their opinions and encourage them to participate in the interviewing of new members; after all, they will have to embrace them if they are selected. We share our opinions on the candidates and collectively we evaluate their suitability.

Experience has taught me that some employment candidates can "talk a great game," but when it comes to actually cooking, they are left wanting. Administering a cooking test can tell you a lot, not only about their cooking skills but also about vital approaches to safety and sanitation.

Michael Ty, CEC, AAC, Executive Chef, Sheraton Desert Inn, Las Vegas, NV

Although interviews are the most widely used method to select team members, a host of problems exists. One of the most significant is that interviews are subject to the same legal requirements of validity and reliability as other steps in the recruitment and selection process. The interview should also follow EEOC guidelines. Interview questions should be tied to job descriptions, and these should only detail the characteristics of the employment position. The basic thrust of equal employment legislation is straightforward: Do not discriminate against people on the basis of their race, color, sex, religion, or national origin. However, subtle interpretations of the laws make this area one of the most actively pursued in the courts. If the interview questions stick to job-related items and are objective and consistently applied to all applicants—men, women, persons of all racial and all national groups—then the interviewer will most certainly stay within the law.

INTERVIEWING GUIDELINES

By putting the potential team member at ease, the interviewer is more likely to get a true picture of the applicant's skills, abilities, and attitudes.

The interview should take place in a pleasant and nonthreatening environment. Begin the interview by welcoming the applicant warmly. An applicant who is at ease will be more likely to answer questions spontaneously. Introduce yourself by name and title. Ask the applicant his or her preferred name and use it throughout the interview. Prepare the atmosphere by initiating a brief conversation on issues unrelated to the interview. Establish and maintain rapport with applicants by displaying sincere interest in them and by listening carefully. Indicate your intention to take notes or complete an evaluation form; be sure to extend this opportunity to the applicant. Strive to understand what is only suggested or implied. A good listener's mind is alert and his or her face and posture reflect this.

Some interviewers tend to talk too much. According to Bill Marvin, in his book *The Foolproof Foodservice Selection System*, "Most Interviewers talk half of the time or more during an interview, but it is the candidate who should be talking 80 or 90 percent of the time. After all, how can you learn about an applicant if you do all the talking?" (4)

Focus your attention fully on the applicant's responses to your questions, the questions, observations, and body language of the applicant, as these often provide clues to that person's attitude and feelings. Answer fully and frankly the applicant's questions. Use questions effectively so as to elicit truthful answers. Questions should be phrased as objectively as possible without an indication of the desired response. During the interview separate facts from inferences. Use open-ended questions that give the applicant an opportunity to talk and share information about past work experiences, training, or lifestyle.

Avoid biases and traps. This includes favoring people who have interests, backgrounds, or experiences similar to yours.

- Avoid allowing an impressive attitude to make you forget to ask essential questions about skills and knowledge.
- Avoid the influence of "beautyism." Discrimination against unattractive persons is a persistent and pervasive form of employment discrimination.

- Avoid the "halo effect," judging an individual favorably or unfavorably on the basis of one strong point (or weak point) on which you place high (or low) value.
- Avoid allowing first impressions (good or bad) to overrule the information gathered from the interview.
- Avoid making a judgment on the basis of preinterview material and either spending the entire time trying to verify the material or simply rendering the interview pointless.
- Avoid making a decision too soon.
- Avoid the temptation of talking too much about yourself.

If you are not getting honest answers to your carefully prepared questions, it is possible to hire the wrong person. To become an effective interviewer, the dynamics of verbal and nonverbal communication must be mastered so that dishonest applicants can be easily spotted. It has been reported that 80 percent of communication is nonverbal rather than verbal and that 80 percent of *that* communication is manifest in a person's face, particularly in the eyes. An interviewer should be able to recognize the subtle nonverbal cues that indicate an attempt to deceive. Few applicants can lie without feeling tightness in the stomach, along with some involuntary change in facial expression or diverting of the eyes from the interviewer (5). Verbal clues that sometimes can indicate deception include remarks such as "to tell the truth," "to be perfectly honest," or "I wouldn't tell most people this." Sometimes verbal and nonverbal cues are combined, for example, an "honest to God" remark accompanied by a major break in eye contact, a shift in body orientation, or a movement of a hand to the face.

Be sure you have all of the information you want before ending the interview. Keep in mind the qualities needed for the job. Cover all major skills that are needed on the job. As a final step in the interview process, ask the applicant if there are further questions or more information to be discussed before closing the interview.

INTERVIEW QUESTIONS

To evaluate the qualifications of potential team members, the chef supervisor must ask a series of questions. However, certain questions are in violation of EEOC guidelines. Other questions are inappropriate, and inexperienced interviewers may unwittingly ask them. The following are examples of appropriate and inappropriate questions:

Name

- Inappropriate: Inquiries about name that would indicate applicant's lineage, ancestry, national origin, or descent. Inquiry of previous name of applicant where it has been changed by court order or otherwise. Inquiries about preferred courtesy title: Mr., Mrs., and Ms.

- Permissible inquiries: "Have you worked for this organization under a different name?" "Is any additional information relative to change of name, use of an assumed name, or nickname necessary to enable a check on your work and educational record? If yes, please explain."

Marital status

- Inappropriate: "Are you married, divorced, or separated?"
- Permissible inquiries: Whether applicant can meet specific work schedules or has activities, commitments, or responsibilities that may hinder the meeting of work attendance requirements.

Age

- Inappropriate: "How old are you?"
- Permissible inquiries: Requiring proof of age in the form of a work permit or a certificate of age if a minor. If it is necessary to know that someone is over a certain age for legal reasons, this question could better be stated, "Are you 21 or over?"

National origin

- Inappropriate: "Are you native born or naturalized?" "Have you proof of your citizenship?" "What was your birthplace?" "Where were your parents born?"
- Permissible inquiries: If it is necessary to know if someone is a U.S. citizen for a job, this question could be asked directly without asking anything that might reveal national origin. If it is necessary to require proof of citizenship or immigrant status, employment can be offered on the condition that proof be supplied.

Mental or physical handicap

- Inappropriate: "Do you have or have you ever had a life-threatening disease?" Questions regarding treatment for alcohol or drug abuse or an on-the-job injury. "Have you ever been treated for a mental condition?"
- Permissible inquiries: For employers subject to the provisions of the Rehabilitation Act of 1973 and the Americans with Disabilities Act of 1990, applicants may be invited to indicate how and to what extent they are handicapped. All applicants can be asked if they are able to carry out all necessary job assignments and perform them in a safe manner. The employer must indicate that compliance with the invitation is voluntary or

that the information is being sought only to remedy discrimination or provide opportunities for the handicapped.

Religion

- Inappropriate: "What is your religious affiliation?" "What clubs/associations are you a member of?" "Can you work Saturdays or Sundays?"
- Permissible inquiries: None. However, an applicant may be advised concerning normal hours and days of work required by the job to avoid possible conflict with religious or other personal conviction.

Conviction, arrest, and court records

- Inappropriate: Any inquiry relating to arrests. Any inquiry into or a request for a person's arrest, court, or conviction record if not substantially related to functions and responsibilities of the particular job in question.
- Permissible inquiries: Inquiry into actual *convictions* that relate reasonably to fitness to perform an actual job.

Military record

- Inappropriate: The type of discharge.
- Permissible inquiries: Type of education and experience in the service as it relates to a particular job.

Credit rating

- Inappropriate: Any questions concerning credit rating, charge accounts, ownership of car, etc.
- Permissible inquiries: None.

The following questions can provoke responses that help determine a person's motivation, initiative, insight, and planning abilities:

On motivation

How will this job help you get what you want?
What have you done to prepare yourself for a better job?

The underlying intent of these types of questions is to determine the applicant's priorities and how motivated they may be.

On initiative

How did you get into this line of work?
When have you felt like giving up on a task? Tell me about it.

The intention here is to determine if the person is a self-starter or can complete an unpleasant assignment.

On insight

What is the most useful criticism you have received?
From whom? Tell me about it.
What is the most useless?

From answers to these questions it is possible to develop an understanding of the applicant's ability to take constructive action on weakness and determine how the applicant can take criticism.

On planning

Tell me how you spend a typical day.
If you were the boss, how would you run your present job?

Reactions to these questions may tell how easily the applicant will fit into your corporate culture and team. They will also help elicit if they have a vision or can get bogged down by details.

Other general questions

Tell me about yourself.
What practical experience have you had in this area?
What is your major strength? Weakness?
What types of people annoy you?
What have you done that shows initiative and action?
How do you spend your spare time?
What personal characteristics do you feel are necessary for success in the foodservice industry?
Where would you like to be in one year?
Why do you want to work for us?
Why do you want to leave your present job?

Questions about the foodservice organization

What do you know about our organization?

Why do you want to work for us?

Why would you like this particular job?

How can you benefit our organization?

What experience(s) have you had that suit you for our organization?

What position would you like to hold with us in five years? In ten years?

What interests you about our organization?

What kind of chef supervisor do you prefer?

What do you feel determines a person's progress in a good organization?

What are your ideas about how the foodservice industry operates today?

In addition to verbal and nonverbal responses during the interview, much can be learned from the actions and appearance of the applicant. These positive actions include:

- Arriving early for the interview
- Being alert and responsive
- Being dressed appropriately
- Being well groomed, clean hair and nails
- Having good eye contact
- Listening carefully
- Speaking well of other people
- Sticking to the point

Obviously the person who arrives late for an interview, is inappropriately dressed and unclean, looks away, complains about other people, or exhibits inappropriate responses presents a negative image. The interview session provides the chef supervisor with an opportunity to form an impression about the applicant's abilities and general disposition and to make a reasoned judgment as to his or her suitability for the kitchen team.

MAKING THE DECISION

In reviewing all the pertinent data elicited from the screening step and the interview, the questions become, is this the person I want for my team and is he or she qualified and suitable? References have been checked to indicate accuracy of presented resume materials. It must be remembered that reference checking assumes that the past will indicate the future and that performance in one job has some continuity with the next. This is not always the case. What you see is what you get, and leopards don't change their spots. These applicants will never look or behave better than they have throughout the evaluation process.

Determine the applicant's temperament. How well will this person fit into your kitchen team? Can this person be trained and developed? What is his or her energy level? The foodservice industry has its demanding busy service periods. Is the applicant a team player? If all of the applicant's hobbies or interests center around individual activities such as reading or listening to music or other solitary activities, this might be an applicant who prefers being alone. Applicants who have a background that includes team activities will in many cases have a grasp of the imperatives of teamwork. Within a kitchen team, ideal members are those who are "people oriented."

Remember also that the foodservice organization can only hire what they can afford. If the team vacancy that exists pays less than the potential team member is worth and if there are no immediate promotional opportunities for this person to advance into, then this person will most certainly soon be looking for a better paid position elsewhere.

Obviously, most of the team positions that chef supervisors are called upon to fill are for cooks. Therefore a simple cooking test may be appropriate. Much can be learned of an applicant by asking them to cook a simple and inexpensive dish. This test can quantify the applicant's skill level much more than an impressive resume containing a list of awards won at food shows ever will. It will also demonstrate the applicant's energy level, organizational abilities, application of safety and sanitation procedures, use of correct equipment, and attitude toward customer service. All of this information can be gathered from making a dish as simple as an omelette.

As is usual with many aspects of decision making regarding hiring new team members, not all of them will fit into each component of the job specification: You like everything about them, but in one or two areas they fail to match the specifications. Sometimes it is necessary to evaluate the risk of hiring against what is generally known as *can do* and *will do* factors. "Can do" concerns the individual's knowledge, skills, and attitudes. "Will do" concerns the person's motivation, interests, and personality characteristics. Some element of risk is involved when the elements of "can do" are not entirely fulfilled. Experienced chef supervisors can calculate the risk by determining that training and development will fix the "can do" part because the "will do" elements outweigh other factors. Therefore, the availability of training and development may permit the hiring of potential team members who can be made qualified.

Other factors in the hiring decision include:

Compensation: The rate of pay available affects the degree of selectivity.

Labor relations: Unions may influence who is selected.

Training and development: Training costs in terms of time and expense may be reduced or increased.

SUMMARY

Recruitment and selection procedures effectively and carefully pursued and applied correctly will combine to facilitate hiring the best possible candidate for the kitchen team. Recruiting and hiring decisions should be based on one question: Will this person fit into our team and our TQM philosophy?

The chef supervisor has an important role to play and should be the final decision maker in the process of selecting new team members.

Legal issues relative to the recruitment and selection process should be scrupulously followed. Chef supervisors should be aware of the legislation pertaining in this area.

Finding the "neatness of fit" between the foodservice organization and the potential new team member should be planned so as to reduce turnover and decrease training costs. Knowing the sources and methods of recruitment facilitates this process.

Job descriptions should be used to format the essential and desirable skills of new team members. The EEOC criteria with regard to employment applicants must be followed strictly so all applicants are afforded the same employment opportunities. Discrimination in employment opportunity is illegal and ignorance of the various laws is no defense.

Careful and effective screening of applicants will reduce the risk of selecting unsuitable team members. Screening requires the chef supervisor to actively check references.

Interviewing permits face-to-face evaluation of potential new team members. Therefore, interviewing skills are necessary, along with an understanding of the various types of interview processes. Guidelines for effective interviewing include:

- Putting the applicant at ease
- Focusing attention on applicant's responses to questions
- Using open-ended questions
- Avoiding biases that affect judgment
- Avoiding the halo effect
- Not allowing first impressions to overrule information gathered from the interview
- Knowing what questions are inappropriate and those that are permissible

Making the decision to hire the applicant is based on an evaluation of the data gathered through the application form, the screening stage, and the face-to-face interview. Additionally, a cooking test may be appropriate to determine skill levels. Elements of the decision to hire are based on this information, recognizing that past performance is not totally predictive of the future. Chef supervisors can only hire what the organization can afford.

DISCUSSION QUESTIONS

1. Why are job descriptions used?
2. What are the methods most commonly used in the foodservice industry to recruit new team members?
3. What is active recruitment?
4. How can seeking out "qualified" persons contribute to reducing costs?
5. What are the guidelines of the Equal Employment Opportunity Commission as they apply to recruitment and selection of employees?
6. Why should great care be taken in designing job application forms?
7. Why can inadequate reference checking lead to high employee turnover?
8. Why is the most crucial step in selecting potential team members the face-to-face interview?
9. What are the primary differences between a structured and an unstructured interview?
10. Why are open-ended questions used during a job interview?
11. What are five questioning areas an interviewer should not engage in during a job interview?
12. How might a chef supervisor ascertain the skill level of a cook applicant?

NOTES

1. Vincent H. Eade, *Human Resources Management in the Hospitality Industry*, Garsuch Sciarisbrick Pub., Scottsdale, AZ, 1993, p. 103.
2. Lloyd L. Byars and Leslie W. Rue, *Human Resource Management*, 4th ed. Irwin, Boston, 1994, p. 183.
3. E. R. Worthington and Anita E. Worthington, *People Investment*, Oasis Press, Grant's Pass, OR, 1993, p. 108.
4. Bill Marvin, *The Foolproof Foodservice Selection System*, John Wiley, New York, 1993, p. 5.
5. Robert F. Wilson, *Conducting Better Job Interviews*, Barron's, New York, 1991, p. 25.

18

Discipline and the Kitchen Team

Outline

- Introduction
- Chef supervisor's role
- Approaches to discipline
- Administering discipline
- Approaches to positive discipline
- Exit interviews
- Summary
- Discussion questions

Objectives

When you complete this chapter, you should be able to:

1. Define discipline in its broader sense as it applies to the role of the chef supervisor.
2. Describe the discipline parameters in which the chef supervisor operates relative to unions and the EEOC.

3. Outline the steps in the progressive approach to discipline.

4. State the guidelines for administering discipline in a fair and equitable way.

5. Distinguish between positive and negative approaches to discipline.

6. Define the strategies and rationale for conducting exit interviews.

INTRODUCTION

Occasionally, a team member will do something that requires disciplinary action by the chef supervisor. It may be an issue of job performance; too many absences; outright violation of an order, rule, or procedure; or some illegal act such as stealing, fighting, gambling, or involvement with illegal drugs.

The words *discipline* and *disciple* share the same root, which means to "mold" or "teach." True discipline should teach a correct action. Yet many chef supervisors think of discipline merely as punishment or reprimanding a team member for a mistake. The word disciple literally means follower. Therefore, good discipline is based on leadership, which includes the ability to guide, coach, correct, and affirm the actions of others. Discipline is an inner force that develops within each team member and causes them to want to follow high standards in life and the workplace. Effective discipline is not just about reprimanding or inflicting penalties. True discipline involves an entire program that teaches and guides individuals to become loyal, motivated, responsible team players.

Discipline in a broader sense concerns the process of socialization. Team members are given the quality values and rules necessary for survival and growth of the foodservice organization. This process is complete when the team member comes to accept those values and rules as legitimate. Within the kitchen team, the rules serve a purpose and each member benefits by obeying.

Application of discipline has come to be split into two distinct areas. On the one hand there is the traditional notion of discipline as punishment and on the other hand is the positive discipline approach. Positive discipline is about exploring other ways for compliance with the rules. It is about reversing the concept of discipline as punishment only and placing emphasis on development along with encouraging responsibility and self-directed behavior. It is an extension of the training and coaching process.

CHEF SUPERVISOR'S ROLE

No chef supervisor enjoys the act of disciplining a team member, but this is an unavoidable part of the job. The kitchen may be running smoothly, with each team member doing his or her job well. Then a team member is careless, an accident occurs, and the chef supervisor must take corrective action. Good leadership ability minimizes the need to be punitive. If the team members respect the chef supervisor, then it is likely that there will be a good team atmosphere and it is easier to head off problems. Kitchen team members who feel you are interested in their welfare will not be disruptive.

The vast majority of team members accept rules and directions as a condition of employment and generally do not set out to break rules. These same team members will observe how the chef supervisor reacts with members who get out of line. Each individual is concerned with getting fair treatment. Morale within the team is lowered when it's observed that some individuals get away with violating rules or if they witness undue harsh discipline.

Before any discipline actions are contemplated, the ground rules for performance and conduct should be clearly communicated to the team. This set of policies and procedures is part of induction and orientation programs. (These were detailed in Chapter 13, Induction and Orientation Training.) However, just because they were included it is unwise to assume they have been read and are understood. There are some rules that need constant reiteration. These concern issues of safety and sanitation and should be policed constantly. Team members must know from the outset what the penalties are for any rule infraction in this area. This information should not be in the form of threats and warnings. They should be stated clearly and succinctly: "Knowing the consequences has its own security: people know where the boss stands, and they know what will happen if they go beyond the limits" (1). The reasons for a particular rule should always be explained. Acceptance of a rule is heightened when team members understand the reason for it. Rules and procedures should always be written and the language used should be clear and unambiguous. If there has been a lax enforcement of a rule, then the rule must be restated along with the consequences of its violation before disciplinary action can begin. While an individual must be advised in advance of all rules and their violation, some conduct can be reasonably expected to be generally known as unacceptable.

APPROACHES TO DISCIPLINE

Discipline should not only be fair and consistent but also conform to legal requirements. Despite worker protection laws, the Equal Employment Opportunity Commission (EEOC) reports that a high percentage of all charges filed are for discriminatory dismissals (2).

Chef supervisors who operate in a union environment have to take extra care when disciplining team members. Binding labor contracts set forth rules and procedures that must be followed and they set penalties on management and workers for failing to abide by the rules. Even minor deviations from labor contract procedure can overturn an otherwise justified disciplinary action. With these contracts there is usually a provision for impartial review or an arbitration process. Additionally, with union organized establishments workers often have an increased awareness of their rights that may cause individuals to challenge the chef supervisor's disciplinary decisions. This does not mean that any form of discipline is impossible under union contracts. On the contrary, it may be easier. The nature of collective bargaining requires both union and management to be rigid and specific regarding rules and procedures.

Discipline and the hot stove rule   A hot stove with its radiating heat gives a *warning* that it should not be touched. Those team members who ignore the warning and touch it, like those who violate a rule, are assured of being burnt. The hot stove burns immediately. Therefore, disciplinary policies should be administered quickly:

- The hot stove gives warning and so should discipline.
- The hot stove burns each person who touches it and in the same manner. Discipline should also be impartial.

Team members should be disciplined for what they have done, not because of who they are.

The hot stove rule outlines four principles:

- An unpleasant experience
- Immediate action
- Consistent punishment
- Impartiality

Generally, discipline is imposed in a progressive manner. By definition, progressive discipline is the application of corrective measures by increasing degrees. It should motivate team members to take corrective action on misconduct voluntarily. This progressive approach is aimed at nipping the problem in the bud by utilizing only enough corrective action to remedy the problem. The sequence and severity of the disciplinary action varies with the type of offense and the circumstances surrounding the misconduct. Following is a typical sequence of progressive discipline:

1. *Oral reprimand*: When a team member makes an immediate change in the way something is done or breaks a minor rule, an oral reprimand may be appropriate. In general these reprimands should be made in private, away from other team members. The rule is to "discipline in private, praise in public." Ensure that you make clear and specific what should be stopped (or started). Remember, most people fear public embarrassment more than the discipline action itself. In the course of the reprimand, be firm and fair. Do not argue or debate side issues, but treat the individual with respect. There are times, however, when it is necessary to reprimand instantly without first considering an individual team member's sensitivity. This concerns misconduct in the critical area of food sanitation and safety. Because of potential hazardous risks to public health, the chef supervisor should react immediately. When this happens, it is

Chef Talk: "Using the Correct Language"

Working as an executive chef in a highly unionized hotel requires careful disciplinary strategies. Not least among them is knowing all the elements of the union/hotel contract and using appropriate language in the disciplinary process. I learned an important lesson on this subject when I dismissed a dishwasher.

Following a late night banquet, I was summoned to the pot wash area in the kitchen. There I met "Joe," a dishwasher who was employed as a night porter. His job was to wash and sanitize the kitchen pots, pans, and utensils and prepare the kitchen for the breakfast chef. When I came upon Joe he was staggering around the dish room, dripping wet. (He had fallen into the large pot sink and had been rescued by the manager, who had summoned me.) There was a strong smell of alcohol from him. I asked him what had happened. How had he fallen into the sink? In his response he was barely coherent, his eyes rolling, he could hardly stand upright. He was clearly in no condition to work. I informed him that the best thing was for him to go home and come to see me the following day. Joe arrived the next day, and I informed him that I was recommending his discharge. I felt comfortable with my decision. He had exhausted all previous disciplinary steps and had been warned verbally and in writing with each warning appropriately documented.

However, I was not prepared for what was to follow. Within a week I was summoned to the general manager's office. There I found not only the manager but Joe and his union representative. Following preliminary discussion to establish the sequence of events leading up to the disciplinary action, I was asked by the union official why I had dismissed Joe. At this stage I was feeling rather agitated by what I considered to be a waste of time, going over what I felt was an obvious open and shut termination action. I responded, "because Joe was drunk on duty."

The union official turned to me and asked me what credentials I possessed that enabled me to make such a judgment, "Was I a qualified medical doctor?" I was taken aback. Looking at the union official, I said, "You know what my credentials are!"

The end result of that meeting was that Joe had to be reinstated with full pay because I had accused him of being "drunk." What I should have said was, "his condition would lead any reasonable person to believe he was under the influence of alcohol." Joe's excuse to the union was that on that particular night he had taken medication for an ear infection, which gave him the appearance of being under the influence of alcohol.

Within six weeks Joe was again discovered on duty in a similar condition. This time I made sure I had a colleague with me to witness the situation. Joe was dismissed, but this time I used the correct language.

Noel C. Cullen, Ed.D., CMC, AAC, Boston University, Boston, MA best to soften the reprimand as much as possible. The important point is to stop the team member from continuing the harmful action. As with all elements of discipline, actions requiring reprimands should always be documented.

2. *Written reprimand*: For the second offense the team member receives a written reprimand. This typically informs the team member that his or her conduct is in violation of rules or procedures and that further violations will result in suspension or loss of pay. Additionally, this reprimand is placed in the team member's personnel file. Copies of this reprimand are also given to the union steward if this is applicable. If the team member is probationary, the letter will usually indicate that improved performance is necessary. Probation is usually handled in writing so that a written record exists in the event that termination is necessary if the required improvement does not occur.

3. *Suspension*: Violations of rules and minor illegal acts often are treated with a temporary layoff or suspension. This suspension is without pay and consistent with the seriousness of the offence. The details are written and given to the individual. This written communication indicates also that another violation will call for discharge.

4. *Termination*: When after the third offense it appears that there is little chance of bringing the individual's performance up to an acceptable level, termination may be the best course of action. It is presumed that the team member has been given every opportunity to conform.

Some infractions are so serious that discharge is permitted with the first violation. Cases involving instant dismissal are rare. They usually involve illegal acts or serious conduct that threatens the safety and security of other individuals or the foodservice organization. Team members must be given an opportunity to improve, and specific reasons for discharge must be documented. This category also includes requested resignations. When it appears that a team member's interests are not being met by the foodservice organization, it may be appropriate to request him or her to seek employment elsewhere: "The decision to discharge an employee must be based on quality and quantity of evidence, not hearsay, personal prejudices, speculation, or rumors" (3).

Major violations that frequently require dismissal include the following:

- Possession of, drinking, smoking, or being under the influence of intoxicants or narcotics on the foodservice establishment's property
- False statements or misrepresentation of facts on employment application forms
- Sleeping on the job
- Stealing company or personal property
- Fighting on company property
- Issues that threaten the well-being of team members or guests

- Gross discourtesy to guests
- Gross negligence involving sanitation/safety
- Excessive absenteeism without prior notification
- Sexual harassment
- Refusing to follow reasonable job-related directives from the chef supervisor

Violations requiring progressive discipline are:

- Tardiness
- Absence for one day without notifying supervisor
- Leaving the kitchen without permission
- Use of abusive language
- Not performing to set quality standards
- Disorderly conduct during working time
- Racial slurs
- Obscene or immoral conduct

The above violations are basic and are not intended to be all inclusive or cover every situation that may arise.

ADMINISTERING DISCIPLINE

Discipline should be administered as soon as possible after the infraction has taken place or has been noticed. For the discipline to be most effective, it must be taken immediately without involving emotional or irrational decisions. Notation of rule infractions in a team member's record does not constitute advance warning and is not sufficient to support disciplinary action. A team member must be advised of the infraction for it to be considered a warning. Noting that the team member was warned about the infraction and having him or her sign a form acknowledging the warning are both good practices. Failure to warn a team member of the consequences of continuous rule violation is one reason often cited for overturning a disciplinary action.

It must be recognized by the chef supervisor that each act of discipline is different and that each team member must be handled differently. The better the chef supervisor knows all team members and how they react, the better they can handle disciplinary actions. Sometimes other reactions are experienced. For example, rather than being motivated to improve performance, a team member may be motivated to retaliate or "get even." The following guidelines will help ensure a positive reaction:

Discipline and the offense   Match the discipline to the offense. A trivial rule infraction does not require harsh or unreasonable discipline. A team member's previous record must be considered. Determining the appropriateness of the discipline action involves serious consideration of:

1. The circumstances surrounding the incident
2. The seriousness of the incident
3. The previous record of the team member
4. The disciplinary action taken in similar situations
5. Existing rules and disciplinary policies
6. The provisions in the labor contract (if applicable)

> *Know the facts*: Investigate thoroughly. Determine who was involved in the incident, what happened, where it happened, and what the team member's involvement was.
>
> *Interview*: Discuss the discipline problem with the team member in private. Keep it as informal as possible in order to allow discussion to proceed calmly.
>
> *Listen*: First ask the team member to tell his or her side of the story. Ask questions to get further details; try not to interrupt until the individual has finished. Listen with an open mind. Do not prejudge the situation.
>
> *Stay calm*: Control your feelings and emotions. Do not argue. Do not engage in any type of name calling. You may win the argument, but you will lose the loyalty and contribution of an important team member.
>
> *Avoid entrapment*: Do not set out to "get" a team member. Do not get involved unless you are sure something is wrong.
>
> *Be firm but fair*: Being firm does not suggest getting tough. Being firm but fair involves explaining to a team member why behavior is unacceptable. Do not humiliate the team member in any way.
>
> *Document*: Make notes on what happened and what the resulting action was. Records of disciplinary action are important for the purpose of demonstrating later on that there was a fair and equitable resolution of the incident.
>
> *Inform others*: Be sure to inform the team member of your intended course of action. Remember you are not the final voice in matters of discipline. The foodservice organization and the union (if applicable) should be informed. Matters of serious discipline are much too important for one person.

It is always a good idea for the chef supervisor to discuss intended disciplinary actions with the foodservice establishment's management or with members of the Human Resources Department. These are the people who have to support the chef supervisor's actions. It is also wise and prudent to discuss intended disciplinary action with a trusted colleague. This will help to establish a better perspective for the action.

Terminating a Team Member

Before a decision is reached to terminate a team member, the following questions should be answered:

1. Was the team member forewarned of the possible disciplinary consequences of his or her actions?
2. Were the work requirements required of the individual reasonable in relation to the safe, orderly, and efficient conduct of the foodservice organization?
3. Were all reasonable efforts expended to fully and fairly determine the facts?
4. Was the team member given ample opportunity for improvement?
5. Were all other options of disciplinary action considered?
6. Was the team member afforded "due process" and a fair hearing?
7. Are there any unusual or mitigating circumstances surrounding the case?
8. Is this action nondiscriminatory?

For most supervisors dismissing a team member can be a painful experience. Often it gives supervisors a feeling that they have failed the individual in some way. The best way to think of termination of a team member is to consider it as an act of "unhiring."

Regardless of the reasons for dismissal, it should be accomplished with consideration of the individual. Every effort should be made to ease the trauma a dismissal can create. The following guidelines can help in the termination discussion:

1. Make the discussion private, brief, and businesslike.
2. Be tactful, honest, and straightforward.
3. Give any information regarding severance pay or other benefits information.
4. Outline the period the team member has before he or she must leave the organization.
5. Avoid any personality differences between you and the team member.

Being dismissed can be a terrific blow to a team member. It is important to allow the team member to leave with self-esteem intact.

APPROACHES TO POSITIVE DISCIPLINE

One approach to disciplinary action is positive discipline, or discipline without punishment, an idea originally developed by John Huberman, a Canadian psychologist. Punitive and positive disciplines differ in both attitude and procedure (4). Most of the time individuals are unaware that they are doing something they are not supposed to do. Despite the fact that they receive good induction and orientation training and that rules and procedures are clearly posted or contained in employee manuals, there are still things they don't know. They may observe some other team member doing something and believe it's all right for them to do it. A positive approach to discipline therefore is continuous education. When discipline is applied positively, it is used to teach and mold. Team members will see that it is for their welfare. Positive discipline shows the team member that obeying the rules and safety or sanitation regulations benefits them as well as the organization.

What then is "positive discipline?" The philosophy behind positive discipline is that most people come to work wishing to do a good job. They appreciate being treated as adults. They want to learn, welcome responsibility, can be self-directed, and are capable of self-discipline. The dynamics of positive discipline is a team effort where the team members and the chef supervisor engage in joint discussion and problem solving to resolve incidents of rule infractions.

Positive discipline focuses on the early correction of team member misconduct. While positive discipline seems similar to progressive discipline, its emphasis is on giving team members reminders rather than reprimands. The steps in positive discipline are:

Step 1: This is an oral reminder. In a private discussion with the chef supervisor, the team member is encouraged to explain the reason for the misconduct. In a friendly way the rules and procedures are restated along with the reasons for having them. The chef supervisor refrains from reprimanding or threatening the team member with further disciplinary action. This meeting may be documented, but a written record is not placed in the team member's file unless the misconduct occurs again. During this meeting the team member agrees not to repeat the misconduct.

Step 2: If improvement is not made, following step 1, a second meeting takes place with the offending team member. During this private meeting the chef supervisor adopts the role of counselor. At this stage, however, a written reminder is given to the team member that summarizes the discussion and the agreement arrived at. It is then signed by both the team member and chef supervisor.

Step 3: When steps 1 and 2 fail to produce the desired results, the team member is placed on "decision-making" leave with pay. The purpose of this paid leave is to allow the offending team member time to decide whether to remain part of the team, whether to return and abide by the rules and conditions or to leave. If the team member returns, it is on the basis of an agreement ¹o conform to the organization's rules and that further infractions will be followed by termination. The foodservice organization pays for this specified leave in order to demonstrate its desire to retain the team member. Paying for the leave eliminates any negative effects that suspension without pay has with individuals.

Step 4: If the agreed improvements do not take place, then the team member has broken the agreement. There is then a clear reason for termination.

Positive discipline works. Organizations that have used it report success (5):

> Many people who use it report that about 75 percent of the time employees decide to come back and follow the rules. They may not maintain their turnaround indefinitely but three months or even three weeks of productive behavior is preferable to finding and breaking in somebody new. And it is infinitely better than the hostile employee you are likely to end up with after an un-paid layoff.

EXIT INTERVIEWS

Team members who leave voluntarily often provide feedback on their experience with the organization that can be useful in averting further employee turnover. Exit interviews enable chef supervisors to compile data about the kitchen work environment, along with establishing the effectiveness of induction and orientation training programs. They are used to establish the primary reasons people leave (6).

Exit interview data can help in determining if there is a trend for voluntary departures. To get the most accurate data from departing employees, the interview is best conducted by a supervisor other than the chef. Another approach is to turn the whole procedure over to the Human Resources Department. Some of the questions appropriate for this interview are:

- "What did you like most about working here? What did you like least?"
- "If you were a consultant to our organization, what changes/improvement would you recommend?"
- "What was it like working for chef . . . ?" If the answer is vague or answered weakly "on the grounds that nobody is perfect," you may want to ask: "What would have made chef . . . a better supervisor, in your opinion?"
- "Where are you going to be working?" This question is to attempt to gather information about competitors and find out if professional recruiters are poaching from your kitchen.

To get as much information as possible from the interview, probe for specific details from each answer. It is important that no team member should leave the foodservice organization without being interviewed. Those team members who leave voluntarily have to be replaced. This process is expensive not only in terms of dollars and time but often also in terms of team morale.

SUMMARY

Discipline should not be interpreted only as punishment. It is also about molding and teaching team members to become loyal, motivated, responsible workers.

Discipline is an inner force that develops within team members and causes them to want to follow high standards in life and the workplace. Effective discipline is not just reprimanding or inflicting penalties. Discipline is split into two distinct areas: discipline as punishment and the positive discipline approach. The leadership abilities of the chef supervisor may minimize the need to be punitive.

Chef supervisors should ensure that each member of the kitchen team understands the policies and procedures of the foodservice organization. Disciplinary actions must be in accordance with EEOC legislation and other discriminatory laws. Chef supervisors should know and understand all union labor contract procedures and agreements relative to employee discipline.

Discipline should be administered in a consistent, fair, and equitable way. Progressive discipline involves the steps of oral reprimand, written reprimand, suspension, and termination. Administering discipline requires the chef supervisor to gather the facts and treat the offender with all "due process" and know the advance steps before termination.

Positive discipline approaches require the chef supervisor to act in a way that invests in the team member by shifting responsibility to the individual. Its philosophy is that most people are self-disciplined and with counseling and guidance team members who break rules can become productive. An important element of the process is the third step, which provides offending team members with a paid period to decide their future with the organization, thus placing the responsibility on them for the next steps.

Exit interviews with team members who voluntarily leave provide the organization with information that can assist in profiling the kitchen as a workplace and the chef as a supervisor.

DISCUSSION QUESTIONS

1. Why does true discipline involve more than punishing or reprimanding?
2. What are the two distinct application areas of discipline?
3. What is the effect on the kitchen team morale with regard to selective application of discipline?
4. What are the rules within the kitchen that require constant reiteration?
5. Why do minor deviations from labor contract procedures overturn otherwise justified disciplinary actions?

6. What is meant by the hot stove rule as it pertains to discipline?
7. What are the steps of progressive discipline?
8. What are the five major rule violations that frequently require team member dismissal?
9. What are the consequences of failing to warn a team member of continued rule violations?
10. What are the guidelines for administering discipline in a fair and equitable way?
11. What are the fundamental differences between positive and negative discipline?
12. What benefits can accrue to the chef supervisor and the foodservice organization as a result of exit interviews?

NOTES

1. Jack E. Miller, Mary Porter, and Karen E. Drummond, *Supervison in the Hospitality Industry*, 2nd ed., John Wiley, New York, 1992, p. 257.
2. E. R. Worthington and Anita E. Worthington, *People Investment*, Oasis Press, Grant's Pass, OR, 1993, p. 56.
3. Vincent H. Eade, *Human Resources Management in the Hospitality Industry*, Garsuch Sciarisbrick Pub., Scottsdale, AZ, 1993, p. 204.
4. George L. Frunzi and Jack Halloran, *Supervision: The Art of Management*, 3rd ed., Prentice-Hall, Englewood Cliffs, NJ, 1991, p. 380.
5. Jack E. Miller, Mary Porter, and Karen E. Drummond, *Supervison in the Hospitality Industry*, 2nd ed., John Wiley, New York, 1992, p. 259.
6. Barbara A. Pope, *Workforce Management*, Business One Review, Chicago, IL, 1992, p. 89.

19

Problem Solving and Decision Making

Outline

- Introduction
- The decision-making process
- Empowerment and decision making
- Problems
- The Pareto principle
- Rules of problem solving and decision making
- Summary
- Discussion questions

Objectives

When you complete this chapter, you should be able to:

1. Describe the primary elements of sound decision making and problem solving.
2. Outline the elements in the decision-making process.
3. Evaluate the links between decision making, empowerment, and total quality management.
4. State reasons why problems recur within the kitchen.

5. Define the steps used to identify problems relating to issues of quality and customer satisfaction.

6. Use the strategies of the Pareto principle to chart cause and effect of problems.

7. Describe elements of open and closed problems.

INTRODUCTION

To succeed and become a more effective supervisor, the chef must learn to make sound decisions and solve problems. This is much easier said than done. Why? Because problems abound in the kitchen. Nothing is concrete, and new challenges confront the chef supervisor every day. The only constant is change. The problem may be customer satisfaction, motivating the kitchen team, time use, competition, money, personal relationships, or health. These problems recur periodically, and their solutions involve decisions. How well and creatively those problems are solved and what the basis of the decision-making process is determine the effectiveness of the chef supervisor.

Problem solving does not come from divine inspiration (although that might be helpful); it is a skill that can be learned. Making decisions is a part of everyday life. Some are made by default: A decision is delayed to the point that some other event removes the opportunity for decision making. Others are made on the basis of feelings or emotions and are often made in haste. Good decisions, however, are made on the basis of careful thought using facts and logic. There is no substitute for good decision making. Decisions are choices between two or more options. Before a choice can be made, the exact nature of the problem must be understood. The chef supervisor must know exactly what the problem is before attempts can be made to correct the situation.

Chef supervisors need to be decisive. When the time for action arrives, action must be taken. Decisions are not made in a vacuum. Each decision impacts the team and future decisions.

THE DECISION-MAKING PROCESS

To avoid jumping to conclusions, a rational procedure should be followed when making decisions. This procedure will enable the chef supervisor to make decisions based on facts and logic, not on emotion. In any decision there are three basic options:

1. To proceed
2. To oppose
3. To take no action (let the problem solve itself)

The starting point in the process is to analyze the situation. Ensure that the real problem has been analyzed. Break up the problem into small parts.

The following elements make up the decision-making process:

1. *Objective*: What is the desired result of the decision?
2. *Examine*: Determine the problem through careful investigation.
3. *Evaluate*: Gather the facts.
4. *Determine*: What are the alternatives and other options?
5. *Choose*: What is the best option?
6. *Implement*: What is the best choice?

1. *Objective*: This refers to the desired end result. It should not contain the method by which you arrive at the decision.
2. *Examine*: This is the "why" portion of the decision. Once all potential causes of the problem have been located, the cause can be determined.
3. *Evaluate*: Make a list of possible solutions to the problem. Narrow this list to a handful of best solutions. The initial step in the process is to make a broad list that can later be narrowed.
4. *Determine*: What are the best alternatives? Evaluate potential best solutions. The greater the number of alternatives, the more likely it is that the best choice will be among them.
5. *Choose*: Making a choice does not complete the decision-making process. Choosing involves writing a detailed plan outlining the action steps. This typically requires who is responsible, the start dates and end dates, what is involved, what changes will take place, and how these changes will take place.
6. *Implement*: Implement the solution and evaluate its progress. Follow up using the plan developed in step 5. Monitor it at every stage. Evaluation provides the decision maker with information to judge the quality of the decision.

Using this six-step model is the starting point: "Often defining the problem is the important step. If the problem is not clearly defined, all the good intentions and committed efforts that follow will not guarantee that you will find the right solutions, let alone implement them" (1).

EMPOWERMENT AND DECISION MAKING

Empowerment is a concept represented by many elements: personal, team, and organizational. Foodservice organizations today are searching for quality and continuous improvement—doing more with less. An empowered kitchen team will recognize that the necessary changes and solutions will not come from top management alone. The chef supervisor and the kitchen team need to initiate decisions that solve problems in their own area: "To ensure high levels of employee commitment, organizations of the 21st century will involve key employees in the decision-making process when determining or-

Chef Talk: "Finding Gilman"

Why are there so many challenges in the course of a business day? Many are small, some are big, some are with clients, and others are with employees. For some unknown reason, the restaurant industry seems to be a "hotbed" for such challenges, day in and day out. The solutions to problems often surprise even the experienced manager.

Faced with heavy bookings during the holiday season, I was disappointed to learn that two of our key apprentices were leaving to join our competition. Disappointment turned to anger when I learned that they had left without giving formal notice. After a quick assessment of the situation, a frantic search began to fill these positions with at least one good cook and to "make do" for the rest of the season. We began the task of advertising and interviewing hopeful candidates in a hurried fashion.

I was in the midst of negotiating the terms of purchase on a new manufacturing facility for our soup and sauce production. A building had been located and architects had been summoned for the initial design work. Though the facility seemed perfect for our needs, the architects informed us that possibly a firm with food knowledge would be more appropriate for the design work. Yes, just one more challenge was added to my stack.

Upon returning to the restaurant, I learned that we still had not lo-

cated a replacement for the apprentices. Entering the kitchen, I noticed a new face at the pot sink. Before I could even say good morning, he extended his hand and introduced himself. "Gilman" thanked me for giving him the opportunity to be a part of our company. Seeing how excited he was about the pot washing position, I opted to discuss his choice of our company. He stated without a thought, "Opportunity is why I'm here. I will begin a kitchen career in any position, pot sink, dishwasher, it doesn't matter. I won't stop, however, until I become a chef!" I discovered that he had come from a rich Cajun and Creole heritage and a long line of good cooks. But the shocker was that this was a career change for Gilman. He had graduated five years earlier from Louisiana State University in architecture. After working in his field at one of the most respected firms in Baton Rouge, he came to realize that his true love was cooking. A quick glance at the pot sink that morning turned out to be a golden opportunity, not only for Gilman, but for our company as well. Gilman realized his dream of becoming a chef. As an added bonus, we discovered our own resident architect on staff. With Gilman's architectural background and our knowledge of food and food production, imagine the team. I will never walk past the pot sink again without stopping and shaking a hand or two. Who knows what gem lies in that stack of dirty pots.

John Folse, CEC, AAC, Lafitte's Landing Restaurant, Donaldsonville, LA ganizational design" (2). This is done when the team adopts its own process of empowerment.

While the new approach to an empowered kitchen team will still require a chef supervisor, the role of the chef supervisor shifts from the traditional one of decision making to that of facilitating the process rather than deciding the outcomes. This new approach is one that is not easy to adopt. It takes time, patience, and leadership to implement. The leader of empowered teams is not the person who gives the orders but the one in charge of the development of the team members, the person who creates the environment for performance, learning, and development (3). This new type of leader is called a facilitative leader, and the most important ingredient of the concept of empowerment is the direct relationship between the kitchen team and the chef supervisor.

Decision making is the core process of working with empowered teams. There are different levels of participation in decision making. The lowest level is telling people what to do. One of the highest levels is when the kitchen team makes decisions together. The next critical step in team decision making is to take the chef supervisor out of the process altogether. The purposes of empowered problem solving in a TQM framework are the following:

1. To improve the foodservice organization's performance by successfully solving problems that cause dissatisfaction for internal or external customers (the dining room team members are an example of the kitchen's internal customers)
2. To ensure that problem solvers do not jump to solutions before the causes of the problem have been analyzed
3. To provide a process that can be used by the kitchen team to maximize each member's contribution.
4. To implement solutions to problems that effectively eliminate the problems through prevention

The more you consult the team, the more time it takes. However, there is a trade-off: The more people are involved in making a decision, the more committed they will be to implementing it (4). The common outcomes of empowerment through TQM include:

1. Reduced problems
2. Improved quality of food preparation
3. Cost reductions
4. Increased sanitation and safety awareness
5. Increased production
6. Improved and better decisions
7. Better team work
8. Greater team member responsibility
9. Greater respect
10. Continuous customer satisfaction

Empowered decision making solves problems. Allowing individuals to make decisions from the bottom up is by far a better approach to improving the culinary operation and satisfying customers' needs.

PROBLEMS

What is a problem? A problem is a situation that a person judges as bad or as something that needs to be corrected. A problem can be experienced in a number of ways but usually is looked upon as a shortfall, a deficit, a lack, a disharmony, a puzzlement, an inconvenience, a discomfort, or a pain of some sort. A problem implies that a state of wholeness does not exist and "should" exist (5).

The causes of many problems in the kitchen are generally linked with the quality of the food served. Associated with this are problems of timely service and production. Obviously, no two establishments have the same level or number of individual problems in these two areas. However, almost certainly when all of these problems are analyzed, they will be "people issues," such as level of training, attitudes, or skills. Very often the easiest problems to solve are ones that concern products or equipment. In spite of the best planning efforts problems occur. Problems occur because circumstances change or the unexpected happens. Some problems could have been foreseen and prevented, and others are largely outside the control of the chef supervisor. When improperly handled, problems can contribute to increased costs and can lower the morale of the kitchen team.

The reasons that problems occur in the kitchen are generally centered around the following:

1. *Team members may fail to do certain things*. They may forget to inform the chef supervisor that food materials have run out or that they have failed to arrive.
2. *Team members may do some things but fail to complete the job*. They listen to complaints concerning food items from waitstaff or customers but fail to follow through by solving the problem.
3. *Team members may do the wrong things*. They get confused during service, prepare the wrong order, or overcook or undercook dishes.
4. *Team members may do tasks poorly*. Food quality is reduced or there is indifference to TQM and/or customer service.
5. *Team members may be poorly motivated*. Lack of leadership within the team affects motivational levels.

The following questions may be used to identify some problems relative to issues of quality and customer service:

- Has the quality level of each menu item been established with each team member?
- Has the customer profile for the menu items been clearly identified?

- Has the foodservice establishment confirmed its menu acceptance by customers?
- Were the customers involved in determining the menu?
- Is there a clear relationship between customer expectations and the kitchen team?
- Are the customer satisfaction levels measurable? If not, can they be made measurable?
- Have all team members been trained to fulfill their roles?
- Has team responsibility been identified in each quality step?
- Has the menu been evaluated to ensure consistent quality levels during busy periods?
- Is there a shortfall between "actual" and "target" quality levels?
- Is there an opportunity to achieve better than target at no additional cost?
- Does the target level reflect competitive best practices?
- Can everyone on the kitchen team contribute to solving the problem?

In the empowered kitchen team, each member has the responsibility that was traditionally given to the executive chef. If any member sees a problem or has an idea, he or she is responsible for bringing it to the team. Each member should be looking for ways to grow and develop and contribute to solving problems.

THE PARETO PRINCIPLE

Many aids and mechanical methods and procedures exist that allow for problem analysis. These range from what is known as "mind mapping" to mathematical probability ratings. Perhaps the best known problem analysis method is the Pareto principle. Using the Pareto principle allows for collecting data, charting it, and grouping problems to determine cause and effects.

Vilfredo Pareto, an Italian economist who conducted extensive research on income distribution, discovered that in his native country 80 percent of the wealth was held by only 20 percent of the population. In international comparative research he established the same ratio. He eventually realized he had discovered a universal law: 80 percent of anything is attributed to 20 percent of its cause. For example, 80 percent of the important decisions are accomplished in 20 percent of the time. The 80-20 rule has come to be called the *Pareto principle*.

In problem solving this can also be determined as 80 percent of the effect can usually be attributed to 20 percent of the cause. Therefore, the Pareto principle may be used to chart those 20 percent of key problem causes that lead to 80 percent of the problems and cure them. An analysis of customer complaints, for example, can identify areas of concern that are directly related to the bulk of complaints. Diagrams and charts are used to present the frequency of occurrences of complaints so as to determine where the bulk of problems with customer service lies. Over a period of time, data can be accu-

Table 1   Complaints in a Restaurant

Summary of Data	Number of Complaints	Rank	Percentage of Complaints
Food cold	13	3	17
Service unfriendly	2		
Food undercooked	1		
Food overcooked	4	4	—
Flatware dirty	1		
Dining room cold	3		
Long wait to be seated	27	1	36
Room crowded	2		
Portions too small	1		
Decor	1		
Service slow	19	2	25
Noise level high	1		
Total	75		78

mulated from customer comment cards. Table 1 and Figure 5 are examples of using the Pareto principle.

From the data listed in the table and figure it is possible to establish where most of the complaints are (6). From the total number of 75 complaints, 59 are divided between three areas. This represents 78 percent of all the complaints. Therefore, corrective action can be taken to reduce almost 80 percent of the total complaints. Solutions to the three areas can be determined: (1) ways to speed up seating, (2) ways to speed up service, and (3) ways to ensure the customer receives hot food.

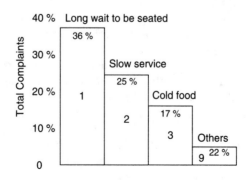

Figure 5   Percentage of total complaints.

Chef Talk: "Fixing a Problem"

In 1979 I went to work in Atlantic City, New Jersey. I had two months to get ready to open the first food service facility within our new hotel/casino. I found this to be a very exciting challenge, but I also found that I was confronted with a situation far beyond my expectations. There were no menus, no purchasing specifications, no storeroom par stocks for opening inventory, and no china, glass, or silver for catering, restaurants, and employee feeding.

What I did find, however, was a handful of dedicated chefs, ready to tackle the problems, looking for leadership and direction. We created menus, established recipes, set up our stewarding department with chemical supplies, china, glass, and silver par stocks. We established work schedules for all areas and developed payroll procedures.

Within two months of opening we hosted a banquet for two thousand people at a New Year's Eve Gala Event. During the evening, the exhaust system in our banquet kitchen broke down. I called two of our assistant directors to manually hold the exhaust system dampers in place until we had served the function and were able to shut down the system.

We work in an industry that is full of excitement. We solve problems every day, put out little fires, only to find others starting up in another area.

Solving problems is about good leadership and training programs and being able to make decisions. Employee involvement, discipline, and professional and technical expertise are the most important factors in solving problems.

Heiko Bendixen, CMC, AAC, Director of Foodservice, Showboat Hotel and Casino, Atlantic City, NJ

RULES OF PROBLEM SOLVING AND DECISION MAKING

Solving problems is something that is done as part of regular daily activities in the kitchen or in our personal lives. Problem solving can be both challenging and frustrating. It has often been said that problems are opportunities to be creative. On the other hand, there are so many difficulties with problem solving that it is necessary to use a sequential process. Knowledge gained from experience is a valuable asset, and its importance should not be underestimated. Fear of failure can also be a powerful force in decision making. There is no such thing as a riskless decision or a set of personal traits that guarantee correct decision making. Most people make decisions on the basis of "risk avoidance." Sometimes risk avoidance blocks a person from applying innovative solutions and ideas. Other elements that contribute to poor decision making in solving problems include:

- Getting involved with problems beyond the scope or ability of the kitchen team
- Failing to involve others in the solution of the problem
- Relying on previously used solutions only
- Failing to adequately investigate the cause of the problem
- Failing to seek advice
- Not suspending judgment to generate solutions
- Not being open minded
- Allowing other people to think you have the best answers

What is the ideal best solution for a problem? The ideal "best" solution probably doesn't exist. There are many possible solutions for each problem, and some are better than others. The best solution is nothing more than the best compromise under the circumstances.

The essential elements of problem solving are:

1. Recognizing the problem
2. Specifying the problem
   What is the problem and what is *not* the problem?
   Where is it and where is it *not*?
   Where did it happen?
   How big is the problem?
   Does it change with time and if so how?
3. Identifying possible causes
   What aspects stand out from the answers to the questions listed above?
   What aspects can be eliminated?
   Using my experience and that of the team, what could have caused the problem?
4. Testing causes
   Could the cause or causes have accounted for the entire problem?
   Are they within my control?
5. Alternative solutions
   What could I or my kitchen team do that would remove or reduce the cause?
   What would the consequences of each action be?
   Which is the best solution?
6. Implementing plan
   What must I do to implement the solution?

7. Reviewing effects
Is the problem solved?
Were there any unforeseen consequences to the actions?

Open and Closed Problems

Closed-ended problems are those in which the boundaries and constraints are fixed. They usually have one solution.

Examples

- Where should we locate?
- What supplier should we use?
- Accounting problems

Open-ended problems are those where boundaries and constraints can be questioned and may change during the solution.

Examples

- What dishes should we feature on our new menu?
- How do we solve our quality problems?
- What are tangible rewards for outstanding performances?

Potential problems

1. Recognize the potential problem:
What could go wrong?
2. Specify the potential problems:
What is likely to go wrong?
Where is it likely to go wrong?
When is it likely to happen?
How big a problem will it become?
How is it likely to happen?
3. Decide the action:
Can I prevent it from happening?
If so, what action can I take to prevent it?
If not, what action can I take to reduce its effects if and when it happens?
4. Plan the action:
What steps can I take now to prevent it and reduce its effects?
What steps can I take later to reduce its effects and prevent it from happening again?
5. Implement the action:
Often defining the problem is the key to successful problem-solving skills. If the problem is not clearly defined, all the other steps and efforts will be rendered useless.

SUMMARY

One of the most important duties of the chef supervisor is to make decisions and solve problems. Good decisions help the foodservice organization, whereas poor ones weaken it.

Decisions should be made on the basis of careful thought using facts and logic. Decisions are choices between two or more options. The decision-making process includes three basic options:

1. To proceed
2. To oppose
3. To take no action (let the problem solve itself)

Decision making follows six steps:

1. Set the objective for the decision.
2. Examine the problem.
3. Evaluate the facts.
4. Determine alternatives.
5. Choose the best option.
6. Implement the choice.

Empowerment is about giving decision making to the kitchen team. Decision making is given to the team in order to solve problems at the root source. The chef supervisor facilitates this process. Common outcomes of team-empowered decision making includes reduction of problems, greater responsibility, reduced costs, and better decisions.

The causes of many problems within the kitchen are generally linked to food quality, and most of these problems are "people" issues. These include:

1. Failing to do things
2. Failing to complete the job
3. Doing the wrong things
4. Doing tasks poorly
5. Poor motivation

By taking a proactive stand to solving potential problems, the kitchen team may avoid many problems of quality.

The Pareto principle is an effective method for determining where problems lie. Using this system can help discover where most of the problems are.

Using a structured and sequential set of steps allows for a more thorough decision-making and problem-solving procedure. These include:

- Recognizing problems
- Specifying problems
- Identifying possible causes
- Open and closed problems and other potential problems

DISCUSSION QUESTIONS

1. What are the three basic options in decision making?
2. What are the elements of the six-step model used to define problems?
3. How does the role of the chef supervisor change within the concept of team empowerment?
4. What are the links between decision making, team empowerment, and total quality management?
5. Why do most problems in the kitchen center around people issues?
6. What are the steps used to identify problems of quality and customer service?
7. What are the elements of the Pareto principle?
8. What are the uses of the Pareto principle relative to identifying and solving problems?
9. Why do most people make decisions on the basis of risk avoidance?
10. What is the difference between an open and a closed problem?

NOTES

1. Richard N. Chang and P. Keith Kelly, *Step by Step Problem Solving*, Richard Chang Associates, Irvine, CA, 1993, p. 83.
2. Florence Berger, Mark D. Fulford, and Michelle Krazmien, "Human Resources Management in the 21st Century: Predicting Partnerships for Profit," *Hospitality Research Journal*, Vol. 17, No. 1, 1993, p. 94.
3. Cynthia D. Scott and Dennis T. Jaffe. *Empowerment*, Crisp, London, 1991, p. 66.
4. Ibid., p. 80.
5. Donald J. Noone, *Creative Problem Solving*, Barron's, Hauppauge, NY, 1993, p. 22.
6. Adapted from *Total Quality Training* by Brian Thomas, McGraw-Hill, London, U.K., 1992, p. 121.

20

Team Performance Appraisal

Objectives

When you complete this chapter, you should be able to:

1. State the elements upon which chef supervisors evaluate team member performance within the kitchen.
2. Describe the benefits and the impact of performance appraisals on the development of the kitchen team.

3. Outline important methods of team member evaluation.

4. Describe the prior steps of appraisal interviews and outline the steps in conducting these interviews.

5. Outline the procedures for evaluating weak team member performance.

INTRODUCTION

Performance appraisal is the systematic process of developing criteria for job performance. This involves outlining criteria to team members along with assessing team members' job performance relative to the criteria and communicating the results to the team members (1).

Many chef supervisors look upon performance appraisals as an unpleasant task. However, performance appraisals present the chef supervisor with opportunities to make valuable contributions not only to the team, but also to each individual member, thus improving the culinary operation. It is not unusual for those chef supervisors who rise from the ranks to find it uncomfortable to evaluate another team member's performance.

Performance appraisal and evaluation is the on-going responsibility of all chef supervisors. They are required to consider how well members of the kitchen team are doing their jobs. Through appraisal it may be decided who should be recommended for promotion, transfer, reassignment, further training, salary increases, or even termination. One of the most important aspects, however, is encouraging team member performance improvement. In this regard, performance appraisals are used to communicate to team members how they are doing and to suggest needed changes in behavior, attitude, skills, or knowledge. This type of feedback clarifies for each team member the job task and overall quality expectations held by the chef supervisor. Additionally, appraisals often serve to validate the selection procedures used during the recruitment stage. (These were described in Chapter 17.)

Performance appraisals should be conducted periodically to let team members know how they are doing and to outline to them whether their performance is satisfactory or unsatisfactory. This typically is done through an appraisal interview.

EVALUATING PERFORMANCE

Performance evaluation is never an end in itself. It is the preliminary step prior to conducting meaningful feedback discussions, making appropriate administrative recommendations, and determining where performance improvement is required. Evaluation of team members includes the following aspects of performance:

- The quality of work performed
- The amount of work performed

- The quality of sanitation or safety procedures
- Culinary skill
- Personal grooming or appearance
- Attendance
- Cooperation
- Ability to work unsupervised
- Knowledge of rules and company procedures
- Food cost control procedures
- Team player
- Leadership potential

Nearly everyone is interested in how they are viewed by the chef supervisor. In the absence of specific feedback, team members often form their own conclusions by comparing their experiences with others around them. This can sometimes lead to wrong conclusions. Clearing up doubt or uncertainty is a major purpose of the performance appraisal (2):

> A productive appraisal, along with providing a review of the employee's work, serves as a work session between supervisor and employee in which you take the time and effort to meet with an individual employee and set new goals and objectives for the coming year. A productive appraisal recognizes that *people* are the most valuable resource of any organization.

Benefits of good performance appraisals include:

- Team members learn what their strengths and weaknesses are within the team.
- New goals and objectives are agreed upon between the chef supervisor and team member.
- The relationship between the chef supervisor and the team member is brought to a new level.
- The team member becomes an active participant in the team objectives.
- The team may be restructured for maximum efficiency.
- The team member's commitment to the team is renewed.
- New training needs are identified.
- Time is set aside for discussing issues other than money.
- Team members feel they are taken seriously as individuals.

Performance appraisals also provide written records to substantiate actions. Therefore, they can serve as an information and team member feedback system.

More and more administrative decisions taken by management are being subjected to review by outside parties. To verify the appropriateness of decisions made, it is necessary to document all meetings for review purposes. Performance appraisals serve as excellent records. Such documentation can also serve to confirm understandings between the chef supervisor and the team member.

METHODS OF EVALUATION

An evaluative decision is made by comparison. Whatever is being evaluated is compared to something else, and it exceeds or equals or falls short in comparison (3). There are many methods of evaluation. Each has its merits. Indeed, many foodservice organizations use more than one. Some of these methods include:

1. *Essay appraisal*: In its simplest form, this technique requires the chef supervisor to write a paragraph or more covering a team member's individual strengths and weaknesses and his or her potential for further development. A major weakness of this method is its variability in length and content. Essay evaluations are difficult to combine or compare.
2. *Graphic rating scale*: Typically a graphic scale assesses a team member on the quality and quantity of work—outstanding, above average, or unsatisfactory—and on a variety of other factors that vary but usually include traits like reliability and cooperation.
3. *Critical-incident appraisal*: A critical-incident appraisal requires the chef supervisor to maintain a log of critical incidents of positive or negative behavior. So, for appraisal purposes the discussion with the team member is based on actual behavior. One of the drawbacks to this method is that it requires the chef supervisor to write down incidents on a regular basis.
4. *Behaviorially anchored rating scales*: These scales (commonly referred to as BARSs) require that a job analysis has been conducted that identified performance behavior appropriate for different levels. The BARS method is objective. Each team member is rated against a predetermined specific set of behaviors identified on a job-by-job basis. The downside to this evaluation method is that it can be costly to initiate and time consuming for the chef supervisor.

Even though there are a variety of performance appraisal methods to choose from, it is still possible to end up with inaccurate information on the kitchen team. To avoid this, chef supervisors should be trained in the techniques of performance appraisals. A common error in the performance appraisal process is the "Halo effect" (discussed in Chapter 17). This occurs when the evaluator allows a single prominent characteristic of a team member to influence his or her judgment. Personal preferences, prejudices, and biases can also cause errors in performance appraisals. Chef supervisors with biases or

```
┌─────────────────────────────────────────────────────────┐
│ Team member:        John Smith                          │
│                                                          │
│ Job Title:            Kitchen Team Member               │
│                                                          │
│ Department:          Kitchen                            │
│                                                          │
│ Check all items relevant to team member's position. Rate│
│ each item on a scale of 1–5. Circle number at right:    │
│                                                          │
│               1 = Needs much improvement                │
│               2 = Needs some improvement                │
│               3 = Satisfactory                          │
│               4 = Very good                             │
│               5 = Excellent                             │
│                                                          │
│ Part I:    General work habits and attitude             │
│                                                          │
│ Sanitation and safety          1    2    3    4    5    │
│ Attendance and punctuality     1    2    3    4    5    │
│ Meets deadlines                1    2    3    4    5    │
│ Cooperates with team members   1    2    3    4    5    │
│ Accepts suggestions            1    2    3    4    5    │
│ Uses equipment properly        1    2    3    4    5    │
│ Prioritizes work well          1    2    3    4    5    │
│                                                          │
│ Part II: Job performance                                │
│                                                          │
│ Quality of work                1    2    3    4    5    │
│ Ability to solve problems      1    2    3    4    5    │
│ Uses original ideas            1    2    3    4    5    │
│ Communications ability         1    2    3    4    5    │
│ Time management                1    2    3    4    5    │
│ Hands-on skills                1    2    3    4    5    │
│ Interpersonal skills           1    2    3    4    5    │
│ Ability to work on a team      1    2    3    4    5    │
└─────────────────────────────────────────────────────────┘
```

Figure 6   Appraisal evaluation form.

prejudices tend to look for team member behaviors that conform to their biases. Figure 6 is a simple generic example of a graphic rating scale.

APPRAISAL INTERVIEWS

The performance appraisal process is not complete until there is a conference between the team member and chef supervisor. These interviews allow discussion about the period since the last appraisal. They typically review the previous year and set a course for the coming year. These discussions help answer such questions as: "How am I doing?" "Where can I go from here?" and "How do I get there?" The first step in beginning an appraisal interview is to give the team member a few days notice of the interview date so that he or she may prepare for it. Chef supervisors should preview relevant data for the interview during this time period. Select a time and a place for the interview that will be private and free from interruptions. The spirit that should permeate this interview is one of teamwork, a collaborative problem-solving approach. Traditionally team members view a performance appraisal as an ordeal they must go through before they can find out whether or not they will receive a negative or positive evaluation.

Start the interview by creating the impression that you consider it very important. Next, help the team member to feel that the interview is a valuable, constructive, cooperative process by placing emphasis on his or her development. Avoid any impression that the interview was arranged only for the purposes of warning or reprimanding. Assure the team member that its purpose is to give constructive and objective feedback.

The interview portion of the performance appraisal should consist of a thorough review of the team member's goals for the appraisal period, the degree to which these goals were accomplished, and setting new goals for the subsequent period. The discussion should be based on observed behavior and performance, not on the team member's personal characteristics. Team members accept criticism when it is based on fact rather than vague remarks. This is where the *actual* appraisal evaluation method is used. This may be a behaviorally anchored rating scale (BARS), a graphic rating scale, or a critical-incident appraisal method. Try to keep the interview friendly, natural, and informal. Remember, the interview is also used to give positive feedback.

Suggestions for conducting the interview

- Arrange the meeting area so you and the team member can sit face to face, without a desk between you, or with both of you sitting at the same side of the desk.
- Make the area comfortable, with the right temperature and comfortable chairs.
- Create a nonthreatening environment and display a supportive attitude.
- Ensure you have all relevant data concerning the team member.
- Select for the interview only those accomplishments and problems relevant to the discussion.
- Focus feedback on the behavior rather than on the individual.
- Get the team member to commit to future goals and set benchmarks for accomplishment.
- Ask team members for their opinions on work-related issues. Interviews are two-way streets. Encourage continued conversation.
- Allow for individual differences in your ratings. Don't compare an average but competent team member with a superstar.
- Evaluate honestly and carefully. Don't say, "I don't like your attitude." It is more appropriate to say, "Your behavior shows that you seem to resent

doing the work that is asked of you. If that is true, you need to change your behavior." (Give specific examples.)

- Some questions encourage while others limit. State questions so that the team member will think and give detailed responses. Generally avoid closed-ended questions that require yes or no answers. Actively listen and avoid forming conclusions on too little data.

An interview cannot be conducted only as a series of questions. It is appropriate for the chef supervisor to add thoughts on the various topics discussed. This will be either confirmation or clarification of the team member's understanding of the points discussed. Always allow the team member ample time to respond to any questions posed.

Closing the interview   When all the points have been covered that were planned, close the discussion. Three important issues need to be addressed at this stage:

1. Summarize the key points and check for team members' understanding. Invite them also to summarize.
2. Compare the points agreed upon.
3. Team members should have a chance to review their problems and outline any concerns or work-related problems that they may have.

Following the interview closing write a brief summary of the discussion. This should include action plans or action points (in some instances it is appropriate to have the team member sign off on this). If it was agreed to do anything during the course of the interview, follow through. If something that was agreed to is later not acted upon, it can have a serious impact on the team member's morale. It sends a message that you don't care. Follow-up is important with all team members, but it is crucial when dealing with weak team members. They need continued guidance and support from the chef supervisor.

Documenting appraisal interviews serves a secondary purpose. It can also be used to protect the chef supervisor and the foodservice organization if they are accused of bias or improper behavior by an individual or by another manager and a lawsuit is brought: "Any incidents that are out of the ordinary or that involve a significant clash of tempers or personalities should be included in the documentation" (4).

COMPENSATION

Hourly wages or salaries are usually established collaboratively between upper management and the chef supervisor (unions may be involved if there is an agreed-on procedure in this area). Productive performance appraisals focus entirely on issues of strengths and weaknesses and the development of new goals and objectives. Once money becomes part of the discussion, interest in improvement tends to dissipate. If the team member does bring up the question of money during the appraisal interview, state that you will discuss it later and that now you want to concentrate on performance only. If the issue of money persists, explain that you are bound by company guidelines and that you do not make the final decision about salary increases. However, indicate clearly that your recommendation in this area will in large part be based on the outcome of this current appraisal interview.

Appraising the poor team member   Performance appraisals do not always bring good news to a team member. Good and bad employees must be told how they are doing. Handling the bad news requires some special techniques (5):

- Have the relevant documentation available to demonstrate previous discussions on poor performance.
- Give specific examples of where work failed to match set quality standards. Show where work failed to match the work of other team members.
- Prepare a list of changes you wish team members to make in their performance.
- Be positive about the team member's ability to improve. Arrange for further training sessions.
- Set short-term goals that are within the ability of the individual. Progressively build upon successes.
- Be honest with team members. Spell out clearly what they have to do and outline the consequences if they do not improve.
- Make a short-term agreement with the team member on measurable performance improvements set against a specific time period. Agree to meet again after the short time period to assess progress.

End the meeting on a positive note. Point out the team member's accomplishments. Reaffirm your willingness to continue to work with the team member until he or she reaches a satisfactory performance level. It is vital to get the team member's attention if the performance is unsatisfactory. Chef supervisors should not gloss over prior performances and go easy on the team member. What may be viewed by the chef supervisor as a tough review may be seen as an acceptable appraisal by the team member unless the unsatisfactory behavior is clearly stated.

SUMMARY

A sound performance appraisal system draws on both the chef supervisor and the team member. Together they negotiate performance expectations for the future. Through appraisal it may be decided who should be recommended for promotion, transfer, reassignment, further training, salary increases, or termination. Performance appraisals are used to communicate to team members their strengths and weaknesses on the job, and together with the chef supervisor plans for future development can be made. Performance appraisals should be conducted periodically. They usually include aspects of work quality, attitude, and cooperation.

When used correctly and appropriately, performance evaluations may be an asset in identifying gaps in the training stage and act as information-gathering systems and morale boosters for the kitchen team.

Performance evaluation methods vary: supervisor-produced essays, graphic rating scales, critical incident appraisal, and behaviorally anchored rating scales (BARSs). Every effort should be made to eliminate areas of bias and prejudice when evaluating team members.

Appraisal interviews are used to apprise the team member of acceptable or unacceptable behavior. They should contain a thorough review of the team member's performance outlined during a matter-of-fact, friendly interview. When the interview is concluded, both parties "sign off" on agreed goals. Issues discussed and agreed upon should be documented.

DISCUSSION QUESTIONS

1. What are the positive outcomes of team member performance appraisal?
2. How can performance appraisals be used to validate selection procedures?
3. What elements of team member performance are usually evaluated?
4. What are the benefits of performance appraisals relative to working relations between the chef supervisor, the foodservice organization, and the individual team member?
5. Why is it appropriate to maintain a written record of performance appraisal interviews?
6. Describe the procedures commonly used for conducting appraisal interviews.
7. What is the halo effect?
8. What important factors should be considered for conducting appraisal interviews?
9. What are the three important issues to be addressed at the conclusion of the interview?
10. How should the question of compensation be treated by the chef supervisor during the interview?
11. What is the methodology used to appraise weaker team members?

NOTES

1. Donald W. Myers, Wallace R. Johnson, and Glenn Pearce, "The Role of Interaction Theory in Approval Feedback," *SAM Advanced Management Journal*, Summer 1991, p. 28.

2. Marion E. Haynes, *Stepping up to Supervisor*, Los Altos, CA, 1990, p. 84.
3. Randi Toler Sachs, *Productive Performance Appraisals*, AMACOM, New York 1992, p. 5.
4. Ibid., p. 43
5. Alfred W. Travers, *Supervision, Techniques and New Dimensions*, Prentice-Hall, Englewood Cliffs, NJ, 1993, p. 181.

Final Thoughts: Chefs and the Future?

We close with a few words about this book. The aim of this book was to create an information, educational, and training resource for all culinarians. It is set in the present, written for the future, but with an eye to the past.

There is a growing perception in many areas of the foodservice industry that we are going through a paradigm shift, a totally new way of thinking about old problems. It occurs when a great many new conceptual frameworks put pressure on old ones. Total quality management (TQM) is one such pressure.

In the Foreword of this book I outlined the changing nature of the chef's job. It is my belief and conviction that chefs must become and be perceived as more than *just* culinarians. To survive in the changing business realm of the future, chefs must formally acquire leadership and supervisory skills along with a thorough understanding of business concepts such as TQM. Total quality management will not go away; its name may change, but its customer-driven competitive philosophy most certainly will not. I am convinced this is good news for chefs. Chefs can now aspire to being truly "chefs" in more than the culinary sense.

Central to the successful implementation and application of TQM is the leadership of people—a new way of harnessing the collective brainpower of employees, empowering them and building them into a team completely focused on the growth of the organization by satisfying customers.

Many of the reasons for writing this book are rooted in my belief that chefs are going through a paradigm shift. The role of the chef can no longer be viewed only from a historical perspective. In the past "Czar" chefs presided over a kitchen from a culinary standpoint only, and this was acceptable then. This person was expected to be a master of the culinary art. Management and business considerations were handled by others.

Enter the 1990s. Chefs can no longer perceive themselves only as culinarians. Business and supervisory skills will move the chef to the next level. This means knowing and understanding how to unleash the creative powers of the entire kitchen team to meet these new challenges.

Coping with change and uncertainty can be difficult. Senior chefs must come to terms with this new expanded role. Those who do will succeed.

The modern chef supervisor needs an overall framework within which to work, one that provides practical norms while capturing the imagination of each team member, manager, and customer. Our future culinarians will be comfortable with these additional areas of responsibility. When supervisory and management skills are merged with those culinary skills—what a combination.

This paradigm shift therefore requires chefs to think in a new and different way about their roles. Future chef supervisors will be required to create a culture in the kitchen, where not only are quality menu items produced, but people are also empowered and led and in a work environment where team building is central.

I have a tremendous belief in chefs. I know they will meet this new challenge and succeed. It is an exciting prospect. It offers to chefs an opportunity to increase and enhance their image, not only as culinarians, but also as forward thinking professionals.

APPENDIX A

Federal Regulations and Executive Orders

EMPLOYMENT REGULATIONS

National Labor Relations Act (1935) (Wagner Act)

Purpose   To establish a national policy of encouraging collective bargaining, guaranteeing certain employee rights, and detailing specific employer unfair labor practices and to establish the National Labor Relations Board (NLRB) to enforce these provisions.

This act was further amended by the Labor-Management Relations (Taft-Hartley) Act of 1947 and the Labor-Management Reporting and Disclosure (Landrum-Griffin) Act of 1959, which establishes a balance between management and union power to protect the public interest and provides detailed regulations for internal union affairs.

Applies to   Private employers and unions.

Penalties   The NLRB has the power to investigate, dismiss charges or hold hearings, issue cease and desist orders, or pursue cases via Circuit Courts of Appeals or U.S. Supreme Court.

Regulatory agency   National Labor Relations Board.

Title VII of the Civil Rights Act (1964)

Purpose   The principal federal law relating to most types of employment discrimination; its purpose is to give everyone an equal chance to obtain employment. The law has a number of objectives, specifically:

- Outlaws certain discriminatory employment practices
- Creates a federal agency to enforce the law and give it regulatory powers
- Sets penalties for violators of the law
- Requires state laws to uphold Title VII
- Requires that certain records be maintained by designated persons or agencies
- Does not alter state or federal veterans' preference laws

Title VII prohibits employment discrimination based on race, religion, sex, color, or national origin. Employers are also prohibited from discriminatory practices regarding:

- Recruiting and hiring
- Job advertising
- Ability and experience
- Occupational qualification
- Testing
- Prehire inquiries
- Employment status
- Compensation
- Merit, incentive, or seniority plans
- Insurance, retirement, and welfare plans
- Promotion and seniority
- Dress and appearance
- Leave of absence benefits
- Discharge
- Retirement
- Union membership
- Persons opposed to discriminatory practices or exercising their rights under Title VII

Applies to   Private or public employers who have 15 or more employees, private and public employment agencies, hiring halls, or labor unions with 15 or more members.

Penalties   Court-decreed affirmative action programs and back pay.

Regulatory agency Equal Employment Opportunity Commission.

Freedom of Information Act (FOIA) (1966)

Purpose To reduce privacy protection by authorizing the release of private information under certain conditions. This act could apply to employee access to personal records, employee information provided to other businesses, and disclosure of personnel information to third parties. This act was created to allow access to records held by federal agencies. Many states have laws that impact on both privacy protection and freedom of information protection.

Applies to Federal agencies and federal records. But the FOIA may be used by anyone as a means of accessing federally maintained information used for decision making.

Age Discrimination in Employment Act (1967, 1978, 1986)

Purpose The act promotes the employment of older persons based on ability rather than age; it prohibits arbitrary age discrimination in employment for workers 40 years or older; it helps employers and workers resolve age-related employment problems.

Applies to Private employers with 20 or more workers; all governments regardless of number of employees. Federal employment has no upper age limit. Applies also to employment agencies and unions with 25 or more members.

Penalties Court-decreed affirmative action programs, back pay, fines up to $10,000, and possible imprisonment.

Regulatory agency Equal Employment Opportunity Commission.

Immigration Reform and Control Act of 1986

Purpose The act requires employers to hire only citizens and aliens who are authorized to work in the United States.

Applies to All employers who hire someone to perform labor or services for wages or other pay.

Penalties Fines range from $100 for record keeping violations to $10,000 per unauthorized employee for hiring unauthorized persons.

Regulatory agency The U.S. Immigration and Naturalization Service.

Drug-Free Workplace Act (1988)

Purpose   Requires each employer-holder of government contracts to certify to the federal contracting agency that it will provide a drug-free workplace by publishing a company policy statement describing unlawful behaviors, required employment conditions, violation penalties; by publicizing the program within the company; and by taking appropriate disciplinary or rehabilitation steps for violators. This act does not mandate drug testing.

Applies to   Employers with employees that hold or seek federal contracts of $25,000 or more and on federal grants.

Penalties   Suspension or termination of grants and/or debarment from federal procurement process for up to five years.

Regulatory agency   The Federal Contracting Agency.

Americans with Disabilities Act (1990)

Purpose   Provides broad nondiscrimination protection for individuals in employment, public services, public accommodations, and services operated by private entities, transportation, and telecommunications. Title I states that no entity covered by this act shall discriminate against a qualified individual because of a disability with regard to a job application procedure or in the hiring, advancement, or discharge of employees, employee compensation, job training, and other terms, conditions, and privileges of employment.

Applies to   As of July 1992 all businesses with 25 or more employees, and in July 1994 all businesses with 15 or more employees.

Penalties   Administrative enforcement and/or individual suits to include injunctive relief and back pay but not compensatory and punitive damages. These latter remedies may be pursued under the Civil Rights Act of 1991.

Regulatory agency   Equal Employment Opportunities Commission.

Civil Rights Act (1991)

Purpose   Extends punitive damages and jury trials to victims of employment discrimination based on the employee's sex, religion, disability, as well as race. Under previous acts employees could only seek back pay.

Applies to   All businesses with 15 or more employees.

Penalties   Punitive damages caps as follows: $50,000 for businesses with 100 or fewer employees; $100,000 for firms with 101 to 500 workers; and a maximum limit of $300,000 for businesses with over 500 employees.

Regulatory agency   Equal Employment Opportunity Commission.

Family and Medical Leave Act of 1993

Purpose   Permits employees to take up to 12 weeks of unpaid leave per year from work for the birth or adoption of a child; for the case of a seriously ill child, spouse, or parent; or for a serious illness afflicting the worker. Employers must guarantee the worker can return to the same or a comparable job. Employers must also continue health care coverage during the leave period. During the leave time workers are not eligible for unemployment or other government compensation.

Applies to   Employers that have 50 or more employees within a 75-mile radius. Employees who have not worked at least one year and have not worked 1250 hours or 25 hours a week in the previous 12 months are not covered by the law. This law takes effect in August 1993.

Regulatory agency   Equal Employment Opportunity Commission.

COMPENSATION REGULATIONS

Most compensation benefits are based on the provision of the Old Age, Survivors, Disability and Health Insurance Program (OASDHI). More than 90 percent of the U.S. labor force is covered by these programs, which include Social Security, unemployment, Medicare, and Medicaid benefits. The OASDHI also covers welfare services such as Aid to Families of Dependent Children (AFDC).

Workers' Compensation (each state has its own laws)

Purpose   It financially compensates workers or their dependents for work-related injuries, diseases, or death. Since the employer is responsible for any job-related damage a worker may sustain, laws have been enacted at the state level to institute insurance programs to cover employees.

Applies to   Most employees except farm workers, home workers, and federal employees.

Regulatory agency   A state industrial commission.

Unemployment Compensation—Title IX of the Social Security Act (1935)

Purpose   The act provides for financial assistance to workers who have been laid off through no fault of their own. Funds are raised through state employment compensation taxes. Each state maintains its own program. The program provides benefits only to employees whose employers are paying the tax. States may establish certain eligibility requirements such as a minimum length of time worked or having earned a minimum set wage.

Applies to   Any employer with one or more employees who worked some part of 20 or more weeks must pay federal or state unemployment tax. Also covered are employers paying wages of $1500 or more in any calendar quarter. Some states may have more rigid requirements than the federal minimum.

Regulatory agency   The state unemployment commission.

Social Security Act (1935)

Purpose   The act was originally created to provide a minimum income for retired workers. Amendments have increased coverage to compensate dependents of a deceased worker and totally disabled workers; hospital and medical insurance coverage to include Medicare for people over 65. Funding is through taxes collected from both employers and employees based on income earned. These taxes are authorized by the Federal Insurance Contributions Act (FICA).

Applies to   Most workers in the United States. Some civilian federal employees are covered instead by a federal retirement system.

Regulatory agency   Social Security Administration in the U.S. Department of Health and Human Services.

Minimum Wage Act (1938)—Amendment to the Fair Labor Standards Act (1938)

Purpose   This federal law specifies a minimum hourly wage and standard work week. Additionally, the law establishes overtime pay, equal pay, required records, and child labor standards.

Applies to   All enterprises affecting interstate commerce. It includes laundries and dry cleaners, construction firms, hospitals, public and private schools, and a retail or service establishment with annual gross sales of not less than $362,500 and any other business with annual gross sales of at least $250,000.

Penalties   Back pay, fines up to $10,000, and possible imprisonment.

Regulatory agency   The U.S. Department of Labor's Wage and Hour Division.

Equal Pay Act (1963)—Amendment to the Fair Labor Standards Act (1938)

Purpose   The Equal Pay Act is part of the Fair Labor Standards Act. It prohibits differential wages paid to men and women doing substantially the same work. If both sexes are doing the same work with similar skills, responsibility, working conditions, and effort, then the pay must be equal.

Applies to   All businesses affecting interstate commerce, including local, state, and federal agencies.

Penalties   Back pay, fines up to $10,000, and possible imprisonment.

Regulatory agency   The U.S. Department of Labor's Wage and Hour Division.

Employment Retirement Income Security Act (1974) (ERISA)

Purpose   The act was enacted to ensure that private employee pension plans will actually provide something when the recipients retire and become eligible for the benefits. ERISA is a complex regulation requiring retirement plan managers to adhere to specific fiduciary duties, maintain records and reports, and remain within specified investment restrictions.

Applies to   Employees with pension plans. ERISA requires companies with pension plans to subscribe to specific regulations regarding the administration of the plans, but it does not require employers to have any pension plans.

Regulatory agency   The Pension Benefit Guaranty Corporation, a federal agency, administers the plan termination insurance program (which ensures that employees obtain vested retirement rights if the plan fails). The Internal Revenue Service Office of Employee Plans and Exempt Organizations handles tax implications and the Department of Labor's Labor-Management Services Administration handles other aspects of managing ERISA. Congress has considered creating a single entity to be in charge, the Employee Benefits Administration.

Individual Retirement Accounts (Revenue Act of 1978)

Purpose   The original purpose of the act was to enable small businesses to have employee retirement plans without the administrative burden of ERISA. The IRA allowed a business to pay $7500 or up to 15 percent of an employee's gross salary (whichever is smaller) to a bank, savings and loan, mutual fund, or insurance company for investment for the employee. In 1981 it was expanded to allow employees to contribute an additional $2000 to their company retirement fund or to their own IRA.

Applies to   Any employer or employee. For an individual to be eligible, he or she must have compensation included in his or her income during the year.

Regulatory agency   The Internal Revenue Service.

Occupational Safety and Health Act (1970) (OSHA)

Purpose   The act created regulations and enforcement practices to render the work environment safe and healthy for workers.

Applies to   Any firm affecting interstate commerce having one or more employees.

Penalties   Violation citations and fines up to $10,000 for each violation.

Regulatory agency   The Occupational Safety and Health Administration in the Department of Labor.

APPENDIX B

Glossary of Terms

Active listening Encouraging the speaker to continue talking by giving interested responses that show that you understand the speaker's meaning and feelings.

Affirmative action Actions or programs designed to improve employment opportunities for members of protected groups, such as minorities, the aged, and the handicapped.

Androgogy Concept of adult education.

Apprentice A worker serving a special training period that combines formal schooling with job experience in preparation for entry into a skilled job.

Authority The rights and powers to make the necessary decisions and to take the necessary action to get the job done.

Autocratic leadership A leadership style characterized by a high concern for task (getting the job done) and a relatively low concern for people.

Body language Expression of attitudes and feelings through body movements and positions.

Brainstorming Generating ideas within a group without considering their drawbacks, limitations, or consequences.

Budget As a planning tool it commits organizational resources to projects, programs, or activities, and results are measured in quantifiable terms over predetermined time periods. As a control device it compares actual performance against expectations.

Case study A form of training that provides trainees with materials that describe particular situations, where the trainees are to analyze the case and make recommendations.

Closed-end questions   Interview questions that require specific and usually restricted responses.

Coaching   Individual, corrective on-the-job training for improving performance.

Collective bargaining   The process of negotiating and administering a union contract.

Communication   The process of passing along information and understanding from one person to another person or group.

Critical incident technique   A form of performance appraisal that has supervisors observe and record outstanding employee behavior, good or bad.

Culinarian   Person who works in a kitchen preparing food.

Cultural empathy   Being sensitive to cultural differences and similarities by seeking to understand others' approach to life and their ways of thinking and living.

Decision   Conscious choice between alternatives.

Delegation   The process of distributing work to others and providing them with the appropriate resources and authority to do the task.

Democratic leadership   A leadership style characterized by a high concern for both people and task accomplishment.

Demotivator   An emotion, environmental factor, or incident that reduces motivation to perform well.

Discipline   The punishment of employees for violating the rules or performance requirements of the organization. The process of socializing employees to accept and follow the rules and values of the organization.

Dissatisfiers   Factors in the job environment that produce dissatisfaction, usually reducing motivation.

Diversity   The physical and cultural dimensions that separate and distinguish individuals and groups: age, gender, physical abilities and qualities, ethnicity, race, and sexual preference.

Downward communication   The process of passing along information and understanding from the higher levels of the organization to the lower levels.

Due process   The means by which employees are given a chance for fair treatment by their employers. The process includes such protective measures as having reasonable work rules, a chance to defend against any accusations, and review by higher levels of management.

Employee rights   The concept that employees are to be treated fairly and with dignity by their employers and if there are violations of those rights, employees should have recourse against the employers.

Empowerment   Giving employees permission to make decisions. In the foodservice industry, empowering employees to satisfy the customer.

Ethnocentrism   A belief that one's own culture or ways of doing things is best.

Exempt employee   An employee who under the provisions of the Fair Labor Standards Act is exempt from the overtime pay requirements of the act, generally considered to be persons employed in a bona fide executive, administrative, or professional capacity.

Exit interview   An interview of a terminating employee to learn the employee's honest reactions or his or her reasons for leaving the organization, usually conducted on the last day of employment.

Expectancy theory   A motivation theory that holds that individuals are motivated to act when they believe their actions will bring about desirable results for themselves.

Facilitator   A new dimension to the supervisor's job that gives emphasis to the supervisor taking appropriate measures to make it easier for workers to do their jobs as well as removing obstacles that hinder performance.

Foodservice organization   Any establishment preparing and serving food and utilizing professionals.

Grievances   The real or imagined complaints of workers against management or working conditions, often related to union-management relations.

Grievance procedure   The procedure set up either by management or by management and the union to fairly resolve employee complaints.

HACCP   Hazard Analysis Critical Control Point. A food preparation safety system that targets high risk foods and preparation at critical points and seeks to maximize safe food handling.

Halo effect   The tendency to assume that because one or a few things are done well by a person, all things about that person are good.

Handicapped worker   Any person who has or is considered to have a physical or mental impairment that substantially limits one or more of such person's major life activities.

Hierarchy of needs theory   Abraham Maslow's motivation theory that identifies and arranges in order of dominance the five levels of human needs.

Hot stove rule   The disciplinary technique that is designed to ensure fair treatment to all employees by comparing the taking of disciplinary action to what happens when one touches a hot stove.

Human relations movement   A belief that the workplace is a social setting, and as such, more attention has to be given to human needs, motivation, and interpersonal relations.

Hygiene factors   Frederick Herzberg's concept that the job-related factors of working conditions, interpersonal relations, organizational policies and procedures, quality of supervision, and pay can cause worker dissatisfaction.

Induction training   The absorbing of new team members into the culture and philosophy of the organization.

Insubordination   The refusal by an employee to follow a direct order of a supervisor.

Job description   A written statement that sets forth in general terms the duties of the position and related responsibilities so people can understand what is done by the person holding that particular job.

Job interview   A purposeful conversation between an employer and a job applicant that deals with the exchange of relevant information about job-related matters.

Job rotation   Periodically moving team members to different jobs for such purposes as cross-training and relieving worker boredom.

Job satisfiers   Frederick Herzberg's concept that the job-related factors of achievement, recognition, responsibility, advancement, and opportunity for growth give employees satisfaction on the job and thus serve as motivators.

Job specifications   A written listing of the specific requirements to perform the job.

Job talk   A training technique of imparting information from the supervisor to the team member. Relies on an illustrated lecture.

Leadership   The ability to influence others to do something voluntarily rather than because it is required or because there is fear of the consequences of not doing it or expectation of reward for doing it.

Learning objective   The training goals stated in measurable or observable terms.

Management by objectives (MBO)   A results-oriented management technique that seeks employee involvement leading to supervisor and employee mutually setting goals and evaluation criteria and that will serve as the basis for evaluating that person's contribution to the overall organizational goals.

MBWA   Management by wandering around.

Mise en place   Preparation, everything ready; in kitchens refers to preparation prior to food service. A collection of items necessary to prepare menu items.

Morale   Group spirit with respect to getting the job done.

Motivation   The stimulating or causing of purposeful activity that is directed to satisfying needs or wants.

Negative discipline   Maintaining discipline through fear and punishment.

Nonexempt employee   An employee who under the provisions of the Fair Labor Standards Act is entitled to overtime pay for hours worked in excess of the statutory requirements.

Nonverbal communication   Communication without words. Use of gestures, facial expressions, or body language.

On-the-job training   Training that is done at the workplace under regular working conditions.

Open-end questions   Interview questions that allow for a range of responses.

Organization   A collection of individuals who are working together to reach common goals.

Organizing   The prelude to action and the process of mentally and physically preparing and arranging for the necessary resources to accomplish results.

Orientation   The programmed introduction of new employees into the organization by which they learn what is important to the organization, to the supervisor, and to fellow employees.

Participative management   A style of management that seeks to give employees a meaningful involvement in their job and conditions of employment.

Performance appraisal   The systematic evaluation of the employee's work performance and potential with the organization.

Personal space   The area within 2–3 feet of a person.

Planning   The process by which management determines expected outcomes and coordinates resources, personnel, and activities to reach these objectives.

Policies   The written statements of the goals and intentions of the top management of the organization.

Positive discipline   A punishment-free formula for disciplinary action that replaces punishment with reminders and features a decision-making leave of absence with pay.

Procedures   The written statements that spell out the details of what is to be done and how.

Productivity   A measure of the relationship that exists between outputs, such as so many pieces per hour, to inputs, such as hours worked to produce the items.

Pygmalion effect   J. Sterling Livingston's concept that the performance level of subordinates is affected by the supervisor's expectations and abilities.

Quality   The concept that the product or service meets the stated and implied specifications.

Rating scale   A form of performance appraisal that requires the rater to make a selection from several predetermined choices.

Re-engineering   The re-design of work processes and the implementation of the new design.

Role model   One who serves as an example for the behavior of others.

Role playing   A form of training that attempts to create common and realistic learning situations (such as performance reviews or disciplinary actions) by having employees act out their assigned roles.

Rules   A form of control that spells out the code of conduct that is required by the organization, and, in many cases, states the penalties for violation.

Sexual harassment   Unwelcome advances, requests for sexual favors, and other verbal or physical conduct of a sexual nature when compliance with any of these acts is a condition of employment, or when comments or physical contact create an intimidating, hostile or offensive working environment.

Scientific management   The concept developed by Frederick Taylor that holds that work is most efficiently performed when management scientifically studies each job, determines the basic elements of each, standardizes the methods and tools used, selects workers suited to the specific jobs, provides for job specialization, and sees to strong supervisory support.

Situational leadership   Adaptation of leadership style to the needs of the situation.

Socialization   The process by which people learn and come to accept the appropriate values and behaviors for various situations.

Supervisor   An employee who is in a management position and has authority to perform such management duties as assigning work, hiring, firing, and making promotions and transfers, or can effectively recommend such actions.

Supportive leadership   A leadership style characterized by a high concern for people and a relatively low concern for task accomplishment.

Theory X   Douglas McGregor's concept that some supervisors assume a generally negative view of workers, believing that the typical employee is lazy, dislikes work, and must be closely supervised.

Theory Y   Douglas McGregor's concept that some supervisors assume a generally positive view of workers, believing that the typical employee is willing, personally responsible, and responds best to a minimum of supervision.

Total quality management (TQM)   A business and management philosophy/process in which all efforts are expended through concerted effort directed at servicing customers by continuous improvements, utilizing and maximizing human resources.

Training   The planned and organized activity that seeks to provide employees with the necessary skills and attitudes to function effectively on the job.

Transactional analysis   Theories and techniques that can be used by individuals and groups to determine the basis from which another individual is communicating or interacting.

Unstructured interview   A form of interview where the question and sequence are accommodated to the applicant's unique background and responses to questions.

Upward communication   The process of passing along information and understanding from the lower levels of the organization to the higher levels.

Values   Strongly held beliefs that either define right or wrong or indicate preferences.

Win-win problem solving   A method of solving problems in which the chef supervisor and team member discuss the problem together and arrive at a mutually acceptable situation.

Work standards   The established time that a normally capable worker should take to do a specified task.

Worker's compensation   A form of no-fault insurance that entitles workers who are injured or who become ill because of job-related conditions to compensation in the form of money, medical treatment, and vocational rehabilitation, if necessary.

Index